Children's ATLAS of the World

Children's ATLAS of the World

Malcom Watson

Consultant: Clive Carpenter

Miles KeLLy

First published in 2007 by Miles Kelly Publishing Ltd
Bardfield Centre, Great Bardfield, Essex, CM7 4SL, UK

Copyright © Miles Kelly Publishing Ltd 2007

This edition updated and published 2013

2 4 6 8 10 9 7 5 3 1

Author: Malcolm Watson
Consultant: Clive Carpenter

Map Artworker: Julian Baker (J B ILLUSTRATIONS)
Mountain High Maps® Copyright © 1993 Digital Wisdom, Inc.

Publishing Director: Belinda Gallagher
Creative Director: Jo Cowan
Editor: Amanda Askew
Editorial Assistant: Carly Blake
Designers: Simon Lee, Elaine Wilkinson
Cover Designer: Simon Lee
Reprographics: Stephan Davis,
Liberty Newton
Production Manager: Elizabeth Collins

ISBN 978-1-78209-151-6

Printed in Dubai

British Library Cataloguing-in-Publication Data
A catalogue record for this book is available from the British Library

Made with paper from a sustainable forest

www.mileskelly.net
info@mileskelly.net

www.factsforprojects.com

Children's ATLAS of the World

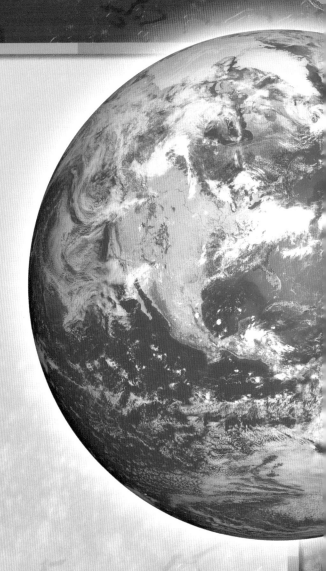

Contents

Using the atlas

Divided into continental areas, this atlas explores the world with amazing facts, statistics and photographs. Highly detailed maps show important cultural and geographical features, such as major towns, places of interest, mountain ranges and rivers.

1 Graticule
The coloured frame that runs around each map. It changes colour for each continental area and provides grid references that enable you to locate features on the map easily.

2 Main heading
Introduces the main countries on the page.

3 Locator globe
Highlights where in the world the countries are.

4 Introduction
Gives an insight into some of the countries that are mapped.

5 Scale
Shows the scale of the map in kilometres and miles.

6 Map
Shows towns, territories and islands, plus physical features such as mountain ranges.

7 Did You Know?
Amazing facts about people and places.

8 Image
Each photograph is accompanied by a detailed caption.

North Africa

4 The Sahara Desert dominates this region at 6000 km in width and 2000 km from north to south. Only a narrow strip of land stands next to the Mediterranean Sea, but the fertile valleys of the Atlas Mountains and the banks of the Nile river have enough water to grow crops.

Algeria, Libya and Tunisia have bec[ome] wealthy by selling oil and natural g[as to] Europe. Egypt was the richest coun[try] in the world when the pharaohs ru[led] more than 3000 years ago. Egypt's well-preserved tombs and temples, especially the Great Pyramid of Giza[,] attract many tourists.

Did You Know?
The Sahara Desert region was wet and fertile 8000 years ago. As the climate has become drier, the desert has expanded.

8 In north Africa, many civilizations live in fortified cities, or ksars. **Aït Benhaddou** is situated near Marrakech [E2], Morocco. Few families live here now as they have moved to modern villages nearby. Scenes from films including Alexander (2004) and The Mummy (1999) have been shot here.

9 ...the Sun will evaporate the equivalent of 110 million bottles of water from the Nile river.

In the next minute...

ATLANTIC OCEAN

Strait of Gibraltar
Tangier · CEUTA (SPAIN)
Tétouan · MELILLA (SPAIN)
Rabat · Kénitra
Casablanca · · Oran
Safi · Fes
Meknès
MOROCCO
Marrakech
Mount Toubkal 4176 m
Agadir ·
Sidi Ifni ·
· Tarfaya
WESTERN SAHARA
MAURITANIA
MALI
Algiers
Ech-Cheliff · Blida · Bejaïa
Sidi Bel Abbès
Constantine · Annaba
Skikda · Bi
Batna ·
TELL ATLAS
SAHARAN ATLAS MOUNTAINS
ATLAS MOUNTAINS
· Béchar
· Ghardaïa
ALGERIA
· Tindouf
Adrar ·
· In Salah
AHAGGAR
Tahat Peak 2918 m
Tamanrasset ·
SAHARA DES
TUN
Gha
NIGER

0 100 200 300 mi
0 200 400 km

62

KEY TO MAPS

Country border

State border

Disputed border

Tarfaya
WESTERN

Country capital
Madrid ●

State capital
Lincoln ■

Town
● Rock Springs

Desert
S A H A R A

Highest peak

Tahat Peak
2918 m

River
Amazon

Dependency/territory
FALKLAND ISLANDS
(UK)

Research station
WILK
Casey ●
(Australia)

Place of interest
◆ *Mount Rushmore*

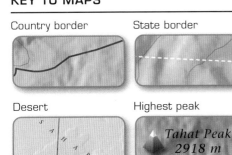

Located on the Nile river, Cairo [F13] is the biggest city in Africa. Built in AD 988, **Al-Azhar University** is the second oldest university in the world, after the University of Al Karaouine Fez, Morocco. Al-Azhar Mosque stands alongside the university.

NORTH AFRICA • AFRICA

14 Facts and Stats

• Egypt's population of 77.8 million would fill 778 Olympic stadiums. Libya's population of 6.4 million would only fill 64 stadiums.

• Cairo [F13] is the biggest city with 15.5 million people. This would fill 155 Olympic stadiums, compared to Tripoli which would only fill 14 [E8].

• The average income per person in Libya is £7140, compared to a world average of £5640.

10 Search and Find

Algeria
• Algiers C6
Egypt
• Cairo F13
Libya
• Tripoli E8

Morocco
• Rabat D3
Tunisia
• Tunis D7

13 World Record
The Sahara sand sea in Algeria has the longest sand dunes in the world, with some more than 300 km.

15 Extreme Weather
The hottest temperature ever recorded was 58°C in Libya's Sahara Desert.

MEDITERRANEAN SEA

Tripoli
Misurata
wiyah
Gulf of Sidra
● Benghazi
Surt ●
● Ajdabiya
● Darnah
● Tubruq

GREAT SAND SEA
QATTARA DEPRESSION

Alexandria ● ● Tanta
Suez Canal
Cairo ●
Giza ● ● Suez
Sinai Peninsula

Port Said ●

ISRAEL

LIBYA

LIBYAN DESERT

ZZAN

WESTERN DESERT

EGYPT

Nile

Gulf of Suez
Sharm al Sheikh ●
● El Minya
Al Ghardaqah ●
Asyut ●

Gulf of Aqaba
RED SEA

● Qena
● Luxor

GILF KEBIR PLATEAU

● Aswan

Lake Nasser

CHAD

SUDAN

11
THE DISTANCE separating Morocco from Spain, Europe, at the Strait of Gibraltar's [C3] narrowest point is only 13 km.

12
EGYPT has huge pyramids, built more than 3000 years ago. Each one held the body of a king.

Desert tribe people, such as the Berbers and Tuaregs, travel by camel from oasis to oasis across the Sahara Desert to trade cloth, salt and spices.

---

9 In the next minute...
Fascinating information about what is happening across the world in only one minute.

10 Search and Find
Each country or state is listed with its capital city and a grid reference.

11 The distance...
Measures the distance from one point to another and how long it would take to travel.

12 Place of interest
Provides extra information about a well-known sight or attraction.

13 World Record
Details a world record that a country holds.

14 Facts and Stats
Helps you to understand facts and figures. The highest peaks are compared to the Eiffel Tower in Paris, France, which is 320 m in height. Rivers are compared to the Nile river, Africa, which is 6670 km in length. Population is compared to an Olympic stadium, which would hold 100,000 people. ·

15 Extreme Weather
Details the highest and lowest temperatures, dramatic storms or high rainfall.

Planet Earth

Earth is a huge ball of rock with two-thirds of its surface covered by seas and oceans. The third planet from the Sun in the Solar System, Earth is the only planet where life is known to exist, due to an atmosphere rich in oxygen and the water on its surface. Beneath the Earth's thin, solid crust is the liquid mantle, and at the centre is the core. The outer part of the core is liquid, but the inner core is solid metal.

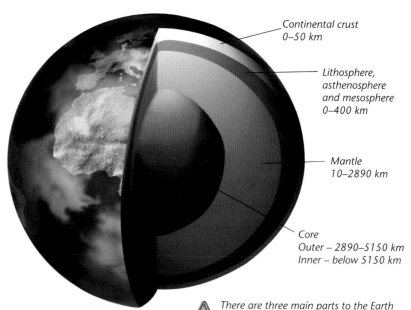

Continental crust
0–50 km

Lithosphere, asthenosphere and mesosphere
0–400 km

Mantle
10–2890 km

Core
Outer – 2890–5150 km
Inner – below 5150 km

There are three main parts to the Earth – the crust, mantle and core. Although the inner core reaches a temperature of 7000°C, it remains solid because the pressure is 6000 times greater than on the surface.

SPINNING EARTH

The Earth spins on its axis – an imaginary line through its centre – at a speed of more than 1600 km/h. It doesn't spin straight up, but leans to one side. As the Earth spins, the view of the Sun from different places on Earth constantly changes. This brings day and night, and the seasons.

In December, the South Pole leans towards the Sun. Places in the southern half of the world have summer. At the same time, places in the northern half have winter.

Seasons

There are four seasons – spring, summer, autumn and winter. Each season brings a change in temperature and weather. The changes in the seasons occur because the Earth tilts towards the Sun. When the Northern Hemisphere tilts towards the Sun, the northern part of the world has summer and the south has winter. Six months later, the opposite occurs – the Southern Hemisphere tilts towards the Sun. Then the north has winter and the south has summer. The tropics around the centre of the Earth are slightly different. They only have two seasons – wet and dry.

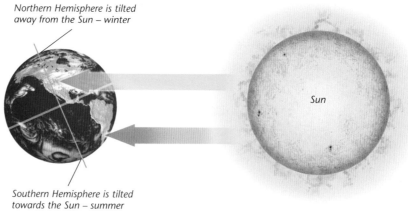

Northern Hemisphere is tilted away from the Sun – winter

Sun

Southern Hemisphere is tilted towards the Sun – summer

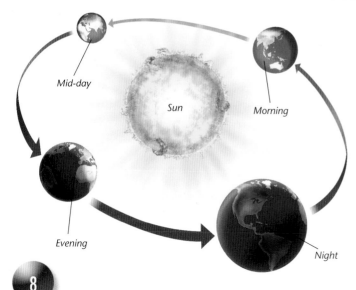

Mid-day

Sun

Morning

Evening

Night

When it is daylight on the half of the Earth facing towards the Sun, it is night on the half of the Earth facing away from it. As the Earth rotates, so the day and night halves shift gradually around the world.

Night and day

The Earth spins a complete turn on its axis every 24 hours. This gives us night and day. The Sun is the source of light for daytime. When it is night, it is dark because the Sun is shining on the opposite side of the Earth. When it is evening or early morning, the Sun is moving away or towards our part of the Earth.

Shaping the land

The Earth's crust is made up of pieces called tectonic plates, which are constantly moving, changing the shape of the land. This can create mountains and volcanoes, as well as cause natural disasters, such as earthquakes. Rocks can also be broken down or worn away by the weather, such as wind and rain, or by the movement of water, such as waves.

A volcano erupts, shooting molten magma into the air.

A sea arch, formed by waves wearing away the rock.

PLATE TECTONICS

The Earth's crust is split into several parts called tectonic plates. The plates float on the molten magma underneath, causing them to constantly move.

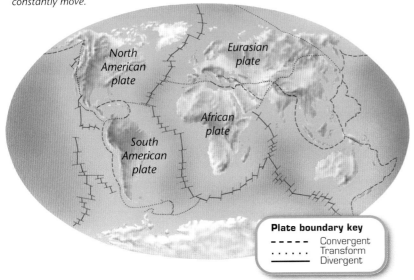

North American plate

Eurasian plate

African plate

South American plate

Plate boundary key
- - - - - Convergent
. . . . . . Transform
Divergent

Divergent plate boundaries
Where two plates move away from each other, molten rock, or magma, rises to fill the gap. This usually occurs beneath the oceans, forming a spreading ocean ridge, such as the mid-Atlantic ridge.

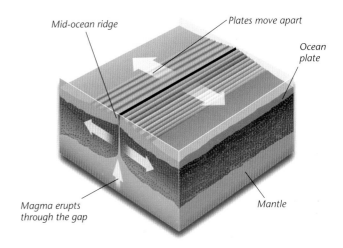

Mid-ocean ridge

Plates move apart

Ocean plate

Magma erupts through the gap

Mantle

Convergent plate boundaries
When two plates crash together, they crumple up and form major mountain chains, such as the Andes, as well as volcanoes. The Earth's crust is thin, so if cracks appear, the magma shoots up as the lava of a volcano. When an ocean plate is driven down into the Earth's magma, it is called subduction.

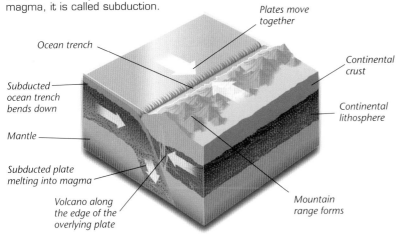

Plates move together

Ocean trench

Subducted ocean trench bends down

Continental crust

Mantle

Continental lithosphere

Subducted plate melting into magma

Volcano along the edge of the overlying plate

Mountain range forms

Transform plate boundaries
If two plates push past each other, pressure can build up, creating a break, or fault, which often causes an earthquake. Some earthquakes are so powerful that buildings collapse. Landslides can also occur, causing great damage. Undersea earthquakes can cause the massive waves of a tsunami, such as the tsunami that struck southeast Asia in 2004, killing 230,000 people.

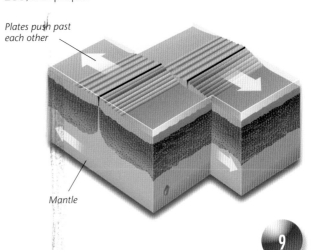

Plates push past each other

Mantle

Climate

The Earth's climate is very simple. Near the Equator, the temperture is hot, and closer to the poles, the temperature is cold. All year round, daytime temperatures at the Equator are around 33°C and there are no seasons. At the poles, the temperature is usually below freezing, and in winter there are long hours of darkness and temperatures drop to −40°C. Rain and snowfall patterns are more complex. Countries at the Equator experience heavy rain, but the poles have very little rainfall.

Global warming

The increased level of carbon dioxide in the atmosphere causes global warming because the gas traps the Sun's heat. Carbon dioxide is emitted when carbon fuels are burnt – this happens in cars and factories. The effects of global warming are becoming evident. Large areas of ice around Antarctica have already disappeared. The Sahara Desert is expanding and droughts are more common in Australia, causing rivers, such as the Murray, to dry up (see below). Sea levels are slowly rising, threatening cities such as New York City and low-lying countries such as Bangladesh with flooding. Using alternative sources of energy, such as wind and solar power, is vital to slow down these changes.

TYPES OF CLIMATE

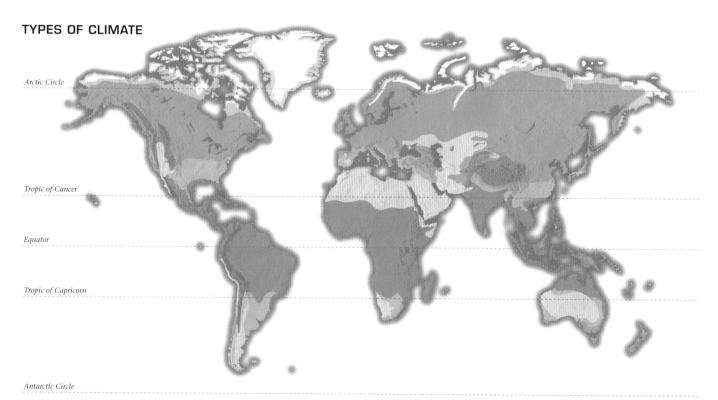

Arctic Circle

Tropic of Cancer

Equator

Tropic of Capricorn

Antarctic Circle

Polar and tundra
The lands around the Arctic Ocean and Antarctica are normally covered in snow. Northern Canada and Russia have a brief summer where the snow melts and the top layer of soil thaws to create a boggy ground called tundra.

Desert
Just north and south of the Equator lie desert areas. They have high daytime summer temperatures and are warm even in winter. Rain is very rare. Few plants grow and crops are only farmed where there are sources of water.

Cool temperate
Near the Arctic Circle, winters are cold and snowy, and summers are short. Closer to the Equator winters are milder, with little snow and warm summers. Forests are abundant and farming is common in the southern areas.

Warm temperate
In areas around the Mediterranean Sea and in some parts of North America, summers are hot and dry and winters are cool, but mild. Rainfall varies, so farming centres around growing citrus and olive trees.

Tropical
Close to the Equator, countries experience high temperatures and high rainfall for almost every month of the year. More animals and plants live in the tropical rainforests of the Amazon, central Africa and Indonesia than any other region.

Mountainous
Mountains have their own climate and snow can even be found at the Equator. At 5000 m in height, the temperature is 30°C colder than at sea level. Mountains also have more rainfall than the land surrounding them.

Population

The population of the world reached 6.7 billion in 2008. With more than 250 babies being born each minute, and many people living longer due to a better quality of life, the population of the world is increasing rapidly. This rise puts pressure on the world's natural resources, and many cities are becoming overcrowded as people move in search of work. China is the most populated country with 1.24 billion people. Tokyo, the capital of Japan, is the largest city in the world with a population of 37.36 million.

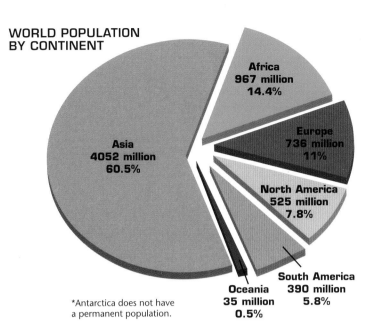

WORLD POPULATION BY CONTINENT

Asia 4052 million 60.5%
Africa 967 million 14.4%
Europe 736 million 11%
North America 525 million 7.8%
South America 390 million 5.8%
Oceania 35 million 0.5%

*Antarctica does not have a permanent population.

TOP 10 COUNTRIES BY POPULATION DENSITY

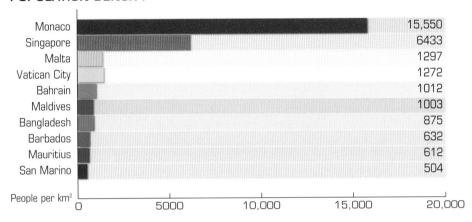

	People per km²
Monaco	15,550
Singapore	6433
Malta	1297
Vatican City	1272
Bahrain	1012
Maldives	1003
Bangladesh	875
Barbados	632
Mauritius	612
San Marino	504

TOP 10 COUNTRIES BY POPULATION

1	China	1,240,000,000
2	India	1,148,000,000
3	USA	304,060,000
4	Indonesia	222,192,000
5	Brazil	183,889,000
6	Pakistan	162,508,000
7	Russia	142,754,000
8	Nigeria	140,003,000
9	Bangladesh	129,247,000
10	Japan	127,931,000

TOP 20 CITIES BY POPULATION

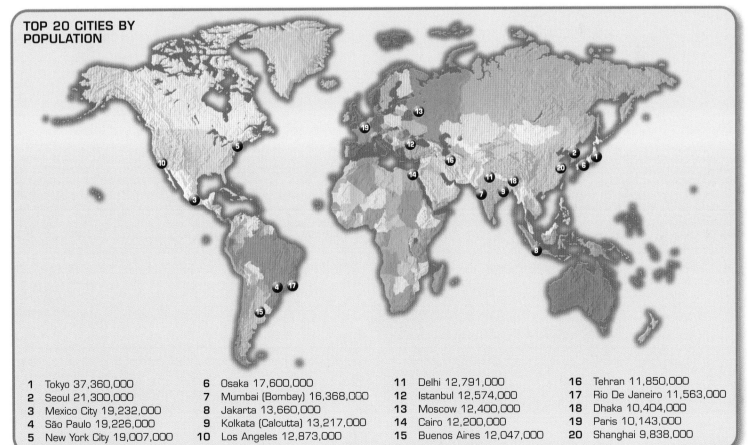

1	Tokyo 37,360,000	6	Osaka 17,600,000	11	Delhi 12,791,000
2	Seoul 21,300,000	7	Mumbai (Bombay) 16,368,000	12	Istanbul 12,574,000
3	Mexico City 19,232,000	8	Jakarta 13,660,000	13	Moscow 12,400,000
4	São Paulo 19,226,000	9	Kolkata (Calcutta) 13,217,000	14	Cairo 12,200,000
5	New York City 19,007,000	10	Los Angeles 12,873,000	15	Buenos Aires 12,047,000

16	Tehran 11,850,000
17	Rio De Janeiro 11,563,000
18	Dhaka 10,404,000
19	Paris 10,143,000
20	Shanghai 9,838,000

The Physical World

ARCT

QUEEN ELIZABETH ISLANDS

Ellesmere Island

GREENLAND (DENMARK)

BEAUFORT SEA

BROOKS RANGE

Victoria Island

Baffin Bay

Back

Baffin Island

NORWEG SEA

Great Bear Lake

Little Bear Lake

Mackenzie

Denmark Strait

Yukon

HUDSON BAY

Gulf of Alaska

Davis Strait

ALEUTIAN ISLANDS

ROCKY MOUNTAINS

GREAT PLAINS

Lake Winnipeg

CANADIAN SHIELD

Newfoundland

MID-ATLANTIC RIDGE

Missouri

THE GREAT LAKES

Mississippi

PACIFIC OCEAN

NORTH AMERICA

NORTH ATLANTIC OCEAN

CANARY ISLANDS (SPAIN)

SIERRA MADRE

Rio Grande

GULF OF MEXICO

ATLAS MOUNT

Hawaii (US)

WEST INDIES

SAH

MID-AMERICA TRENCH

CARIBBEAN SEA

GULF GUIN

Galápagos Islands (Ecuador)

LLANOS

Orinoco

GUIANA HIGHLANDS

MID-ATLANTIC RIDGE

Amazon

Niger

ANDES

SOUTH AMERICA

SOUTH ATLANTI OCEAN

SELVAS

BRAZILIAN HIGHLANDS

PERU-CHILE TRENCH

GRAN CHACO

PAMPAS

WALVIS

FALKLAND ISLANDS (UK)

Cape Horn

Antarctic

LONGEST RIVERS BY CONTINENT

River	Continent	Length km
Nile	Africa	6670
Chang Jiang (Yangze)	Asia	6300
Volga	Europe	3530
Mississippi-Missouri	North America	6020

LOWEST POINTS BY CONTINENT

Area	Continent	Depth m
Lake Assal	Africa	−153
Dead Sea	Asia	−402
Caspian Sea shore	Europe	−28
Death Valley	North America	−86
Lake Eyre	Oceania	−16

HIGHEST POINTS BY CONTINENT

Mountain	Continent	Height m
Mount Kilimanjaro	Africa	5895
Mount Everest	Asia	8848
Mount Elbrus	Europe	5642
Mount McKinley	North America	6194
Puncak Jaya	Oceania	5030

0	1000	2000	3000 m
0	1000	2000	3000	4000	5000

WORLD'S OCEANS

Ocean	Area km²
Pacific	165,240,000
Atlantic	82,440,000
Indian	73,440,000
Southern	23,325,000
Arctic	14,090,000

LARGEST DESERTS

Desert	Continent	Area km²
Sahara	Africa	8,600,000
Arabian	Asia	2,300,000
Australian	Australia	1,550,000
Gobi	Asia	1,300,000
Kalahari	Africa	930,000

LARGEST INLAND WATER BODIES

Lake	Continent	Area km²
Caspian Sea	Asia–Europe	371,800
Superior	North America	82,350
Victoria	Africa	69,500
Huron	North America	59,600
Michigan	North America	57,800

The Political World

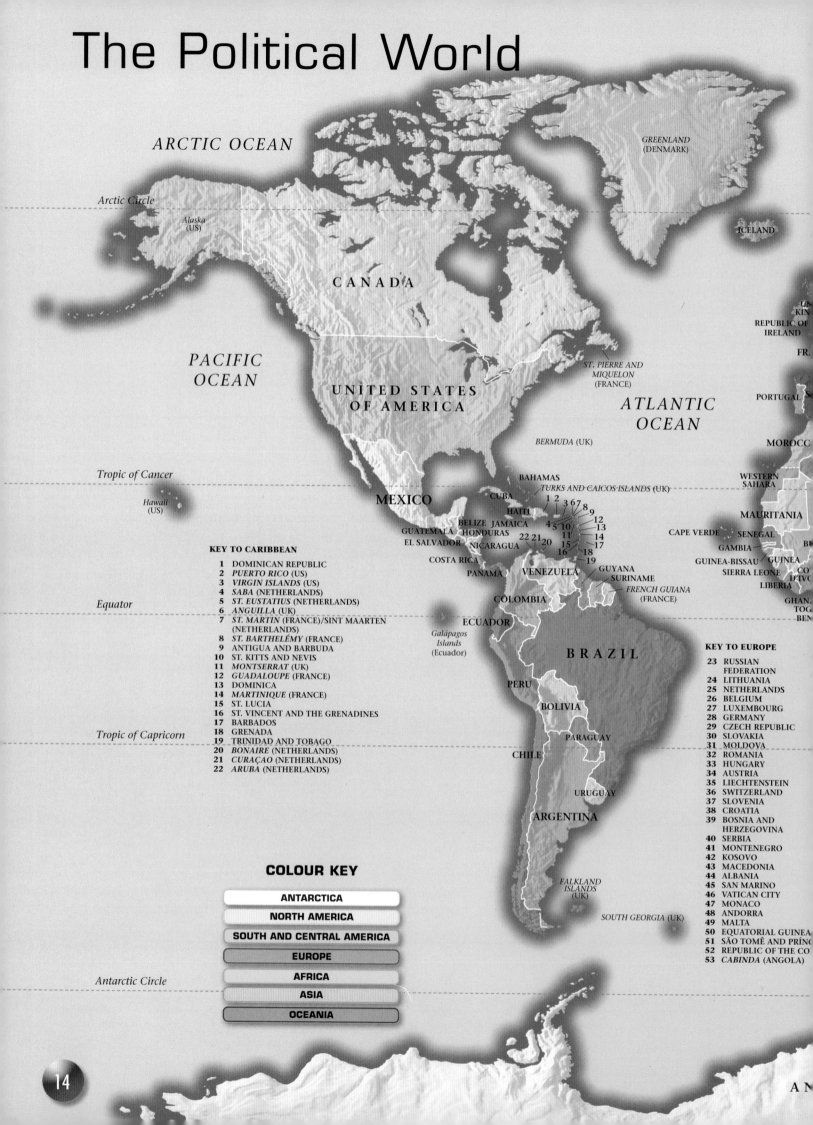

ARCTIC OCEAN

Arctic Circle

Alaska (US)

GREENLAND (DENMARK)

ICELAND

CANADA

PACIFIC OCEAN

UNITED STATES OF AMERICA

ST. PIERRE AND MIQUELON (FRANCE)

ATLANTIC OCEAN

BERMUDA (UK)

Tropic of Cancer

BAHAMAS

TURKS AND CAICOS ISLANDS (UK)

CUBA

MEXICO

HAITI

BELIZE JAMAICA
GUATEMALA HONDURAS
EL SALVADOR NICARAGUA

COSTA RICA

PANAMA

VENEZUELA

GUYANA
SURINAME
FRENCH GUIANA (FRANCE)

COLOMBIA

ECUADOR

Galápagos Islands (Ecuador)

Equator

BRAZIL

PERU

BOLIVIA

PARAGUAY

CHILE

URUGUAY

Tropic of Capricorn

ARGENTINA

FALKLAND ISLANDS (UK)

SOUTH GEORGIA (UK)

Hawaii (US)

UNITED KINGDOM
REPUBLIC OF IRELAND
FR.
PORTUGAL S
MOROCCO
WESTERN SAHARA
MAURITANIA
CAPE VERDE SENEGAL
GAMBIA B
GUINEA-BISSAU GUINEA
SIERRA LEONE CÔTE D'IVO
LIBERIA
GHAN.
TOG
BEN

KEY TO CARIBBEAN

1 DOMINICAN REPUBLIC
2 PUERTO RICO (US)
3 VIRGIN ISLANDS (US)
4 SABA (NETHERLANDS)
5 ST. EUSTATIUS (NETHERLANDS)
6 ANGUILLA (UK)
7 ST. MARTIN (FRANCE)/SINT MAARTEN (NETHERLANDS)
8 ST. BARTHELÉMY (FRANCE)
9 ANTIGUA AND BARBUDA
10 ST. KITTS AND NEVIS
11 MONTSERRAT (UK)
12 GUADALOUPE (FRANCE)
13 DOMINICA
14 MARTINIQUE (FRANCE)
15 ST. LUCIA
16 ST. VINCENT AND THE GRENADINES
17 BARBADOS
18 GRENADA
19 TRINIDAD AND TOBAGO
20 BONAIRE (NETHERLANDS)
21 CURAÇAO (NETHERLANDS)
22 ARUBA (NETHERLANDS)

KEY TO EUROPE

23 RUSSIAN FEDERATION
24 LITHUANIA
25 NETHERLANDS
26 BELGIUM
27 LUXEMBOURG
28 GERMANY
29 CZECH REPUBLIC
30 SLOVAKIA
31 MOLDOVA
32 ROMANIA
33 HUNGARY
34 AUSTRIA
35 LIECHTENSTEIN
36 SWITZERLAND
37 SLOVENIA
38 CROATIA
39 BOSNIA AND HERZEGOVINA
40 SERBIA
41 MONTENEGRO
42 KOSOVO
43 MACEDONIA
44 ALBANIA
45 SAN MARINO
46 VATICAN CITY
47 MONACO
48 ANDORRA
49 MALTA
50 EQUATORIAL GUINEA
51 SÃO TOMÉ AND PRÍNC
52 REPUBLIC OF THE CO
53 CABINDA (ANGOLA)

COLOUR KEY

ANTARCTICA

NORTH AMERICA

SOUTH AND CENTRAL AMERICA

EUROPE

AFRICA

ASIA

OCEANIA

Antarctic Circle

AN

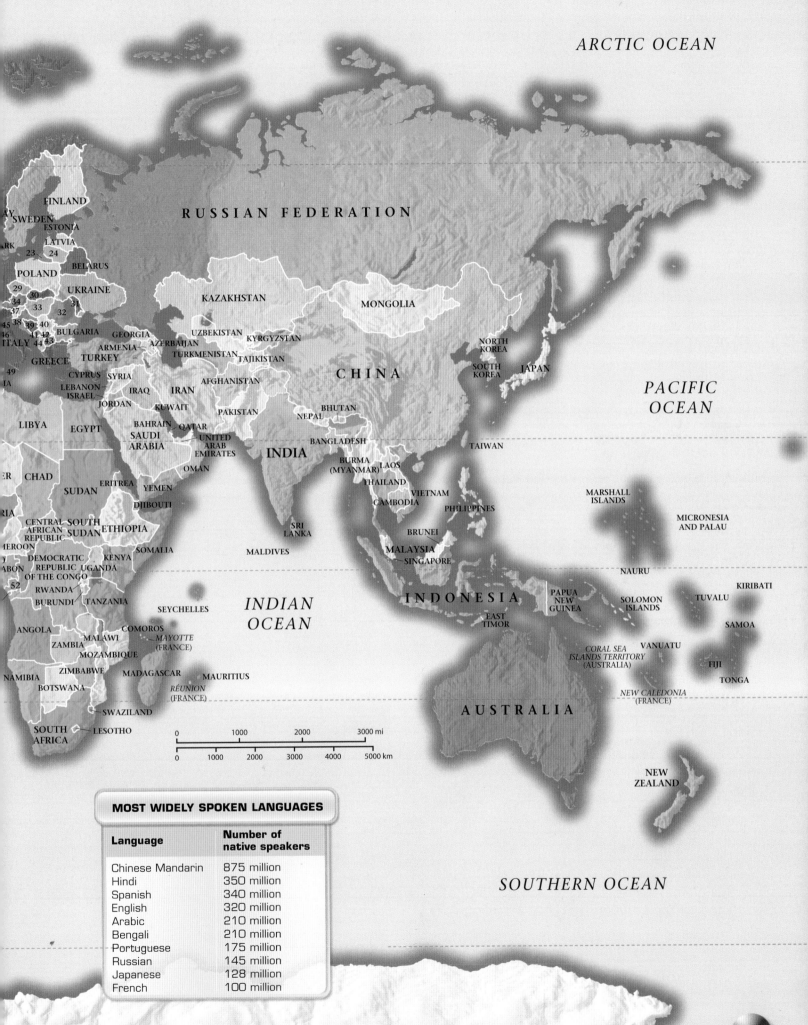

ARCTIC OCEAN

FINLAND
SWEDEN
ESTONIA
ARK
LATVIA
23   24
BELARUS
POLAND
29   30   UKRAINE
34   31
37   33   32
45   38   39-40
46   41 42
ITALY 44   43
BULGARIA   GEORGIA
ARMENIA   AZERBAIJAN
GREECE   TURKEY   TURKMENISTAN
49
CYPRUS   SYRIA
LEBANON   IRAQ   IRAN
ISRAEL
JORDAN   KUWAIT
LIBYA   EGYPT   BAHRAIN   QATAR
SAUDI   UNITED
ARABIA   ARAB
EMIRATES
OMAN
CHAD   ERITREA   YEMEN
SUDAN   DJIBOUTI
CENTRAL   SOUTH
AFRICAN   SUDAN   ETHIOPIA
REPUBLIC
MEROON
DEMOCRATIC   SOMALIA
REPUBLIC   UGANDA
OF THE CONGO   KENYA
52   RWANDA
BURUNDI   TANZANIA
ANGOLA   SEYCHELLES
COMOROS
ZAMBIA   MALAWI   MAYOTTE
MOZAMBIQUE   (FRANCE)
ZIMBABWE
NAMIBIA   MADAGASCAR   MAURITIUS
BOTSWANA   RÉUNION
(FRANCE)
SWAZILAND
SOUTH   LESOTHO
AFRICA

RUSSIAN FEDERATION

KAZAKHSTAN   MONGOLIA

UZBEKISTAN   KYRGYZSTAN
TAJIKISTAN
AFGHANISTAN   CHINA

NORTH
KOREA
SOUTH   JAPAN
KOREA

PAKISTAN
NEPAL   BHUTAN
BANGLADESH
INDIA   TAIWAN
BURMA   LAOS
(MYANMAR)
THAILAND
VIETNAM
CAMBODIA
PHILIPPINES

SRI
LANKA
MALDIVES   BRUNEI
MALAYSIA
SINGAPORE

INDONESIA
EAST
TIMOR

*INDIAN
OCEAN*

*PACIFIC
OCEAN*

MARSHALL
ISLANDS

MICRONESIA
AND PALAU

NAURU

PAPUA
NEW
GUINEA   SOLOMON
ISLANDS   TUVALU   KIRIBATI

SAMOA

*CORAL SEA
ISLANDS TERRITORY
(AUSTRALIA)*   VANUATU

FIJI

*NEW CALEDONIA
(FRANCE)*   TONGA

AUSTRALIA

NEW
ZEALAND

0		1000		2000		3000 mi

0	1000	2000	3000	4000	5000 km

MOST WIDELY SPOKEN LANGUAGES

Language	Number of native speakers
Chinese Mandarin	875 million
Hindi	350 million
Spanish	340 million
English	320 million
Arabic	210 million
Bengali	210 million
Portuguese	175 million
Russian	145 million
Japanese	128 million
French	100 million

SOUTHERN OCEAN

RCTICA

Antarctica

Antarctica is 98 percent covered by ice that is about 1.6 km thick. Although it is the coldest place on Earth, the region is heavily affected by global warming. The climate is becoming warmer due to an increased level of carbon dioxide, which traps the Sun's heat. Large areas of ice that cover the sea around Antarctica have already broken away and melted. Deep under the ice lie vast amounts of oil, coal and gold, but mining is prohibited.

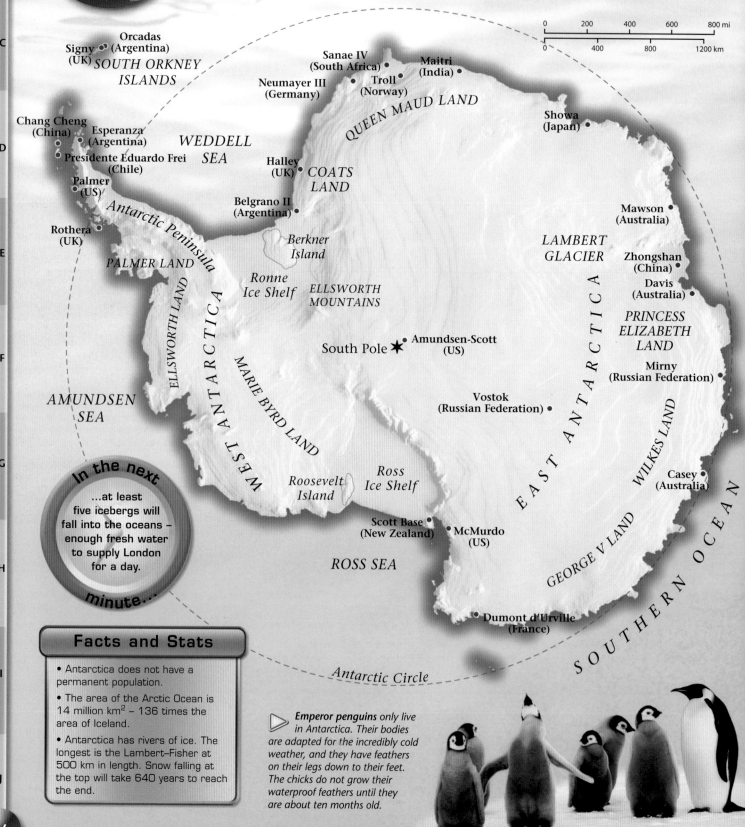

0   200   400   600   800 mi
0   400   800   1200 km

Signy (UK)
Orcadas (Argentina)
SOUTH ORKNEY ISLANDS

Chang Cheng (China)
Esperanza (Argentina)
Presidente Eduardo Frei (Chile)
Palmer (US)
Rothera (UK)

Antarctic Peninsula

WEDDELL SEA

Halley (UK)
COATS LAND
Belgrano II (Argentina)

PALMER LAND

Berkner Island

Ronne Ice Shelf

ELLSWORTH LAND

WEST ANTARCTICA

ELLSWORTH MOUNTAINS

AMUNDSEN SEA

MARIE BYRD LAND

South Pole ✷ Amundsen-Scott (US)

Roosevelt Island

Ross Ice Shelf

Scott Base (New Zealand)
McMurdo (US)

ROSS SEA

Sanae IV (South Africa)
Neumayer III (Germany)
Troll (Norway)
Maitri (India)

QUEEN MAUD LAND

Showa (Japan)

Mawson (Australia)

LAMBERT GLACIER

Zhongshan (China)
Davis (Australia)

PRINCESS ELIZABETH LAND

Mirny (Russian Federation)

Vostok (Russian Federation)

EAST ANTARCTICA

WILKES LAND

Casey (Australia)

GEORGE V LAND

SOUTHERN OCEAN

Dumont d'Urville (France)

Antarctic Circle

In the next ...at least five icebergs will fall into the oceans – enough fresh water to supply London for a day. **minute...**

Facts and Stats

- Antarctica does not have a permanent population.
- The area of the Arctic Ocean is 14 million km² – 136 times the area of Iceland.
- Antarctica has rivers of ice. The longest is the Lambert–Fisher at 500 km in length. Snow falling at the top will take 640 years to reach the end.

▷ **Emperor penguins** only live in Antarctica. Their bodies are adapted for the incredibly cold weather, and they have feathers on their legs down to their feet. The chicks do not grow their waterproof feathers until they are about ten months old.

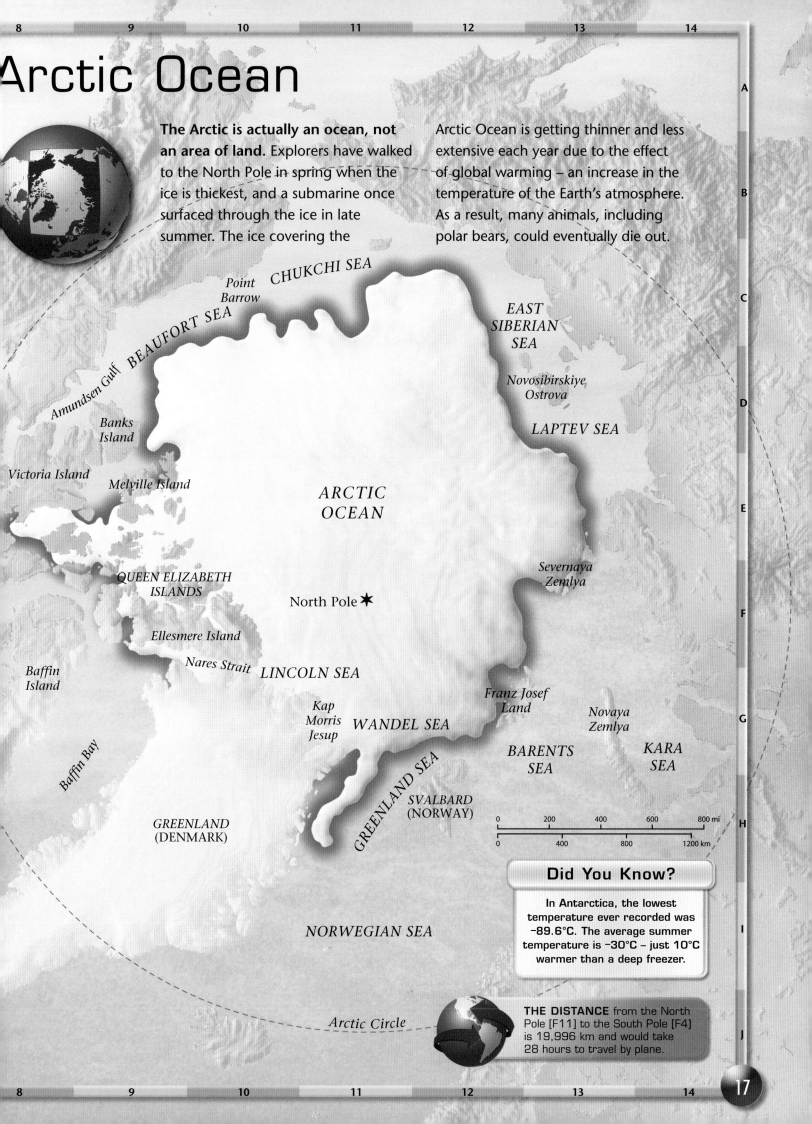

Arctic Ocean

The Arctic is actually an ocean, not an area of land. Explorers have walked to the North Pole in spring when the ice is thickest, and a submarine once surfaced through the ice in late summer. The ice covering the Arctic Ocean is getting thinner and less extensive each year due to the effect of global warming – an increase in the temperature of the Earth's atmosphere. As a result, many animals, including polar bears, could eventually die out.

CHUKCHI SEA

Point
Barrow

EAST
SIBERIAN
SEA

BEAUFORT SEA

Amundsen Gulf

Novosibirskiye
Ostrova

Banks
Island

LAPTEV SEA

Victoria Island

Melville Island

ARCTIC
OCEAN

QUEEN ELIZABETH
ISLANDS

Severnaya
Zemlya

North Pole ✷

Ellesmere Island

Nares Strait   LINCOLN SEA

Baffin
Island

Franz Josef
Land

Kap
Morris
Jesup   WANDEL SEA

Novaya
Zemlya

Baffin Bay

GREENLAND SEA

BARENTS
SEA

KARA
SEA

SVALBARD
(NORWAY)

GREENLAND
(DENMARK)

0	200	400	600	800 mi
0	400	800	1200 km	

Did You Know?

In Antarctica, the lowest temperature ever recorded was –89.6°C. The average summer temperature is –30°C – just 10°C warmer than a deep freezer.

NORWEGIAN SEA

Arctic Circle

THE DISTANCE from the North Pole [F11] to the South Pole [F4] is 19,996 km and would take 28 hours to travel by plane.

North America

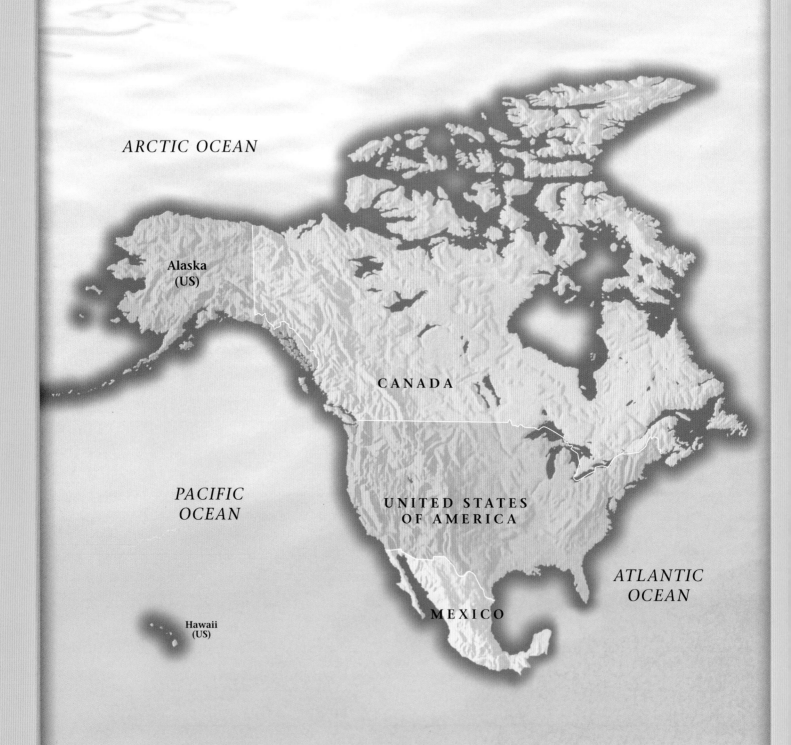

ARCTIC OCEAN

Alaska
(US)

CANADA

PACIFIC
OCEAN

UNITED STATES
OF AMERICA

ATLANTIC
OCEAN

Hawaii
(US)

MEXICO

COUNTRY FACTFILE

Country	Life expectancy	Population in thousands	Population growth %	Population as urban %	Literacy %	Area km²	Population density per km²	Capital city	Currency	Languages
Canada	81	33,477	0.8	82	99	9,970,610	3.4	Ottawa	Canadian Dollar	English, French
Mexico	77	112,338	1.1	78	86	1,958,201	57.4	Mexico City	Mexican Peso	Spanish
United States of America	78	308,467	0.9	82	99	9,629,091	31.9	Washington D.C.	US Dollar	English, Spanish

NB: Central America can be found as part of the South and Central America section.

Northeast USA

The northeast is the centre of the United States' industry and commerce with many large manufacturing companies. Ford and General Motor vehicles, as well as coal mines, steel works, the New York Stock Exchange, Washington White House and the Senate buildings are all situated here. Modern black music started in Cleveland and Detroit, whilst away from the cities there are many beaches, rivers, forests and lakes.

Lake of the Woods

Isle Royale

Lake Superior

CANADA

Red Lake

NORTH DAKOTA

Marquette •

Upper Peninsula

• Moorhead

Duluth •

MINNESOTA

Green Bay

MICHIGA

WISCONSIN

Lower Peninsula

SOUTH DAKOTA

Minnesota

Minneapolis ■ St. Paul
Bloomington
Burnsville

• Eau Claire

Green Bay •
Appleton •
Oshkosh •

Lake Winnebago

Saginaw

Grand Rapids ■

Fl

Lansin

Mississippi

Lake Michigan

Green Bay

• Mankato

Rochester •

• La Crosse

Ann Ar

• Kalamazo

Wisconsin

Waukesha •

Madison ■

• Milwaukee

Cedar

Mason City •

Janesville •

Waterloo •

Rockford •

• Elgin

• South Bend

IOWA

• Cedar Rapids

Aurora •

Chicago •

Sioux City •

Davenport •

Joliet •

Gary •

Fort Wayne •

NEBRASKA

Des Moines ■

Des Moines

ILLINOIS

Wabash

INDIANA

• Council Bluffs

• Peoria

Illinois

Champaign •

Anderson •

Mun

MISSOURI

Decatur •

Mississippi

Springfield ■

Terre Haute •

■ Indianap

• Bloomington

Jeffersonville •

• East St. Louis

Evansville •

There are 30 major league baseball teams in two leagues, the American League (founded 1901) and the National League (founded 1876).1903 was the first time that the World Series, between the winners of the two leagues, was played.

Search and Find

- Washington D.C. H11
Connecticut
- Hartford F12
Delaware
- Dover G11
Illinois
- Springfield. I5
Indiana
- Indianapolis ... H7
Iowa
- Des Moines ... G3
Maine
- Augusta D13
Maryland
- Annapolis ... H11
Massachusetts
- Boston E13
Michigan
- Lansing F7

Minnesota
- St. Paul E3
New Hampshire
- Concord E13
New Jersey
- Trenton G12
New York
- Albany E12
Ohio
- Columbus H8
Pennsylvania
- Harrisburg.. . G11
Rhode Island
- Providence ... E13
Vermont
- Montpelier. .. D12
West Virginia
- Charleston I9
Wisconsin
- Madison F5

Facts and Stats

- The biggest city is New York City [F12] with 19 million people. This would fill 190 Olympic stadiums.
- The biggest lake is Lake Superior [C5] at 82,350 km², This is only 20 percent smaller than Iceland.
- Mount Washington [D12] is the highest mountain at 1917 m – six times higher than the Eiffel Tower.

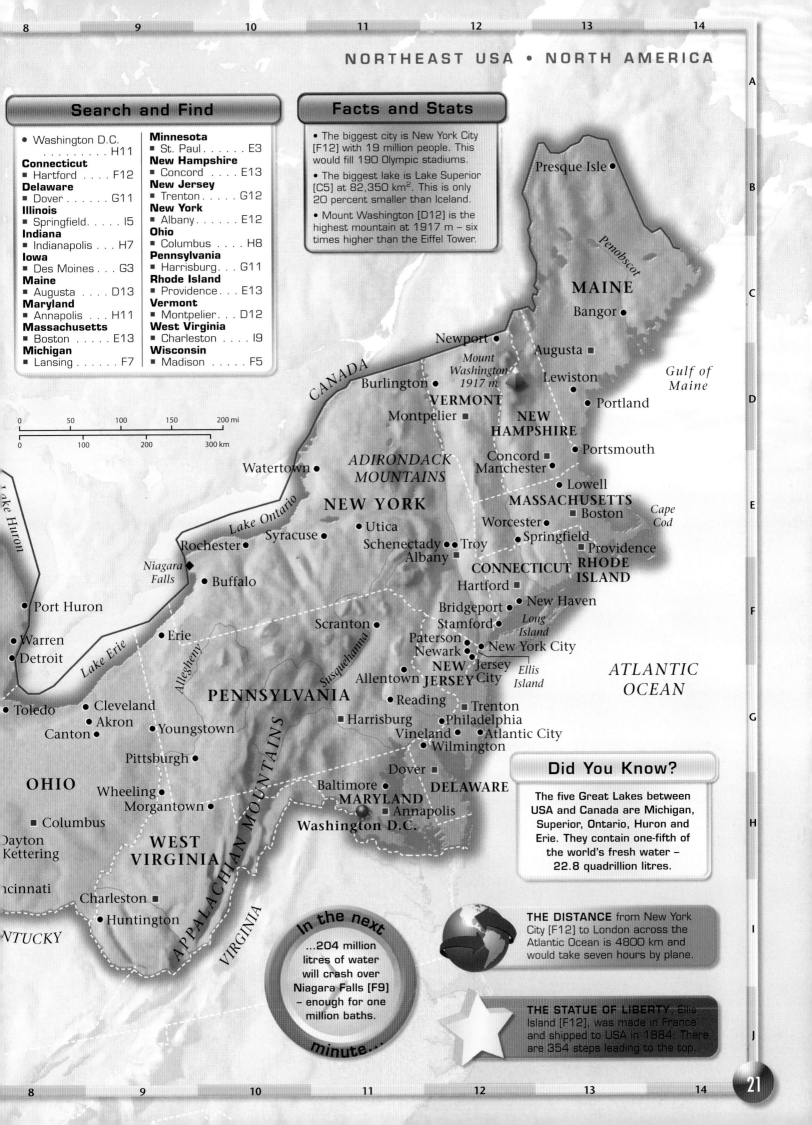

MAINE

Presque Isle •

Penobscot

Bangor •

Gulf of Maine

Newport •

CANADA

Mount Washington 1917 m

Augusta ■

Lewiston •

Burlington •

VERMONT

NEW HAMPSHIRE

Portland •

Montpelier ■

Concord ■

Portsmouth •

Manchester •

Watertown •

ADIRONDACK MOUNTAINS

Lowell •

NEW YORK

MASSACHUSETTS

Worcester •

Boston ■

Cape Cod

Lake Ontario

Syracuse •

Utica •

Schenectady • Troy •

Springfield •

Providence •

Rochester •

Albany ■

RHODE ISLAND

Niagara Falls ◆

Buffalo •

CONNECTICUT

Hartford ■

Port Huron •

New Haven •

Lake Huron

Bridgeport •

Stamford •

Long Island

Scranton •

Erie •

Warren •

Detroit •

Lake Erie

Allegheny

Susquehanna

Paterson •

Newark •

New York City

Jersey City

Ellis Island

ATLANTIC OCEAN

Toledo •

Cleveland •

Akron •

Youngstown •

NEW JERSEY

Allentown •

Canton •

PENNSYLVANIA

Reading •

Trenton •

Pittsburgh •

Harrisburg ■

Philadelphia •

Vineland •

Atlantic City •

Wilmington •

OHIO

Wheeling •

Dover ■

Morgantown •

Baltimore •

DELAWARE

Columbus ■

MARYLAND

Annapolis ■

Dayton •

Washington D.C.

Kettering •

WEST VIRGINIA

APPALACHIAN MOUNTAINS

cinnati •

Charleston ■

Huntington •

NTUCKY

VIRGINIA

Did You Know?

The five Great Lakes between USA and Canada are Michigan, Superior, Ontario, Huron and Erie. They contain one-fifth of the world's fresh water – 22.8 quadrillion litres.

THE DISTANCE from New York City [F12] to London across the Atlantic Ocean is 4800 km and would take seven hours by plane.

In the next
...204 million litres of water will crash over Niagara Falls [F9] – enough for one million baths.
minute...

THE STATUE OF LIBERTY, Ellis Island [F12], was made in France and shipped to USA in 1884. There are 354 steps leading to the top.

Southeast USA

The warm climate of Florida and the Gulf of Mexico coastal areas makes southeast USA popular with tourists. There is Disney World in Florida for fun, Cape Canaveral for space rocket launches, Miami for beaches, New Orleans for jazz, Nashville for country music and the Mississippi river for boat trips. Farming is the main occupation – mainly of tobacco, oranges, rice, peanuts, vegetables and cotton. There are many oil and gas rigs in the Gulf of Mexico to generate energy resources.

GRACELAND, Nashville [C8], is the home of Elvis Presley (1935–1977) and is visited by more than 600,000 fans a year.

THE DISTANCE from the source to the mouth of the Mississippi–Missouri river is 6020 km and would take 20 days floating on a raft.

Extreme Weather

Hurricane Katrina, the largest hurricane ever recorded in the USA, caused 80 percent of New Orleans [H6] to flood. More than one million people were evacuated and 1833 died.

The **Kentucky Derby** takes place in Louisville [B8] on the first Saturday of May. The race is 2 km in length and more than 150,000 spectators attend the two-week-long festival every year.

World Record

The largest space rocket launch site in the world is at Cape Canaveral [H11].

Map labels:

IOWA
ILLINOIS
St. Joseph
Independence
Kansas City
Columbia
Jefferson City
St. Louis
Owensboro
KANSAS
MISSOURI
Cape Girardeau
Paducah
Springfield
Clarksville
OZARK PLATEAU
OKLAHOMA
ARKANSAS
Memphis
Fort Smith
Little Rock
Mississippi
Yazoo
Hot Springs
Pine Bluff
Ouachita
Greenville
Tuscaloc
Texarkana
El Dorado
MISSISSIPPI
TEXAS
Monroe
Meridian
Shreveport
Jackson
Pearl
LOUISIANA
Natchez
Hattiesburg
Red
Alexandria
Prichard
Mobi
Biloxi
Baton Rouge
Lafayette
Metairie
New Orleans
Lake Charles
Marsh Island
Mississippi Delta

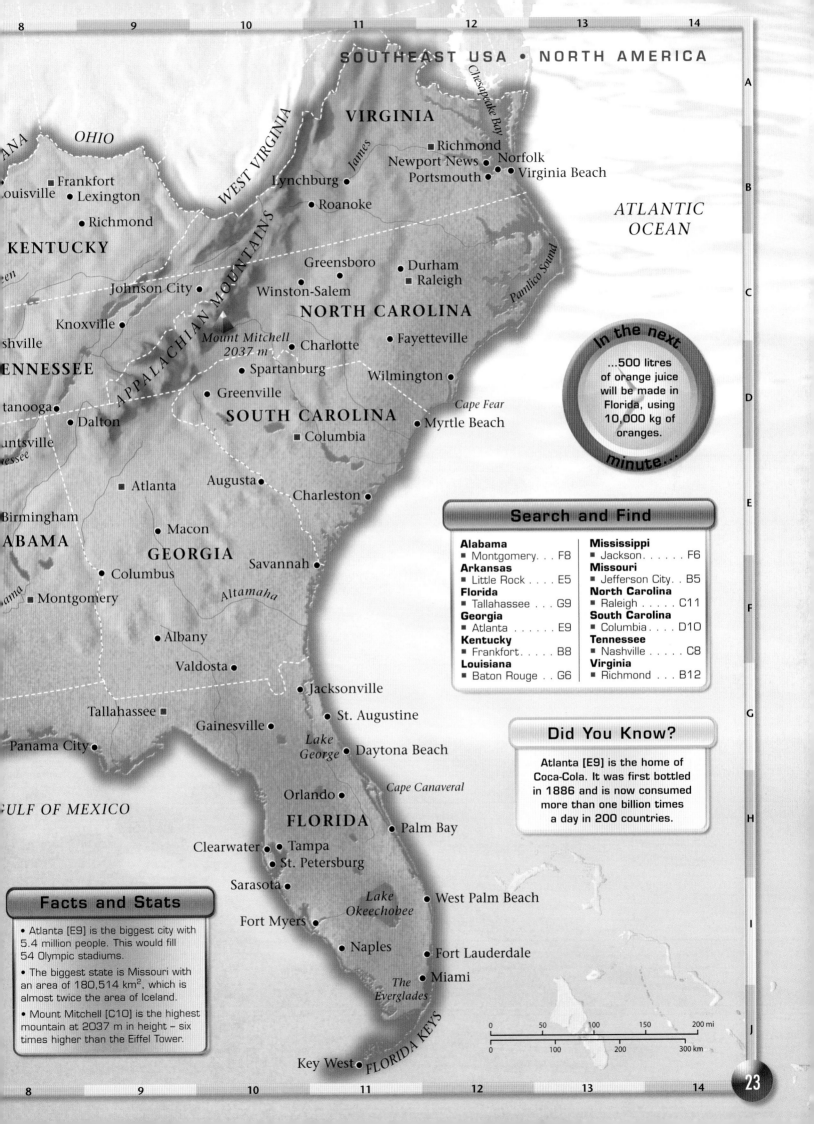

8 **9** **10** **11** **12** **13** **14**

A

VIRGINIA

Chesapeake Bay

OHIO

■ Frankfort
Louisville ● Lexington
● Richmond

■ Richmond
Newport News ● Norfolk
Portsmouth ● ● Virginia Beach

KENTUCKY

WEST VIRGINIA

Lynchburg ●

James

B

*ATLANTIC
OCEAN*

● Roanoke

Johnson City ●

Greensboro ● ● Durham
Winston-Salem ■ Raleigh

Pamlico Sound

C

Knoxville ●
shville

NORTH CAROLINA

*Mount Mitchell
2037 m* ● Charlotte   ● Fayetteville

ENNESSEE

APPALACHIAN MOUNTAINS

● Spartanburg
Wilmington ●

D

tanooga ●
● Dalton

● Greenville

Cape Fear

untsville

SOUTH CAROLINA

● Myrtle Beach

essee

In the next

...500 litres
of orange juice
will be made in
Florida, using
10,000 kg of
oranges.

minute...

■ Atlanta   Augusta ●
● Columbia

E

Birmingham

■ Columbia

Search and Find

ABAMA

● Macon

Alabama
■ Montgomery. . . F8
Arkansas
■ Little Rock E5
Florida
■ Tallahassee . . . G9
Georgia
■ Atlanta E9
Kentucky
■ Frankfort. B8
Louisiana
■ Baton Rouge . . G6

Mississippi
■ Jackson. F6
Missouri
■ Jefferson City . . B5
North Carolina
■ Raleigh C11
South Carolina
■ Columbia D10
Tennessee
■ Nashville C8
Virginia
■ Richmond . . . B12

GEORGIA

Savannah ●

ama

● Columbus

Altamaha

F

■ Montgomery

● Albany

Did You Know?

Atlanta [E9] is the home of
Coca-Cola. It was first bottled
in 1886 and is now consumed
more than one billion times
a day in 200 countries.

Valdosta ●

● Jacksonville

G

Tallahassee ■

● St. Augustine

Gainesville ●

*Lake
George* ● Daytona Beach

Panama City ●

GULF OF MEXICO

● Orlando

Cape Canaveral

H

FLORIDA

● Palm Bay

Clearwater ● ● Tampa
● St. Petersburg

Sarasota ●

*Lake
Okeechobee* ● West Palm Beach

I

Facts and Stats

• Atlanta [E9] is the biggest city with
5.4 million people. This would fill
54 Olympic stadiums.

• The biggest state is Missouri with
an area of 180,514 km², which is
almost twice the area of Iceland.

• Mount Mitchell [C10] is the highest
mountain at 2037 m in height – six
times higher than the Eiffel Tower.

Fort Myers ●

● Naples

● Fort Lauderdale

● Miami

*The
Everglades*

0   50   100   150   200 mi
0   100   200   300 km

J

Key West ● *FLORIDA KEYS*

8 **9** **10** **11** **12** **13** **14**

Northwest USA and Alaska

Inland areas in northwest USA are either stunning mountain scenery or vast ranches. Washington's Seattle is the only large urban area, with the Boeing aircraft factory, and the headquarters of Microsoft, UPS, Starbucks and Amazon. The USA's biggest apple-growing region stretches from the Pacific Ocean to the Great Plains of the Dakotas. Alaska is the USA's largest state. However, vast areas are uninhabited due to long, severe winters. Alaska is one of the leading oil-producing regions in the world.

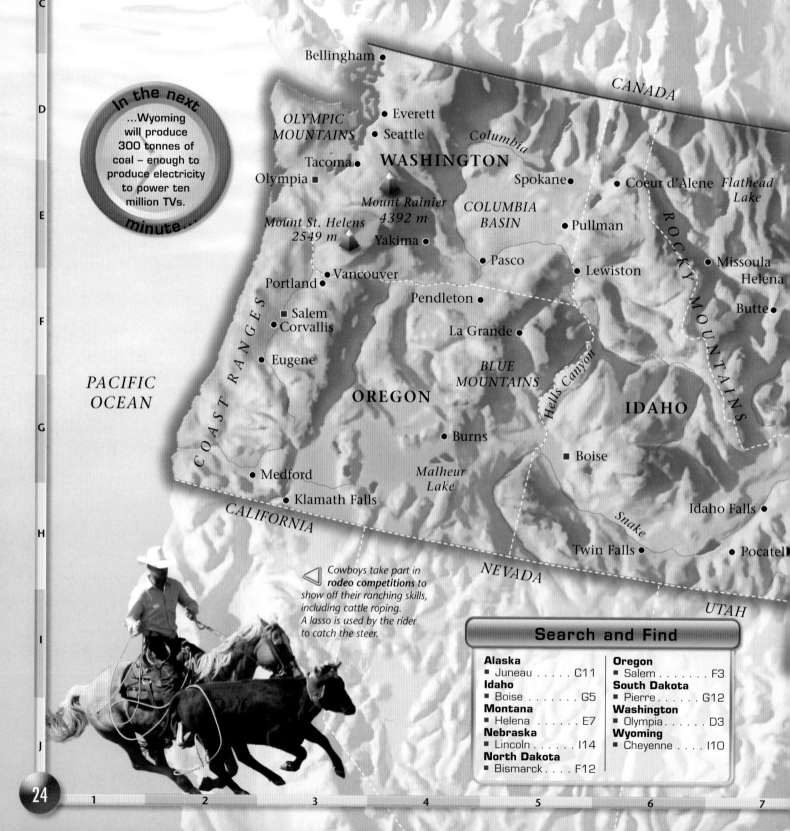

In the next
...Wyoming will produce 300 tonnes of coal – enough to produce electricity to power ten million TVs.
minute...

Bellingham

CANADA

OLYMPIC MOUNTAINS

Everett
Seattle

Columbia

Tacoma

WASHINGTON

Olympia

Spokane

Coeur d'Alene   Flathead Lake

Mount Rainier 4392 m

COLUMBIA BASIN

Pullman

Mount St. Helens 2549 m

Yakima

Pasco

Lewiston

Missoula
Helena

Vancouver

Portland

Pendleton

ROCKY MOUNTAINS

Butte

Salem
Corvallis

La Grande

COAST RANGES

Eugene

BLUE MOUNTAINS

Hells Canyon

IDAHO

PACIFIC OCEAN

OREGON

Burns

Boise

Medford

Malheur Lake

Idaho Falls

Klamath Falls

Snake

CALIFORNIA

Twin Falls

Pocatell

NEVADA

UTAH

Cowboys take part in **rodeo competitions** to show off their ranching skills, including cattle roping. A lasso is used by the rider to catch the steer.

Search and Find

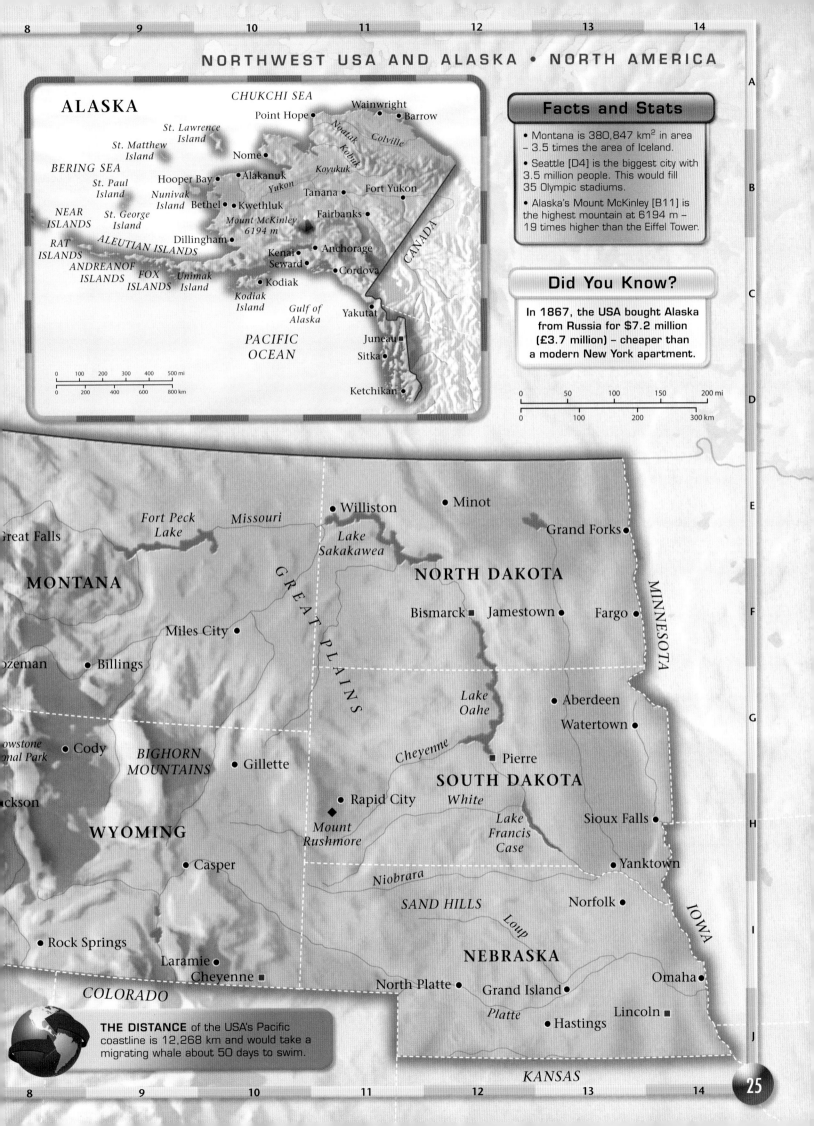

ALASKA

CHUKCHI SEA

Wainwright
Point Hope
• Barrow

St. Lawrence
Island
St. Matthew
Island
Nome
Noatak
Colville

BERING SEA
Kobuk

St. Paul
Island
Hooper Bay
• Alakanuk
Koyukuk
Fort Yukon

Nunivak
Island
Yukon
Tanana

NEAR
ISLANDS
St. George
Island
Bethel
• Kwethluk
Fairbanks

RAT
ISLANDS
Mount McKinley
6194 m

ANDREANOF
ISLANDS
ALEUTIAN ISLANDS
Dillingham
• Anchorage

FOX
ISLANDS
Unimak
Island
Kenai
Seward
• Cordova

Kodiak
Island
• Kodiak

Gulf of
Alaska
Yakutat

PACIFIC
OCEAN
Juneau
Sitka

Ketchikan

CANADA

0 100 200 300 400 500 mi
0 200 400 600 800 km

Facts and Stats

• Montana is 380,847 km² in area – 3.5 times the area of Iceland.

• Seattle [D4] is the biggest city with 3.5 million people. This would fill 35 Olympic stadiums.

• Alaska's Mount McKinley [B11] is the highest mountain at 6194 m – 19 times higher than the Eiffel Tower.

Did You Know?

In 1867, the USA bought Alaska from Russia for $7.2 million (£3.7 million) – cheaper than a modern New York apartment.

0 50 100 150 200 mi
0 100 200 300 km

Great Falls

Fort Peck
Lake
Missouri
• Williston
• Minot

Grand Forks •

Lake
Sakakawea

MONTANA

NORTH DAKOTA

Miles City •

Bismarck ■ Jamestown •
Fargo •

MINNESOTA

ozeman
• Billings

GREAT PLAINS

Lake
Oahe
• Aberdeen

Watertown •

owstone
nal Park
• Cody

BIGHORN
MOUNTAINS
• Gillette

Cheyenne
■ Pierre

ckson

SOUTH DAKOTA

• Rapid City
White

Sioux Falls •

WYOMING

♦
Mount
Rushmore

Lake
Francis
Case

• Casper

Niobrara
Yanktown •

SAND HILLS
Norfolk •

IOWA

• Rock Springs

Loup

Laramie •
Cheyenne ■

NEBRASKA

COLORADO

North Platte •
Grand Island •
Omaha •

Lincoln ■

Platte
• Hastings

THE DISTANCE of the USA's Pacific coastline is 12,268 km and would take a migrating whale about 50 days to swim.

KANSAS

Southwest USA and Hawaii

PACIFIC
OCEAN

The nation's most dramatic landscape belongs to southwest USA, which is covered by the Rocky Mountains. Southern California, Nevada and Arizona are desert – the driest place being Death Valley. Texas is the home of the oil industry, and Nevada's Las Vegas attracts tourists visiting casinos and nearby scenery, such as the Grand Canyon. California has boomed due to the Hollywood film studios, Silicon Valley's large number of computer firms, and some of the most productive farmland in the country. Tropical Hawaii is a popular surfing and beach island 4800 km southwest of California.

Search and Find

Arizona
- Phoenix F7

California
- Sacramento . . . C4

Colorado
- Denver C10

Hawaii
- Honolulu H3

Kansas
- Topeka D13

Nevada
- Carson City . . . C5

New Mexico
- Santa Fe F10

Oklahoma
- Oklahoma City . F13

Texas
- Austin H13

Utah
- Salt Lake City . . C8

OREGON

Mount Shasta
4322 m

Eureka

Redding

IDAH

Winnemucca

Humboldt

Elko

Gr
Salt

COAST RANGES

Reno

Carson City

NEVADA

Santa Rosa

Sacramento

Oakland

Stockton

San Francisco

Palo Alto

Modesto

Yosemite
National
Park

SIERRA NEVADA

Tonopah

GREAT
BASIN

Sunnyvale

San Jose

Salinas

Monterey

Fresno

Mount Whitney
4418 m

Cedar City

DEATH VALLEY

San Luis
Obispo

Bakersfield

Las
Vegas

CALIFORNIA

Hoover
Dam

Grand Can

Santa Barbara

ARIZON

Oxnard

Pasadena

San Bernardino

Los Angeles

Riverside

Prescor

Long Beach

Anaheim

Oceanside

Phoenix

San Diego

Gila

M

Yuma

Did You Know?

If California were its own country, it would have the eighth largest economy in the world.

Mount
Kawaikini
1598 m

Kauai

Kapaa

KAUAI CHANNEL

Oahu

Niihau

Waialua

Kaneohe

Wahiawa

Honolulu

Kalaupapa

Maui

Molokai

Lanai City

Wailuku

Lanai

Kahoolawe

PACIFIC
OCEAN

ALENUIHAHA CHANNEL

Mauna Kea
4205 m

Hilo

0	50	100	150 mi
0	100	200 km	

HAWAII

Mauna Loa
4169 m

Facts and Stats

- Texas is 691,027 km² in area – 6.5 times the area of Iceland.
- Los Angeles [F5] is the biggest city with 12.9 million people. This would fill 129 Olympic stadiums.
- Mount Whitney [D5] is the highest mountain at 4418 m in height – 14 times higher than the Eiffel Tower.

▷ The Colorado river has carved a gorge over millions of years to form the **Grand Canyon** [E7]. It is up to 446 km in length and 1.6 km in depth.

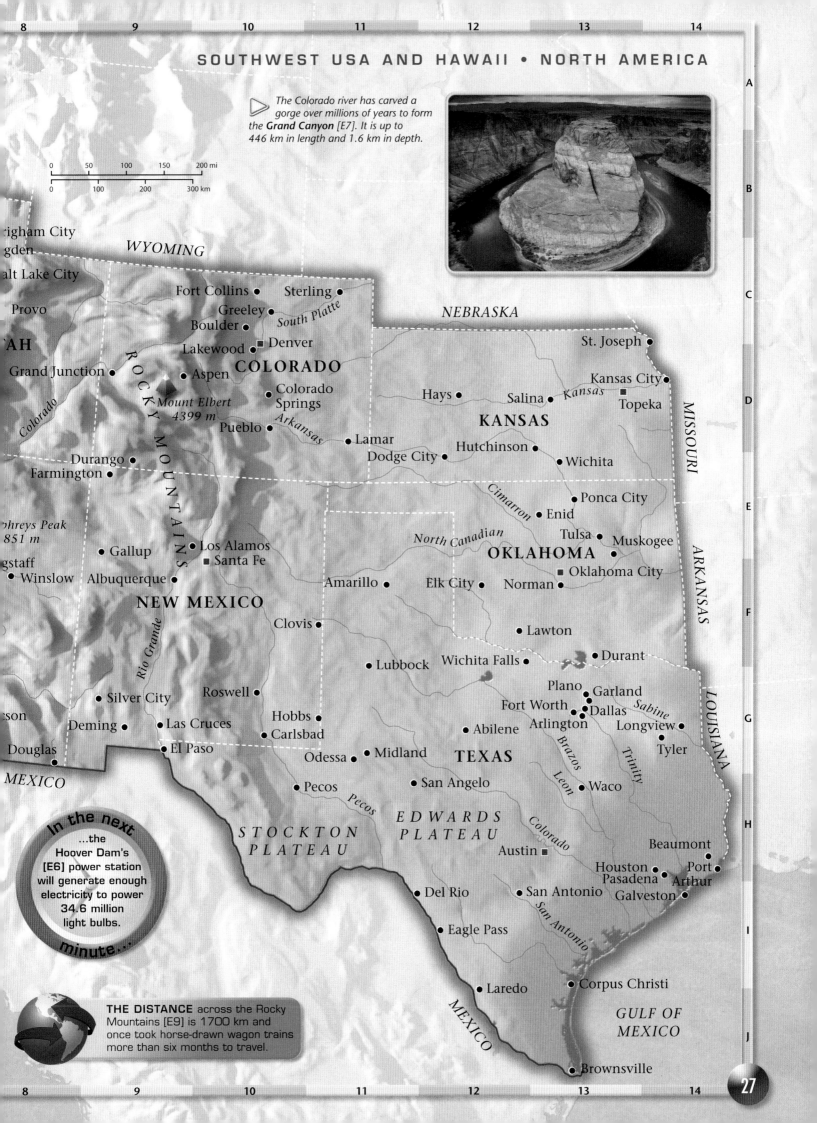

0   50   100   150   200 mi

0   100   200   300 km

WYOMING

righam City
gden
alt Lake City
Provo

Fort Collins • Sterling •
Greeley •
Boulder •
Lakewood ▪ Denver
COLORADO
Grand Junction •
• Aspen
Mount Elbert
4399 m
Pueblo •

NEBRASKA

St. Joseph •
Kansas City •
Colorado Springs
Hays • Salina • *Kansas* ▪ Topeka
KANSAS
Hutchinson •
Dodge City • • Wichita
Lamar •
Arkansas

'AH

Durango •
Farmington •

Cimarron
• Ponca City
• Enid
Tulsa • • Muskogee

hreys Peak
851 m
gstaff
• Winslow
• Gallup
Albuquerque •
NEW MEXICO

• Los Alamos
▪ Santa Fe

North Canadian
OKLAHOMA
▪ Oklahoma City
Amarillo • Elk City • Norman •

son

Clovis •

Rio Grande

Lawton •

Silver City •
Roswell •
Deming •
Las Cruces •
Hobbs •
• Carlsbad
Douglas •
El Paso •

Lubbock • Wichita Falls • Durant •

Plano •
Fort Worth • Garland •
Arlington • Dallas *Sabine*
Longview •
Abilene • Tyler •

MEXICO

• Pecos
Odessa • Midland •
San Angelo •
TEXAS
Leon Waco •
Brazos *Trinity*

Pecos

STOCKTON PLATEAU

EDWARDS PLATEAU
Colorado

In the next minute...
...the Hoover Dam's [E6] power station will generate enough electricity to power 34.6 million light bulbs.

Austin ▪
Beaumont •
Houston • Port
Pasadena • Arthur
Del Rio • San Antonio • Galveston •

Eagle Pass •

San Antonio

THE DISTANCE across the Rocky Mountains [E9] is 1700 km and once took horse-drawn wagon trains more than six months to travel.

Laredo • Corpus Christi •

MEXICO

GULF OF MEXICO

Brownsville •

ROCKY MOUNTAINS

South Platte

Colorado

MISSOURI

ARKANSAS

LOUISIANA

8   9   10   11   12   13   14

A
B
C
D
E
F
G
H
I
J

Canada

Canada is the second largest country in the world. The Rocky Mountains of western Canada reach more than 3600 m above sea level and create stunning scenery. Tourists sail along the coast to see icebergs and to view migrating whales. The largest Canadian cities are Toronto and Montreal in the east, and Vancouver in the west. Quebec differs from the rest of Canada because of the large French-speaking population that lives there. Canada has a wealth of natural resources, including wood and petroleum, and is one of the top ten richest nations.

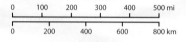

0	100	200	300	400	500 mi
0	200	400	600	800 km	

Did You Know?

Canada has 10 percent of the world's forests. These are inhabited by a wide range of wildlife, including bears and moose.

Facts and Stats

• Canada is the second largest country in the world with an area of 9,970,610 km² – 97 times the area of Iceland.

• Toronto [J11] is the biggest city with a population of 5.6 million – this would fill 56 Olympic stadiums.

Deep in the Canadian Rockies is **Banff National Park** in Alberta, which was founded in 1885, and is Canada's oldest national park. Peyto Lake is a popular attraction as the water turns turquoise in colour as the surrounding glaciers melt.

ARCTIC OCEAN

BEAUFORT SEA

Ba
Isl

ALASKA (US)

• Inuvik

Mackenzie

Kugluktu

• Dawson

Norman
Wells•

MACKENZIE MOUNTAINS

YUKON
TERRITORY

NORTHWES
TERRITORIE

Mount Logan
5959 m

• Whitehorse

Yellowknife•

Gulf of
Alaska

ROCKY

Fort Resolution •

Fort Smit

PACIFIC
OCEAN

COAST

BRITISH
COLUMBIA

Peace

CA

QUEEN CHARLOTTE
ISLANDS

• Hazelton
• Prince Rupert

MOUNTAINS

• Peace Riv

• Grande Prairie

Prince
George

ALBERTA

• Edmc

MOUNTAINS

Vancouver
Island

Fraser

• Red I

Vancouver•
Victoria ■

• Kamloops

Medicine Hat •

• Calgary

Lethbridge•

UNITED STA

8   9   10   11   12   13   14

Aurora Borealis can be seen in the Northern Hemisphere. Also known as the Northern Lights, the bands of shimmering light are caused by atmospheric particles crashing into the Earth's atmosphere.

Search and Find

Alberta
- Edmonton H7

British Columbia
- Victoria I5

Canada
- Ottawa I12

Manitoba
- Winnipeg I9

New Brunswick
- Fredericton . . . I13

Newfoundland and Labrador
- St. John's . . . H14

Northwest Territories
- Yellowknife F7

Nova Scotia
- Halifax I13

Nunavut
- Iqaluit F11

Ontario
- Toronto J11

Prince Edward Island
- Charlottetown . I13

Quebec
- Quebec I12

Saskatchewan
- Regina I8

Yukon Territory
- Whitehorse . . . F5

In the next minute... ...Canadians will consume 25 litres of maple syrup – a natural sugar from the sugar maple tree.

THE DISTANCE from St. John's [H14] to Vancouver [I6] is further than St. John's to Prague, Europe.

GREENLAND (DENMARK)

Axel Heiberg Island

Ellesmere Island

Bathurst Island

Devon Island

Baffin Bay

Prince of Wales Island

Baffin Island

toria and

Iqalukyuuttiaq

NUNAVUT

Southampton Island

Salliit

Iqaluit

LABRADOR SEA

Kangiqtiniq (Rankin Inlet)

Coats Island

Mansel Island

Ungava Peninsula

Hudson Strait

Churchill

HUDSON BAY

Churchill

Nelson

Feuilles

Nain

LABRADOR

Goose Bay

NEWFOUNDLAND AND LABRADOR

Gander

St. John's

Newfoundland

D A

Flin Flon

MANITOBA

Prince Albert

Severn

ONTARIO

Fort Albany

Albany

La Grande Rivière

James Bay

QUEBEC

Anticosti Island

ST. PIERRE AND MIQUELON (FRANCE)

askatoon

Regina

ose

Brandon

Winnipeg

Thunder Bay

AMERICA

Chicoutimi

Gaspé

PRINCE EDWARD ISLAND

Charlottetown

NEW BRUNSWICK

Fredericton

Quebec

Trois-Rivières

St. John

Halifax

Sherbrooke

Montreal

Bay of Fundy

NOVA SCOTIA

Sudbury

Ottawa

Georgian Bay

ATLANTIC OCEAN

Toronto

Oshawa

Kitchener

Hamilton

London

Windsor

Mexico

Mexico lies between the USA and Guatemala, and has two high coastal mountain ranges, between which is a high plateau called the **Altiplano.** Much of the land is mountain or desert, making rural areas very poor as less than one-fifth is suitable for farming. As a result, many people move to Mexico City or the USA for work – more than 20 million people now live in the Mexico City area. Tourists visit both the tropical beaches and the ancient sites of the Aztec and Mayan cultures.

In the next... minute...
...Mexico's farmers will use 10 million litres of water on the land – enough for 2.5 million baths.

World Record
At 430 m above the ground, the Baluarte Bridge in northern Mexico is the world's highest suspension bridge.

TEOTIHUACÁN [H9] was Mexico's biggest Aztec city. Ruins include the Pyramid of the Sun in the Avenue of the Dead.

Tijuana

Mexicali

Ensenada

UNITED STATES OF AMERICA

Ciudad Juárez

Río Gra

Guadalupe Island

Cedros Island

Gulf of California

Hermosillo

Chihuahua

Guaymas

Ciudad Obregón

Los Mochis

Culiacán

La Paz

Duran

Mazatlán

MARÍAS ISLANDS

Socorro Island

PACIFIC OCEAN

The Mayan civilization lasted 2000 years and many magnificent buildings were constructed. **Palenque** [H12] is a site of ancient Mayan ruins, including the Palenque Palace.

The stories of the ancient Mexican cultures are retold through ornately dressed **folk dancers**. The costumes and performances represent ancient Mayan dances for the gods.

Facts and Stats

• Mexico City [H9] has a population of 20.1 million people – this would fill 201 Olympic stadiums.

• The Rio Grande [C7] is 3060 km in length – less than half the length of the Nile river.

• The highest mountain is Volcan Pico de Orizaba [H10] at 5700 m in height. It is 18 times higher than the Eiffel Tower.

THE DISTANCE from east to west across Mexico City [H9] is only 30 km, but it takes more than three hours by car at peak times.

The Xochimilco area of Mexico City [H9] has many **ancient canals**. During festivals, boats are covered with flowers to attract tourists.

UNITED STATES OF AMERICA

Nuevo Laredo

mez Palacio   Monclova
            Reynosa
erreón Monterrey   Matamoros
    Saltillo

MEXICO

Ciudad Victoria

GULF OF
MEXICO

Ciudad Madero
San Luis Potosí Tampico
Aguascalientes

León   Cancún
Querétaro   Mérida
Guadalajara   Chichén
        Pachuca   Itzá
Teotihuacán   Bay of Campeche   Yucatán
        Ecatepec Volcan Pico   Peninsula
Morelia   de Orizaba
Toluca   5700 m   Chetumal
Colima **Mexico City**   Veracruz
    Cuernavaca Puebla Orizaba
                      Villahermosa
        Coatzacoalcos
Chilpancingo   Palenque
        Oaxaca
Acapulco   Tuxtla Gutiérrez

Cozumel
Island

GUATEMALA   BELIZE

Gulf of
Tehuantepec

0   100   200   300 mi
0   200   400 km

South and Central America

BAHAMAS

CUBA

DOMINICAN REPUBLIC

BELIZE

GUATEMALA

HONDURAS

EL SALVADOR

NICARAGUA

COSTA RICA

PANAMA

VENEZUELA

GUYANA

SURINAME

COLOMBIA

ECUADOR

PERU

BRAZIL

BOLIVIA

PACIFIC OCEAN

CHILE

PARAGUAY

URUGUAY

ATLANTIC OCEAN

ARGENTINA

2 1 3 4 5 6 7 9 8 10

KEY
1 HAITI
2 JAMAICA
3 ST. KITTS AND NEVIS
4 ANTIGUA AND BARBUDA
5 DOMINICA
6 ST. LUCIA
7 ST. VINCENT AND THE GRENADINES
8 GRENADA
9 BARBADOS
10 TRINIDAD AND TOBAGO

COUNTRY FACTFILE

Country	Life expectancy	Population in thousands	Population growth %	Population as urban %	Literacy %	Area km²	Population density per km²	Capital city	Currency	Languages
Antigua and Barbuda	76	86	1.3	59	86	442	194.6	St. John's	East Caribbean Dollar	English, Creole
Argentina	77	40,117	1	92	97	2,766,890	14.5	Buenos Aires	Argentine Peso	Spanish
Bahamas	71	354	0.9	87	96	13,939	25.3	Nassau	Bahamian Dollar	English, Creole
Barbados	75	274	0.4	52	99	430	637.2	Bridgetown	Barbadian Dollar	English, Bajan (Creole)
Belize	68	333	2.1	52	77	22,965	14.5	Belmopan	Belizean Dollar	English, Creole, Spanish
Bolivia	68	10,426	1.7	67	87	1,098,581	9.5	La Paz, Sucre	Boliviano	Spanish, Quechua, Aymara
Brazil	73	185,713	1.1	87	89	8,547,404	21.7	Brasília	Real	Portuguese
Chile	78	17,094	0.8	89	96	756,626	22.6	Santiago, Valparaiso	Chilean Peso	Spanish
Colombia	75	46,045	1.2	75	90	1,414,568	40.3	Bogotá	Colombian Peso	Spanish
Costa Rica	78	4302	1.3	65	95	51,100	84.2	San José	Costa Rican Colon	Spanish
Cuba	78	11,241	0.0	74	99	110,861	101.4	Havana	Cuban Peso	Spanish
Dominica	76	71	0.0	71	94	739	96.1	Roseau	East Caribbean Dollar	English, French Creole
Dominican Republic	77	9379	1.3	69	87	48,443	193.6	Santo Domingo	Domincan Peso	Spanish
Ecuador	76	14,483	1.4	67	91	269,178	53.8	Quito	US Dollar	Spanish, Quechua
El Salvador	74	6183	0.3	64	81	21,041	293.9	San Salvador	US Dollar	Spanish
Grenada	73	103	0.6	39	96	344	299.4	St. George's	East Caribbean Dollar	English, French Creole
Guatemala	71	14,362	2	49	69.1	108,889	131.9	Guatemala City	Quetzal	Spanish
Guyana	67	754	0.0	36	92	215,083	3.5	Georgetown	Guyanese Dollar	English, Creole
Haiti	63	9923	0.8	52	53	27,750	357.6	Port-au-Prince	Gourde	French, Creole
Honduras	71	8046	1.9	52	80	112,088	71.8	Tegucigalpa	Lempira	Spanish
Jamaica	73	2706	0.7	53	88	10,991	246.2	Kingston	Jamaican Dollar	English, Creole
Nicaragua	72	5742	1.1	57	68	130,670	43.9	Managua	Gold Cordoba	Spanish
Panama	78	3406	1.4	75	92	75,990	44.8	Panama City	Balboa, US Dollar	Spanish, English
Paraguay	76	6230	1.3	61	94	406,752	15.3	Asunción	Guarani	Spanish, Guarani
Peru	73	30,136	1	77	93	1,285,216	23.4	Lima	Nuevo Sol	Spanish, Quechua
St. Kitts and Nevis	75	52	0.8	43	97	269	193.3	Basseterre	East Caribbean Dollar	English, Creole
St. Lucia	77	166	0.4	48	90	617	269	Castries	East Caribbean Dollar	English, French Creole
St. Vincent and the Grenadines	74	109	0.0	55	96	398	280.2	Kingstown	East Caribbean Dollar	English, Creole
Suriname	71	525	1.1	75	90	163,270	3.2	Paramaribo	Suriname Dollar	Dutch, Sranantonga, Hindi
Trinidad and Tobago	72	1318	0.0	72	99	5128	257	Port-of-Spain	Trinidad and Tobago Dollar	English, Creole
Uruguay	76	3252	0.2	92	98	176,215	18.5	Montevideo	Uruguayan Peso	Spanish
Venezuela	74	27,150	1.5	93	93	912,050	29.8	Caracas	Bolivar	Spanish

Central America and the Caribbean

Central America is a narrow area of land where the mountain chain continues from Antarctica up to Alaska. The only gap, which joins the Atlantic and Pacific Oceans, is the Panama Canal. The manmade canal shortens the journey between the oceans by 13,000 km. The Caribbean islands are mainly agricultural, but their sandy beaches, warm seas and links to the USA and Europe make them popular tourist destinations. Venezuela is one of the world's leading oil producers and is much wealthier than Colombia and Guyana.

In many places in Central America, **weaving** is still done by hand rather than by machine. Colourful rugs and tapestries from the region are sold around the world.

Map labels:
MEXICO
Quezaltenango
GUATEMALA
Guatemala City
Escuintla
San Salvador
EL SALVADOR
Chinandega
León
MAYA MOUNTAINS
BELIZE
Belize City
Belmopan
San Antonio
San Pedro Sula
El Progreso
La Ceiba
HONDURAS
Tegucigalpa
Estelí
NICARAGUA
Managua
COSTA RICA
Puntarenas
San José
Limón
Cerro Chirripó Grande 3819 m
David
CORDILLERA CENTRAL
PANAMA
Panama Canal
Colón
San Miguelito
Panama City
Gulf of Panama
Gulf of Darien
Barranquilla
Cartagena
Sincelejo
Montería
Medellín
Quibdó
Manizales
Pereira
Armenia
Buenaventura
Ibagué
Cali
Popayán
Pasto
ECUADOR
CORDILLERA

Havana
Pinar del Río
Nueva Gerona
Guanabacoa
Cárdenas
Santa Clara
Cienfuegos
Sancti Spíritus
Camagüey
CUBA
Isla de la Juventud
CAYMAN ISLANDS (UK)
Montego Bay
JAMAICA
Spanish Town

Search and Find

Scale:
0 100 200 300 400 mi
0 200 400 600 km

Facts and Stats

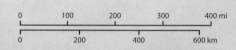

• Colombia has a population of 46 million people – this would fill 460 Olympic stadiums.

• The life expectancy of people in Haiti is only 63 years, compared to 78 years in Cuba and a world average of 68 years.

• The average income per person in Haiti is £430 and £15,060 in the Bahamas, compared to a world average of £5640.

ssau

BAHAMAS

TURKS AND
CAICOS ISLANDS
(UK)

There are two lakes
in the craters of the
Poas volcano, Costa Rica.
Due to geothermal activity,
it is believed that the lakes
are turning into geysers.
Since 1828, the volcano
has erupted 39 times.

olguín
amo
Guantánamo
go Cap-Haïtien
ba Gónaïves
rt-au-Prince
ton
Les Cayes Jacmel
HAITI

DOMINICAN
REPUBLIC

Santiago San Francisco
La Vega   de Macorís
         La Romana
Santo
Domingo

VIRGIN
ISLANDS
(UK)

VIRGIN
ISLANDS
(US)

ANGUILLA (UK)

ST. MARTIN (FRANCE)/SINT MAARTEN (NETH.)

ST. BARTHELÉMY (FRANCE)

ST. EUSTATIUS (NETH.)

PUERTO
RICO (US)

SABA
(NETH.)

Basseterre
ST. KITTS AND NEVIS
MONTSERRAT (UK)

ANTIGUA AND
BARBUDA

St. John's

GUADELOUPE
(FRANCE)

DOMINICA
Roseau

MARTINIQUE (FRANCE)

ST. LUCIA Castries

ST. VINCENT AND
THE GRENADINES Kingstown

GRENADA
St. George's

BARBADOS
Bridgetown

C A R I B B E A N   S E A

ARUBA
(NETHERLANDS)

CURAÇAO
(NETHERLANDS)

BONAIRE
(NETHERLANDS)

Port-of-Spain

TRINIDAD
AND TOBAGO

Pico Cristobal Colon
5800 m
Maracaibo
Barquisimeto
Valera   Acarigua
        Guanare
        Barinas

Caracas   Cumaná
Valencia   Barcelona

uta
San Cristóbal
Bucaramanga
ancabermeja

Ciudad Bolívar Ciudad Guayana

VENEZUELA

Georgetown

Angel Falls

GUIANA
HIGHLANDS

Paramaribo

FRENCH
GUIANA
(FRANCE)

Tunja
Bogotá

Puerto Ayacucho

GUYANA

SURINAME

Villavicencio

COLOMBIA

BRAZIL

Río Meta

Río Vaupés

Río Apaporis

BRAZIL

Caquetá

RU

BRAZIL

...Venezuela
will extract
enough oil from
the Earth to make
220,000 litres
of petrol.

In the next

minute...

World Record
At more than
979 m in height,
Angel Falls [G11] is
the highest waterfall
in the world.

Did You Know?

The Bermuda Triangle is an area
in the Atlantic Ocean, northeast
of the Caribbean. Many ships
and aircraft have disappeared
here without a trace.

THE DISTANCE from one end
of the Panama Canal [F6] to the
other is only 77 km, but it saves
18 days sailing time.

South America

Stretching from the tropical forests of the Amazon to just a short distance from icy Antarctica, South America is a continent of contrasts. The Andes stretch the length of the continent, but the main feature is the Amazon rainforest. The rainforest is home to more plant and animal species than any other habitat in the world. However, more than 50,000 km² of the rainforest is destroyed each year to make room for farmland. The forest not only provides a home to many animals, but it is also the source of many plant-derived medicines. By absorbing carbon dioxide, the forest helps to reduce global warming.

At 6448 km in length, the **Amazon river** crosses the full width of Brazil. A wide range of wildlife live in the river, including the endangered boto, or Amazon river dolphin.

Search and Find

Argentina	• Valparaíso G6
• Buenos Aires . . G8	**Ecuador**
Bolivia	• Quito B5
• La Paz D7	**Paraguay**
• Sucre E7	• Asunción E8
Brazil	**Peru**
• Brasília D10	• Lima D5
Chile	**Uruguay**
• Santiago G7	• Montevideo . . . G8

In the next ...9000 tonnes of the Amazon rainforest will be destroyed – about 100 trees and other plants. minute...

The statue of Jesus, **Christ the Redeemer**, stands at the top of Mount Corcovado, Rio de Janeiro [E10]. At 38 m in height, it is one of the most famous landmarks in the world.

VENEZU

Esmeraldas
Ibarra
Manta Quito
Portoviejo Ambato
Guayaquil Riobamba
COLOMBIA
Negr
ECUADOR
Iquitos
Amazon
AMAZO
BASIN
Piura
Chiclayo
Pucallpa
Trujillo
Porto Velh
Chimbote
Rio Branc
PERU
Huacho
Lima
Callao Huancayo
BOLIV
Ayacucho Cusco
Ica
Lake
Juliaca Titicaca
Arequipa Puno
Cochab.
La Paz Oruro
Sucr
Arica Nevado Sajama
6520 m
Iquique Potosí
Tarija
Calama San Salv
ATACAMA de Ju
Antofagasta DESERT
CHILE
San Miguel
de Tucumán
PACIFIC OCEAN
AR
La Serena Cór
Coquimbo
San Juan
Godoy Cruz
Vina del Mar Cu
Valparaíso Mendo.
Santiago
Rancagua Cerro
Aconcag.
6959 m
Talcahuano Chillan
Concepción
Los Ángeles
Temuco Neuq
Valdivia
Osorno Como.
Puerto Montt Rivada.
PATAGONIA
Pu
Ma
Río
Gal
Punta Arenas
Ush

GUYANA
SURINAME
FRENCH GUIANA
(FRANCE)

Amapá
Macapá
Marajó Island
Amazon
Belém
São Luis
Parnaíba
Manaus
Santarém
Altamira
Fortaleza
Marabá
Imperatriz
Teresina
Mossoró
Natal
Campina Grande
João Pessoa
Araguaína
Recife
Juazeiro do Norte
BRAZIL
Tocantins
Juazeiro
Maceio
Aracaju
Feira de Santana
Salvador
Chiabá
Taguatinga
Brasília
Itabuna
Anápolis
MATO GROSSO PLATEAU
Goiânia
Campo Grande
Uberlândia
Uberaba
Governador Valadares
Belo Horizonte
Rio Préto
Vitoria
Pedro Juan Caballero
Nova Iguaçu
Niteroi
Campinas
Rio de Janeiro
São Paulo
ARAGUAY
Asunción
Santos
Ciudad del Este
Curitiba
CO
esistencia
Corrientes
Florianópolio
TINA
ATLANTIC OCEAN
Salto
Rivera
Porto Alegre
a Fe
Pelotas
Rio Grande
ario
URUGUAY
Buenos Aires
Montevideo
mas
La Plata
amora
ahía
lanca
Mar del Plata
unta Alta

0	200	400	600	800 mi
0	400	800	1200 km	

FALKLAND ISLANDS
(UK)

Horn

SOUTH GEORGIA
(UK)

Facts and Stats

• Brazil's population is 185.7 million and would fill 1857 Olympic stadiums. In comparison, Uruguay's population is only 3.3 million.

• There are only 9 doctors per 10,000 people in Peru, compared to 37 doctors in Uruguay and a world average of 23 doctors.

• The average income per person in Uruguay is £7560 and £810 in Bolivia, compared to a world average of £5640.

Did You Know?

The Amazon river holds two-thirds of all the flowing water in the world and is 270 km in width where it meets the sea.

Extreme Weather

Chile's Atacama Desert [E7] has an average rainfall of less than 0.5 mm a year. The city of Calama [E7] has never recorded a single drop. It's too dry for animals to survive.

USHUAIA [J7] is the most southern city in the world. It has a ski resort and a base for supply ships to Antarctica.

THE DISTANCE from Chile to the next land mass of Australia is 10,400 km and would take 12 hours by plane.

One of the largest **street carnivals** in the world is held every February in Rio de Janeiro [E10]. People dress in elaborate costumes and parades take place in the city centre. More than 200,000 people take part.

Europe

ARCTIC OCEAN

ICELAND

FINLAND

NORWAY SWEDEN

ESTONIA

LATVIA

DENMARK

1

2

RUSSIAN FEDERATION

UNITED KINGDOM

REPUBLIC OF IRELAND

3

POLAND

BELARUS

GERMANY

4

6

5

11

10

7

UKRAINE

ATLANTIC OCEAN

FRANCE

12

9

8

15

16

ROMANIA

13

14

23

17

18

25

24

19

20 22

21

BULGARIA

GEORGIA

AZERBAIJAN

26

SPAIN

PORTUGAL

ITALY

GREECE

KEY

1 RUSSIAN FEDERATION
2 LITHUANIA
3 NETHERLANDS
4 BELGIUM
5 LUXEMBOURG
6 CZECH REPUBLIC
7 SLOVAKIA
8 MOLDOVA
9 HUNGARY
10 AUSTRIA
11 LIECHTENSTEIN
12 SWITZERLAND
13 ANDORRA

14 MONACO
15 SLOVENIA
16 CROATIA
17 BOSNIA AND HERZEGOVINA
18 SERBIA
19 MONTENEGRO
20 KOSOVO
21 MACEDONIA
22 ALBANIA
23 SAN MARINO
24 VATICAN CITY
25 MALTA
26 ARMENIA

COUNTRY FACTFILE

Country	Life expectancy	Population in thousands	Population growth %	Population as urban %	Literacy %	Area km²	Population density per km²	Capital city	Currency	Languages
Albania	78	2832	−0.3	52	99	28,748	98.5	Tiranë	Lek	Albanian
Andorra	83	78	0.3	95	100	468	166.7	Andorra la Vella	Euro	Catalan, Spanish
Armenia	73	3262	0.0	70	99	29,743	109.7	Yerevan	Dram	Armenian
Austria	80	8404	0.03	68	98	83,858	100.2	Vienna	Euro	German
Azerbaijan*	71	9111	0.8	57	99	86,600	105.2	Baku	Manat	Azeri
Belarus	71	9481	−0.4	75	99	207,546	45.7	Minsk	Belarusian Rouble	Belarusian, Russian
Belgium	80	10,951	0.07	97	99	30,528	358.7	Brussels	Euro	Dutch, French
Bosnia and Herzegovina	79	3840	0.0	49	97	51,129	75.1	Sarajevo	Marka	Croat, Serb
Bulgaria	74	7365	−0.8	71	98	110,993	66.4	Sofia	Lev	Bulgarian, Turkish
Croatia	76	4291	−0.05	58	98	56,542	75.9	Zagreb	Kuna	Croat
Czech Republic	77	10,562	0.0	75	99	78,864	133.9	Prague	Czech Koruna	Czech
Denmark	79	5581	0.3	87	100	43,094	129.5	Copenhagen	Danish Krone	Danish
Estonia	74	1318	−0.6	69	100	45,227	29.1	Tallinn	Euro	Estonian, Russian
Finland	79	5401	0.1	85	100	338,145	15.9	Helsinki	Euro	Finnish, Swedish
France	81	62,466	0.5	85	99	547,030	114.2	Paris	Euro	French
Georgia	77	4472	−0.3	68	99	69,492	68.6	Tbilisi	Lari	Georgian
Germany	80	81,752	−0.2	88	99	357,021	229	Berlin	Euro	German
Greece	80	10,788	−0.9	61	96	131,957	81.8	Athens	Euro	Greek
Hungary	75	9982	−0.2	68	99	93,030	107.3	Budapest	Forint	Hungarian
Iceland	81	320	0.7	93	100	102,819	3.1	Reykjavik	Icelandic Krona	Icelandic
Ireland, Republic of	78	4240	1.1	61	99	70,285	60.3	Dublin	Euro	English, Irish (Gaelic)
Italy	82	60,340	0.4	68	99	301,277	200.3	Rome	Euro	Italian
Kosovo	78	1734	−0.5	51	92	10,910	158.9	Pristina	Euro	Albania
Latvia	73	2068	−0.6	69	100	64,610	32	Riga	Latvian Lat	Latvian, Russian
Liechtenstein	82	36.1	0.7	45	100	160	225.6	Vaduz	Swiss Franc	German
Lithuania	76	3054	−0.3	68	100	65,301	46.8	Vilnius	Litas	Lithuanian, Russian
Luxembourg	80	512	1.1	88	100	2586	198	Luxembourg	Euro	Letzeburgish, German, French
Macedonia	75	2057	0.2	67	96	25,713	80	Skopje	Macedonian Denar	Macedonian, Albanian
Malta	80	418	0.4	95	93	316	1327	Valletta	Euro	Maltese, English
Moldova	70	4090	0.0	48	99	33,873	120.7	Chisinau	Moldovan Leu	Romanian (Moldovan), Russian, Ukrainian
Monaco	90	31.1	0.0	100	99	2	15,550	Monaco	Euro	French, Monegasque, Italian
Montenegro	75	620	−0.01	61	97	13,812	45.8	Podgorica	Euro	Serb, Albanian, Montenegrin
Netherlands	81	16,575	0.4	91	99	41,526	399.1	Amsterdam, The Hague	Euro	Dutch, Frisian
Norway	80	4986	0.3	79	100	323,878	15.4	Oslo	Norwegian Krone	Norwegian
Poland	76	38,325	0.02	66	100	312,685	122.6	Warsaw	Zloty	Polish
Portugal	79	10,562	0.0	64	93	92,391	114.3	Lisbon	Euro	Portuguese
Romania	74	19,043	−0.4	57	97	237,500	80.2	Bucharest	Leu	Romanian, Hungarian
Russian Federation	66	142,905	−0.5	78	99	17,075,400	8.4	Moscow	Rouble	Russian, Tatar, Ukrainian
San Marino	83	32.2	1.0	94	98	61	527.9	San Marino	Euro	Italian
Serbia	75	7121	−0.5	56	96	77,468	91.9	Belgrade	Serbian Dinar	Serb, Hungarian
Slovakia	76	5397	0.0	57	100	49,036	110.1	Bratislava	Euro	Slovak, Hungarian
Slovenia	77	2047	0.0	51	100	20,273	101	Ljubljana	Euro	Slovenian
Spain	81	47,190	0.06	78	98	504,782	93.5	Madrid	Euro	Spanish (Castilian), Catalan, Basque, Gallego
Sweden	81	9483	0.2	85	99	449,964	21.1	Stockholm	Swedish Krona	Swedish
Switzerland	81	7786	0.2	74	99	41,285	188.6	Bern	Swiss Franc	German, French, Italian
Ukraine	69	45,779	−0.6	69	99	603,700	75.8	Kiev	Hryvnia	Ukrainian, Russian
United Kingdom	80	62,262	0.6	82	99	244,088	255.1	London	British Pound	English
Vatican City	N/A	0.44	N/A	100	100	0.44	1009.1	Vatican City	Euro	Italian, Latin

* Although Azerbaijan is a member of some European organizations, it is historically and culturally part of western Asia
NB: Cyprus is part of Europe, but the mapping can be found in the Asia section

The British Isles

The United Kingdom (England, Scotland, Wales and Northern Ireland) and the Republic of Ireland make up the British Isles. The UK has become one of the most influential and prosperous countries in the world. By 1900, the British Empire ruled many countries, including Canada, South Africa, India and Australia, which is why so many nations speak English. Ireland declared independence in 1919, but it only came into effect in 1922. Scotland, Wales and Northern Ireland now have their own parliaments. Manufacturing was once the major industry, but most wealth is now generated by banking, insurance and high-tech equipment.

*The **Giant's Causeway** [E7] in Northern Ireland is made up of 40,000 columns created by a volcanic eruption. The columns measure up to 12 m in height. According to legend, the giant Finn McCool began to build the causeway towards Scotland, but he fell asleep before he finished it.*

Search and Find

England	Scotland
• London H10	■ Edinburgh E8
Northern Ireland	**Wales**
■ Belfast F7	■ Cardiff H8
Republic of Ireland	
• Dublin G7	

THE DISTANCE from Land's End [I7] to John o'Groats [C9] once took a cyclist 41 hours and a runner 12 days to complete.

OUTER HEBRIDES

Lewis

Sk

ATLANTIC OCEAN

Giant's Causeway

Londonde

NORTHERN IRELAND

Sligo

REPUBLIC OF IRELAND

B

Arn

Galway

Drogheda

IR
S

Shannon

Liffey

Du

Limerick

WICKLOW MOUNTAINS

Carrantuohill 1041 m

Waterford

Cork

ST. GEORGE'S CHAN

ISLES OF SCILLY

Land's End

Edinburgh [E8], Scotland, is the second most visited city after London. More than 13 million people are attracted to the city each year to see historical sights, such as Edinburgh Castle, or to attend the Edinburgh Festival in August.

A

SHETLAND
ISLANDS

Lerwick

ORKNEY
ISLANDS

John o'Groats

▷ **Snowdonia National Park** [G8], Wales, was created in 1951 and covers 2142 km^2 of land. More than 26,000 people actually live within the area and it receives more than six million visitors a year. The area is a mixture of forest, open land, coast and mountains – making it popular with hikers.

B

C

0   50   100   150 mi
0   100   200 km

Inverness

SCOTLAND

Ben Nevis
1343 m

GRAMPIAN MOUNTAINS

Aberdeen

Perth   Dundee

Falkirk

Glasgow   Edinburgh

Ayr

Newcastle
upon Tyne

Carlisle   Sunderland

Scafell Pike
977 m

PENNINES

Middlesbrough

NORTH
SEA

THE TOWER OF LONDON [H10] has been a castle, a royal palace, a prison, a zoo and the home of the crown jewels.

D

E

...133 passengers will arrive or depart from London's Heathrow Airport, one of the busiest airports in the world.

In the next minute...

Facts and Stats

• London [H10] is the biggest city with 8.3 million people. This would fill 83 Olympic stadiums.

• The Shannon [G6] is the longest river at 386 km in length. However, it is more than 17 times shorter than the Nile river.

• Ben Nevis [D8] is the highest mountain at 1343 m in height – four times higher than the Eiffel Tower.

York

Blackpool   Leeds   Hull

Snowdon
1085 m

Liverpool   Manchester

Chester   Sheffield

ENGLAND

Stoke-on-Trent

Wrexham

Trent

Nottingham

WALES

Derby

Aberystwyth

Leicester   Peterborough   Norwich

CAMBRIAN
MOUNTAINS

Birmingham   Coventry

Ouse

Northampton   Cambridge

Wye

Severn   Ipswich

Swansea   Gloucester   Colchester

Newport   Oxford

Cardiff   Swindon

Thames

London

Avebury Stone Circle   Reading

Stonehenge   Dover

Bristol

Southampton   Portsmouth

Exeter   Bournemouth   Brighton

Plymouth   Isle of
Wight

F

G

Did You Know?

Avebury Stone Circle [I9] is 6000 years old, and is the largest ancient stone monument in the world.

H

I

▷ The **Millennium Bridge**, London [H10], was opened in 2000, and is used as a pedestrian footbridge. It has been designed to hold 5000 people at any one time. St. Paul's Cathedral is situated at its north end and the Tate Modern art gallery is at the south end.

ENGLISH CHANNEL

Guernsey
CHANNEL   Jersey
ISLANDS (UK)

J

Scandinavia

Norway, Sweden, Denmark, Finland and Iceland are Europe's most northerly and least populated countries. Mainland Scandinavia stretches from Norway's mountainous Atlantic coast in the west to Finland's low-lying forested countryside in the east. More than one-third lies within the Arctic Circle where, during a 73-day winter period, the Sun never rises. Norway and Iceland are not members of the European Union. Living standards are high due to vast natural resources, such as oil, gas, timber and iron. Scandinavia has a reputation for stylish designs with brands such as Bang and Olufsen, Ikea and Volvo.

In the next minute...

...Sweden will make more than two million matches – enough to fill 40,000 boxes.

World Record

Finland has more of its territory covered by lakes than any other country – 187,888 lakes cover 10 percent of the country.

Facts and Stats

- Sweden's population of 9.2 million would fill 92 Olympic stadiums.
- The life expectancy of people in Sweden is 81 years, compared to 78 years in Denmark and a world average of 68 years.
- The average income per person in Norway is £19,900, compared to a world average of £3500.

Did You Know?

The first Legoland was opened in Billund [I6], Denmark, in 1968. On average, every person in the world owns 52 Lego bricks.

◁ **Sognefjord [F5], Norway,** is the second largest fjord in the world. Towns are situated on the fjord and the stunning scenery attracts many tourists, which helps to support the economy.

Lofoten Island

Bodø

ATLANTIC OCEAN

Kristiansund • • Trondheim Östersund
Ålesund •

NORWAY

Sognefjord Galdhøpiggen
2469 m

Bergen • • Voss • Lillehammer
Hamar •

Haugesund • • Oslo
Drammen •
Stavanger • Skien • Fredrikstad Karlstad
Öre

Kristiansand •

Linköpi

Skagerrak Göteborg Borås

NORTH SEA

Jönköpi

Ålborg • *Kattegat* Halmstad Vä

DENMARK • Randers
Billund Århus • Helsingborg Karlsham
Esbjerg • **Copenhagen** • Karlskr
Kolding Odense • • Lund
Roskilde Malmö

BORNHOLM (DENMARK

GERMANY

ARCTIC
OCEAN

North Cape

Vadsø •

omsø •

• Narvik

• Kiruna

L A P L A N D

Gällivare •

WEDEN

Rovaniemi •

• Kemi

Luleå •
Piteå •

• Oulu

Skellefteå •

GULF OF BOTHNIA

• Kokkola

Umeå •

rnsköldsvik

• Vaasa

Kuopio •

ndsvall

Jyväskylä •

FINLAND

Pori • • Tampere

• Söderhamn

Hämeenlinna • • Lahti

• Gävle   *Åland Island*   Turku •   Vantaa
• Kotka

Espoo •   •● **Helsinki**

• Uppsala   • Mariehamn

ästerås

● **Stockholm**

• Södertälje

rrköping

tervik

• Visby
Gotland

BALTIC SEA

orgholm
nd

Sweden's **Ice Hotel** near Kiruna [C8] is only open from December to April and is rebuilt each year. The hotel has more than 80 rooms and even has a church. Everything in the hotel, down to the glasses, is made of ice.

RUSSIAN FEDERATION

Search and Find

Denmark
● Copenhagen . . . I7
Finland
● Helsinki G10
Iceland
● Reykjavik I11

Norway
● Oslo G6
Sweden
● Stockholm G8

THE DISTANCE from Norway's North Cape [A9] to the North Pole is shorter than the distance from Oslo [G6] to southern Italy.

LAPLAND [C9] is said to be where Santa Claus lives. In December, many tourists visit the region to see Santa with his elves and reindeer.

0   50   100   150 mi
0   100   200 km

• Isafjördhur

• Olafsfjördhur

Húsavik •   Akureyri •   *Myvatn*

Seydisfjördhur •
Eskifjördhur •

VATNAJÖKULL

Ólafsvik •   **I C E L A N D**

Hvítá   *Thórsá*   Hvannadalshnúkur 2119 m

Akranes •   • Höfn

● **Reykjavik**

Keflavik •   Kopavogur •

NORWEGIAN SEA

ATLANTIC OCEAN   • Vestmannaeyar

0   50   100   150   200 mi
0   100   200   300 km

Spain and Portugal

The Iberian Peninsula is occupied by Spain and Portugal. Africa is less than 16 km from the Strait of Gibraltar, and to the north Spain is bordered by France and the mountain state of Andorra. Spain also includes the Balearic Islands in the Mediterranean Sea and the Canary Islands, including Tenerife and Gran Canaria, which lie 100 km west of Africa in the Atlantic Ocean. Well-known for olive, orange and lemon groves, as well as hot weather and sandy beaches, these countries attract millions of tourists each year.

The costas of Spain are popular coastal regions. **Costa Brava [C13]** in northeast Spain is in the vicinity of Barcelona. S'Agaró is an exclusive resort, and its hotels have even been used in films.

THE DISTANCE from the east to the west side of the border between Spain and Gibraltar [I7] is only 800 m.

BILBAO [B9] is home to many museums including the Fine Arts Museum and the world-famous Guggenheim Museum.

Facts and Stats

• Spain's population of 47.2 million would fill 472 Olympic stadiums. However, the population of Andorra is only 67,000 and would only fill half a stadium.

• The life expectancy of people in Spain is 81 years, compared to a world average of 68 years.

• The average income per person in Andorra is £27,890, compared to a world average of £5640.

Did You Know?

Sardines are the most popular Portuguese seafood. The average consumption for a person is 6 kg a year.

El Ferrol
La Coruña
Gijón
Ovi
Lugo
Santiago de Compostela
CANTABRIAN
León
Sil
Vigo
Orense
Braga
Zamora
Guimaraes
Duero
Tormes
Porto
Salamanca
Aveiro
Coimbra
SIER
Tajo (T
Santarém
Tajo (Tagus)
Cáceres
PORTUGAL
Mérida
Estoril
Lisbon
Badajoz
Almada
Setúbal
Évora
Beja
Guadiana
Guadalqu
Lagos
Huelva
Seville
ATLANTIC OCEAN
Faro
Moron de la Frontera
Arcos
Ron
Jerez de la Frontera
Cádiz
GIBRAL
(UK
Algeciras
Strait of Gibra
CEU
(SPA
MOROCC

8   9   10   11   12   13   14

BAY OF BISCAY

Santander

San Sebastián

Bilbao

TAINS

FRANCE

Vitória-Gasteiz   Pamplona

Pico de Aneto
3405 m

ANDORRA

Logroño

P Y R E N E E S

Andorra
la Vella

Burgos

Gállego

Girona

Palencia

Ebro

Manresa

Soria

Cinca

Terrasa   Mataró

Valladolid

Duero

Zaragoza   Lleida

Barcelona

Costa Brava

Reus   Tarragona

Costa Dorada

Tortosa

govia

GREDOS

Morella

Costa del Azahar

Menorca

vila

Mallorca

Mahón

Guadalajara
Alcalá de Henares

Teruel

Madrid

Cuenca   Castellón de la Plana

Palma

Aranjuez

Turia

Sagunto

Toledo

Valencia

SPAIN

Júcar

Gulf of
Valencia

Ibiza

BALEARIC ISLANDS

Albacete

Ibiza

Alcoy

Formentera

Benidorm

Ciudad Real

Segura

Alicante
Elche

Costa Blanca

Linares

Córdoba

Murcia

Jaén

Lorca   Cartagena

Genil

Granada

SIERRA NEVADA

Motril   Almería

Málaga

arbella   **Costa del Sol**

M E D I T E R R A N E A N   S E A

**MELILLA
(SPAIN)**

Search and Find

Andorra
● Andorra la Vella C12
Portugal
● Lisbon G4

Spain
● Madrid E8

0   50   100 mi
0   80   160 km

In the next
...the bark
of Portugal's and
Spain's cork trees
will produce enough
cork for 136,000
wine bottles.
minute...

Bullfighting is popular in Spain.
Toreros are performers who
fight and kill bulls. There are various
types, including matadors, depending
on the skills used during the fight.
Performances and costumes are
elaborate, attracting tourists from
all over the world.

A
B
C
D
E
F
G
H
I
J

France and Monaco

The third largest country in Europe, France has the fourth highest population. Despite having a rural landscape, more than 85 percent of the population lives in towns, with more than one-sixth in Paris. France has an excellent health, education and social care system, and is the fifth wealthiest country in the world. Northern France is an industrialized, low-lying region, and the south has the snow-capped peaks of the Alps and Pyrenees as well as the sunny beaches of the Mediterranean Sea. Monaco is a tiny, independent, French-speaking country. One of the richest countries in the world, Monaco boasts more than 2000 millionaires and no taxes. Only three hours from the mainland by boat is the mountainous island of Corsica.

Search and Find

France	Monaco
• Paris C9	• Monaco H11

PARIS [C9] is one of the most visited places in the world, with attractions such as the Eiffel Tower and the Louvre.

THE DISTANCE from Calais [A9] to Dover, England, is 41 km and has been swum in less than eight hours.

BAY OF BISCAY

Île d'Ouessant

Brest •
St. Malo •
Quimper •
Laval •
Lorient •
Rennes •
Belle-Île
Angers •
St. Nazaire •
• Nantes
Île d'Yeu
Poitie
Île de Ré
• La Rochelle
Cognac •
Angoulên
Périgue
Bordeaux •
Dordogne
Garonne
Berge
Mont-de-Marsan •
Agen •
Adour
Bayonne •
Montaub
• Pau
Tou
• Tarbes
• Lourdes
P Y R E N E E S
SPAIN
ANDORRA

Cherbo

The Gothic cathedral **Notre Dame de Paris** [C9] was mainly constructed in the 13th and 14th centuries, but is constantly being restored. The famous Emmanuel bell weighs 13 tonnes.

In the next ...France will provide the UK with enough electricity to power one light bulb in every home. **minute...**

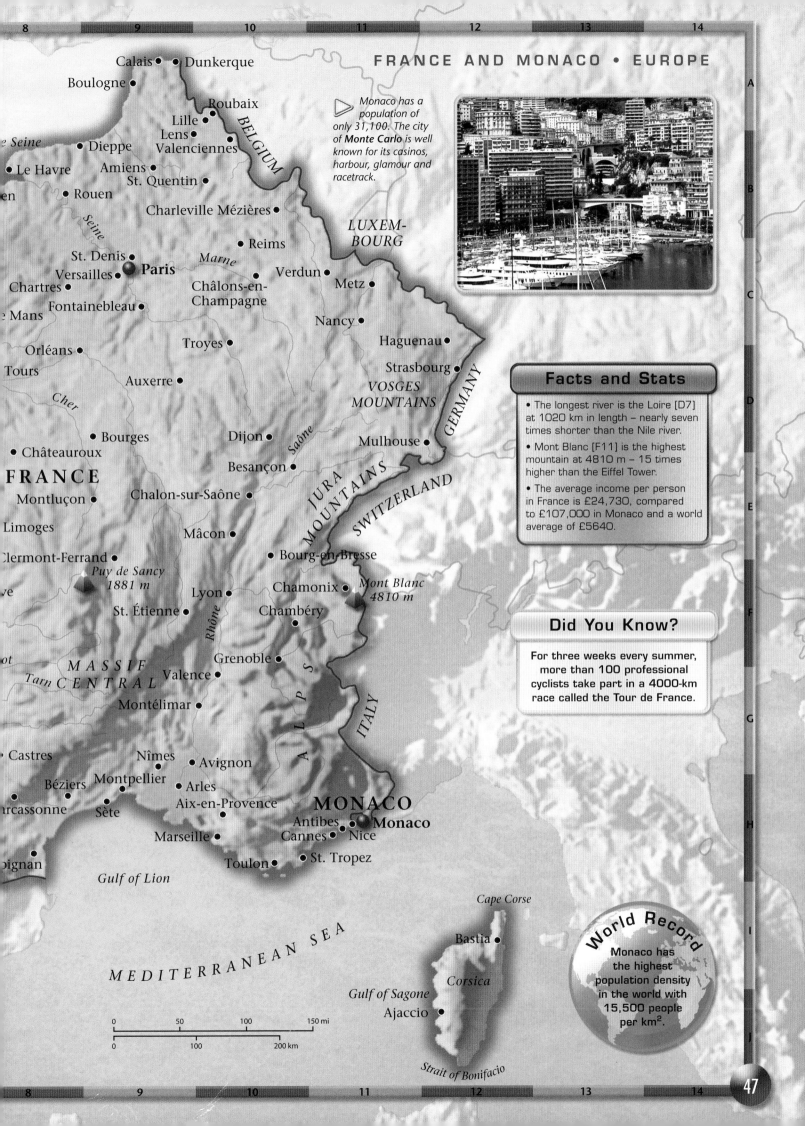

8 9 10 11 12 13 14

Calais • • Dunkerque
Boulogne •
• Roubaix
Lille •
Lens • Valenciennes •
Dieppe •
Le Havre •
Amiens •
St. Quentin •
Rouen •
Charleville Mézières •

e Seine

LUXEM-
BOURG

Monaco has a
population of
only 31,100. The city
of **Monte Carlo** is well
known for its casinos,
harbour, glamour and
racetrack.

• Reims
St. Denis •
Versailles • **Paris**
Chartres •
Fontainebleau •
e Mans

Verdun •
Châlons-en-
Champagne
Metz •

Nancy •

Orléans •
Tours

Troyes •

Haguenau •
Strasbourg •

Auxerre •

VOSGES
MOUNTAINS

Cher

Bourges •
Châteauroux •

Dijon •

Mulhouse •

FRANCE

Besançon •

GERMANY

Montluçon •

Chalon-sur-Saône •

JURA
MOUNTAINS

Limoges •

Mâcon •

SWITZERLAND

Clermont-Ferrand •

Bourg-en-Bresse •

Puy de Sancy
1881 m

Chamonix •
Mont Blanc
4810 m

Lyon •
St. Étienne •

Chambéry •

Rhône

Grenoble •

MASSIF
CENTRAL

Valence •

Tarn

Castres •

Nîmes •

ALPS

ITALY

Montélimar •

Avignon •

Béziers •
Montpellier •

Arles •

rcassonne •

Sète •

Aix-en-Provence •

MONACO

Antibes •
Cannes •

Monaco

Nice •

Marseille •

Toulon •

St. Tropez •

Gulf of Lion

MEDITERRANEAN SEA

Cape Corse

Bastia •

Corsica

Gulf of Sagone

Ajaccio •

Strait of Bonifacio

0   50   100   150 mi
0   100   200 km

Facts and Stats

• The longest river is the Loire [D7]
at 1020 km in length – nearly seven
times shorter than the Nile river.

• Mont Blanc [F11] is the highest
mountain at 4810 m – 15 times
higher than the Eiffel Tower.

• The average income per person
in France is £24,730, compared
to £107,000 in Monaco and a world
average of £5640.

Did You Know?

For three weeks every summer,
more than 100 professional
cyclists take part in a 4000-km
race called the Tour de France.

World Record

Monaco has
the highest
population density
in the world with
15,500 people
per km².

Italy and the Balkans

Northern Italy is highly industrialized and produces many famous brands, such as Ferrari and Armani, while the south is mainly agricultural. Croatia, Bosnia and Herzegovina, Serbia, Montenegro, Kosovo and Macedonia were once part of Yugoslavia, but they have each become independent since 1991. Greece is one of Europe's oldest nations. The dry climate, steep slopes and thin soil limit farming to grapes, olives and citrus fruit. This area was home to the ancient Greek and Roman empires, which produced monuments such as Rome's Colosseum and the Parthenon in Athens, as well as Olympia – home to the first Olympic Games in 776 BC.

Facts and Stats

- Italy's population of 60.3 million would fill 603 Olympic stadiums. Montenegro's population of 620,000 would fill six stadiums.
- The life expectancy of people in Italy is 82 years, compared to 75 years in Serbia and a world average of 68 years.
- The average income per person in Italy is £20,940, compared to £1920 in Kosovo and a world average of £5640.

In the next minute...
...Italy will produce over 12,000 packets of pasta – that's 200 km of spaghetti!

One of the most prominent sights in **Zagreb** [B8], the capital of Croatia, is the cathedral. The spires are 105 m in height and were built after an earthquake in 1880, which damaged much of the original structure.

Did You Know?

It costs the Italian government more money to keep the Tower of Pisa [D5] leaning than it would to straighten it.

SWITZERLAND
AUST...
SLOVEN...
Bolzano
Aosta
Como
Lecco
Trento
Udine
Krar...
Monza
Bergamo
Verona
Vicenza
Ljublj...
Novara
Milan
Brescia
Treviso
Trieste
FRANCE
Turin
Lodi
Padua
Venice
Ko...
Piacenza
Cremona
Mantua
Chioggia
Rije...
Alessandria
Adria
Pu...
Parma
Ferrara
Gulf of Venice
Genoa
Reggio nell'
Savona
Emilia
Bologna
Ravenna
San Remo
La Spezia
Carrara
Forlì
Massa
Pistoia
Rimini
Viareggio
Prato
SAN MARIN...
Pisa
Empoli
Florence
San Marino
Livorno
Arezzo
Ancona
Siena
Piombino
Perugia
ITALY
Elba
Grosseto
Terni
Teram...
Civitavecchia
VATICAN CITY (in Rome)
Pe...
Rome
Latina
Campobasso
Gaeta
Benever...
Gulf of Gaeta
Na...
Salerno
Gulf of Salerno
Sassari
Nuoro
Sardinia
Cagliari
TYRRHENIAN SEA
Palermo
Me...
Trapani
Mount Etna 3326 m
Caltanissetta
Cata...
Agrigento
Sicily
Ragusa
Sir...
Pantelleria
MALTA
Val...

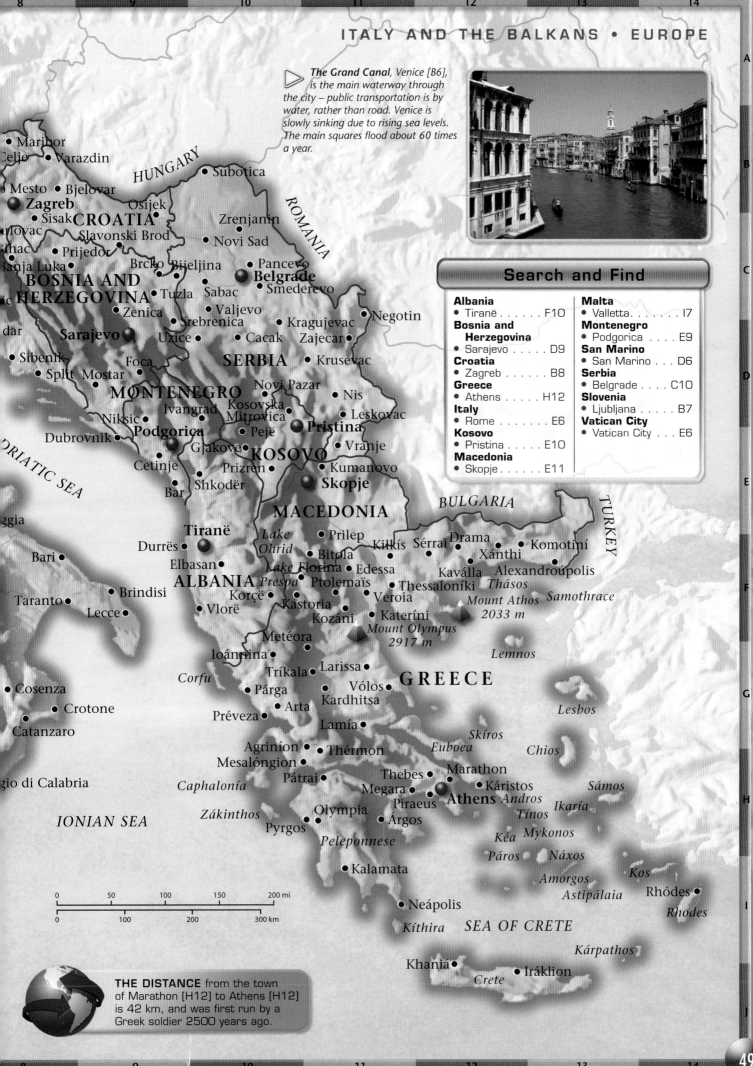

▷ **The Grand Canal**, Venice [B6], is the main waterway through the city – public transportation is by water, rather than road. Venice is slowly sinking due to rising sea levels. The main squares flood about 60 times a year.

Search and Find

Albania		**Malta**	
● Tiranë	F10	● Valletta	I7
Bosnia and		**Montenegro**	
Herzegovina		● Podgorica	E9
● Sarajevo	D9	**San Marino**	
Croatia		● San Marino	D6
● Zagreb	B8	**Serbia**	
Greece		● Belgrade	C10
● Athens	H12	**Slovenia**	
Italy		● Ljubljana	B7
● Rome	E6	**Vatican City**	
Kosovo		● Vatican City	E6
● Pristina	E10		
Macedonia			
● Skopje	E11		

THE DISTANCE from the town of Marathon [H12] to Athens [H12] is 42 km, and was first run by a Greek soldier 2500 years ago.

HUNGARY
ROMANIA
BULGARIA
TURKEY

CROATIA
BOSNIA AND HERZEGOVINA
SERBIA
MONTENEGRO
KOSOVO
MACEDONIA
ALBANIA
GREECE

Maribor
Celje
Varazdin
Mesto
Bjelovar
Zagreb
Sisak
Osijek
Slavonski Brod
Prijedor
Banja Luka
Brcko
Bijeljina
Pancevo
Belgrade
Tuzla
Sabac
Smederevo
Zenica
Valjevo
Srebrenica
Kragujevac
Negotin
Sarajevo
Uzice
Cacak
Zajecar
Sibenik
Foca
Krusevac
Split
Mostar
Novi Pazar
Nis
Ivangrad
Kosovska Mitrovica
Leskovac
Niksic
Pejë
Pristina
Dubrovnik
Podgorica
Gjakove
Vranje
Cetinje
Prizren
Kumanovo
Bar
Shkodër
Skopje
Subotica
Zrenjanin
Novi Sad

ADRIATIC SEA

Tiranë
Durrës
Prilep
Kilkís
Sérrai
Drama
Komotiní
Lake Ohrid
Bitola
Xánthi
Elbasan
Lake Florina
Edessa
Alexandroúpolis
Prespa
Ptolemaïs
Kaválla
Thásos
Samothrace
Korçë
Veroia
Thessaloníki
Vlorë
Kastoria
Mount Athos 2033 m
Kozáni
Kateríni
Mount Olympus 2917 m
Metéora
Ioánnina
Lemnos
Corfu
Tríkala
Larissa
Párga
Vólos
GREECE
Préveza
Arta
Kardhitsa
Lesbos
Lamía
Skíros
Agriníon
Thérmon
Euboea
Chios
Mesalóngion
Thebes
Marathon
Pátrai
Megara
Sámos
Caphalonía
Piraeus
Athens
Andros
Ikaría
Zákinthos
Olympia
Árgos
Tínos
Pyrgos
Kéa
Mykonos
Peleponnese
Páros
Náxos
Kos
Amorgos
Astipálaia
Rhódes
Kalamata
Rhodes
Neápolis
Kíthira
SEA OF CRETE
Kárpathos
Khaniá
Iráklion
Crete

Bari
Brindisi
Taranto
Lecce
Cosenza
Crotone
Catanzaro
io di Calabria
IONIAN SEA

0 50 100 150 200 mi
0 100 200 300 km

Germany and the Low Countries

Luxembourg, Belgium and the Netherlands are the three nations that make up the low countries.

Much of the Netherlands is below sea level, and it relies on massive sea walls called dykes and thousands of pumps to drain the land. Brussels, the capital of Belgium, is home to the European Union's main centre of government, and Antwerp is the centre of the world's diamond-cutting industry. Luxembourg has the highest income per person in the world due to its banking industry. Germany has the third largest economy in the world after the United States and Japan, and produces machinery and cars such as BMW, Mercedes and Porsche. However, the reunification of East and West Germany in 1990 has caused unemployment and slow economic growth.

Search and Find

Belgium	**Luxembourg**
● Brussels E5	● Luxembourg. . . G6
Germany	**Netherlands**
● Berlin D11	● Amsterdam . . . D6
	● The Hague. . . . D5

Amsterdam [D6] is well-known for its network of canals. The tall, leaning buildings were once used for storage. Hooks at the top of each house enabled goods to be pulled up to the top rooms.

Facts and Stats

● Germany's population of 82.8 million would fill 828 Olympic stadiums. Luxembourg's population of 484,000 would only fill 4.8 stadiums.

● Mount Zugspitze [I9] is the highest mountain at 2964 m – nine times higher than the Eiffel Tower.

● The average income per person in Luxembourg is £29,600, compared to a world average of £5640.

COLOGNE [E7] holds one of the biggest carnivals in the world. Every November, more than one million people take part in the festival.

THE DISTANCE from the source of the Rhine river [F7] in the Swiss Alps to its mouth at the North Sea is 1320 km.

NORTH SEA

Terschelling Ameland
Vlieland *Waddenzee*
Texel Groni
Den Helder● Leeuwarden● As
NETHERLANDS
Alkmaar● *Northeast Polder* Emme
Haarlem● **Amsterdam** Zwolle●
Flevoland Polder
Leiden● Apeldoorn●
The Hague ● Hilversum
Delft● Utrecht● Enschede●
● Gouda Arnhem●
Rotterdam● *Waal* Nijmegen●
Dordrecht● Mür
Vlissingen● Breda● Tilburg● 's-Hertogenbosch
Zeebrugge●
Ostend● ● Bruges Eindhoven● Duisburg● Dortm
Ghent● ● Antwerp *Maas (Meuse)* Krefeld●● Ess
Roeselare● Aalst ● Mechelen Düsseldorf● Wupp
Kortrijk● *Scheldt* Leuven Genk Solingen●
Brussels Hasselt● Maastricht ● Colo
● Tournai ● Aachen
Charleroi Namur ● Liège ● Bon
Mons● *Meuse (Maas)* Verviers● Rhine
● Dinant
BELGIUM
FRANCE Bastogne● *HUNSRÜCK* Kobl
LUXEMBOURG
Luxembourg ● Trier
Esch-sur-Alzette● Kaiserslau
Saarbrücken●
FRANCE Karlsru
Baden-B
B
F
● Freibu
im Bre
SW

50

8 9 10 11 12 13 14

A

Sylt
DENMARK

Flensburg •

Schleswig •

Kiel Bay
Fehmarn

Kiel •

Mecklenburg
Bay

Rügen

B

Did You Know?

Each year, Belgium produces and sells 172,000 tonnes of chocolate in more than 2130 chocolate shops.

AN ISLANDS

• Cuxhaven

Lübeck •

Rostock •

Greifswald •

elmshaven

• Bremerhaven

Hamburg •

• Schwerin

Neubrandenburg •

C

...the Netherlands will make 1280 kg of cheese – enough for 64,000 cheese slices.

In the next minute...

enburg

• Bremen

• Lüneburg

Ems

Elbe

abrück

Hannover •

Wolfsburg •

Brandenburg •

Berlin

D

POLAND

Bielefeld •

• Hameln

• Braunschweig

• Potsdam

umm

Magdeburg •

Frankfurt an der Oder

• Paderborn

Dessau •

Elbe

Cottbus •

E

World Record

Germany has the highest paper recycling rate in the world – more than 75 percent of their paper is reused.

• Göttingen

Kassel •

Halle •

GERMANY

Leipzig •

gen

Eisenach •

Weimar •

Meissen •

Görlitz •

Erfurt •

Dresden •

F

• Giessen

Jena •

Chemnitz

Gera •

Freital •

• Fulda

• Zwickau

n • Frankfurt am Main

• Plauen

CZECH REPUBLIC

Offenbach •

Main

ainz

• Darmstadt

Bamberg •

• Bayreuth

G

▷ **Cologne Cathedral** [E7] is one of the tallest and most magnificent Gothic buildings in the world. Its construction began in the 13th century, but wasn't completed until the late 19th century. The cathedral has 12 bells, and 509 steps lead to the top of the south tower, nearly 100 m above the ground.

ms

nnheim

• Würzburg

vigshafen

Fürth • • Nuremberg

idelberg

BOHEMIAN FOREST

• Heilbronn

H

forzheim

Regensburg •

• Stuttgart

Tübingen •

• Ingolstadt

• Reutlingen

SWABIAN JURA

• Ulm

• Augsburg

Passau •

I

Danube

• Munich

Lake
Constance

BAVARIAN ALPS

Mount Zugspitze
2964 m

Berchtesgaden •

AND

AUSTRIA

J

8 9 10 11 12 13 14

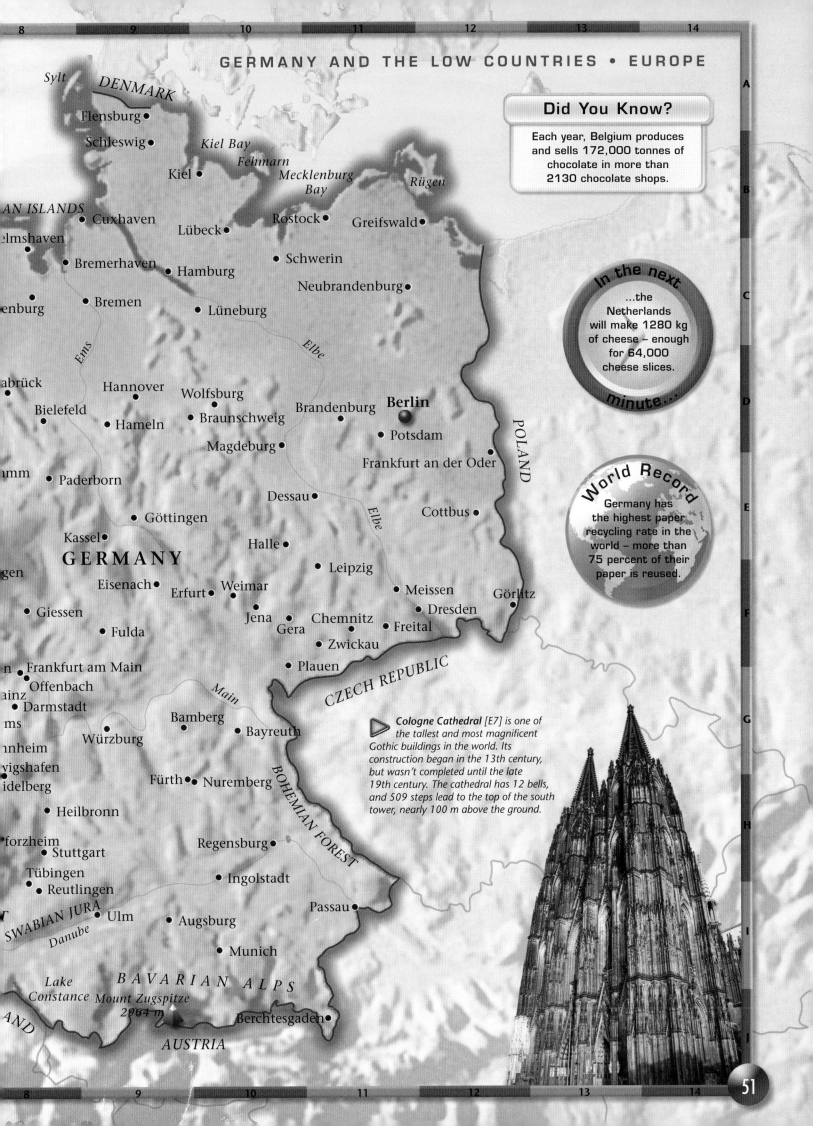

Switzerland and Austria

Landlocked Switzerland, Austria and Liechtenstein are dominated by the Alps, creating stunning mountain scenery. Millions of tourists are attracted to the natural beauty, spectacular mountain vistas and popular Alpine skiing. Switzerland guards its independence and was not involved in either of the two World Wars. As a neutral, independent state, Switzerland is part of the United Nations and many charitable and banking organizations. As a result, it is a very wealthy country. Many composers come from Austria, including Mozart, Haydn, Schubert and Strauss.

The Belvedere Palace, Vienna [E13], was built in the 17th and 18th centuries. Archduke Franz Ferdinand was the last person to live at the palace. It is now a museum and gallery, exhibiting many important collections, including the works of Renoir, Monet and Van Gogh.

In the next ...41,000 kg of chocolate will be eaten worldwide. The Swiss are the world's biggest consumers. **minute...**

FRANCE

Basel · Rhine · Schaffhausen

Aarau · Baden · Winterthur

Olten · Zürich · Lake Constance · GERMANY

Biel · Solothurn

Neuchâtel · St. Gallen · Bregenz

Lake Neuchâtel · Zug · Lucerne · Feldkirch · Innsbruck

Yverdon · Bern · Vaduz

Thun · SWITZERLAND · LIECHTENSTEIN · St. Anton

Fribourg · Interlaken · Chur · Galtür

Lausanne · Saanen · Andermatt · Davos

Lake Geneva · Montreux · BERNESE ALPS · LEPONTINE ALPS

Geneva

Sion · Brig · St. Moritz

Mount Dufourspitze 4634 m · Bellinzona

Zermatt · Locarno

Mount Matterhorn 4478 m · ITALY

ITALY · Lugano

Did You Know?

The Swiss invented the quartz watch, wristwatch and waterproof watch. Switzerland produces expensive watches, such as Rolex, and watch-making is its third largest industry.

Leukerbad, in the heart of the Bernese Alps [G3], is the largest thermal spa in Europe. Dating back to Roman times, the complex contains 3.9 million litres of water and is surrounded by picturesque mountain scenery.

BERN [F3] is the city where Albert Einstein worked, the Toblerone chocolate bar is made, and Emmental cheese is manufactured.

THE DISTANCE of the St. Moritz [G5] bobsleigh run is 1585 m and it takes just 70 seconds to travel from one end to the other.

Search and Find

Austria
- Vienna E13

Liechtenstein
- Vaduz F5

Switzerland
- Bern F3

Extreme Weather

In 1999, the biggest avalanche in Austria for 400 years smashed into the town of Galtür [G6], killing 31 people.

0	50	100 mi
0	80	160 km

CZECH REPUBLIC

SLOVAKIA

Zwettl Stadt

Inn
Braunau
Linz
Krems
Danube
Wels
Amstetten
Klosterneuburg
Steyr
Sankt Pölten
Vienna
Gmunden
Enns
Baden
Salzburg
Hallein
Bad Ischl
Wiener Neustadt
Neusiedler See
Kufstein
chwaz
Kitzbühel
AUSTRIA
Mount Grossglockner 3797 m
Kapfenberg
Leoben
HOHE TAUERN
NIEDERE TAUERN
Knittelfeld
Judenburg
Mur
Graz
Gleisdorf
HUNGARY
Spittal
Wolfsberg
Drau
Villach
Klagenfurt
ITALY
SLOVENIA

Facts and Stats

- The population of Liechtenstein is only 36,100 and wouldn't even fill half an Olympic stadium.
- Switzerland's Mount Dufourspitze [H3] is the highest mountain at 4634 m in height – 14 times higher than the Eiffel Tower.
- The average income per person in Switzerland is £42,570 compared to a world average of £5640.

▷ Switzerland is split into federal states, or cantons. Bern is the second largest Swiss canton, and is dominated by mountains, glaciers and waterfalls. The small village of **Gstaad** near Saanen [G2] is a popular ski resort with fantastic Alpine scenery.

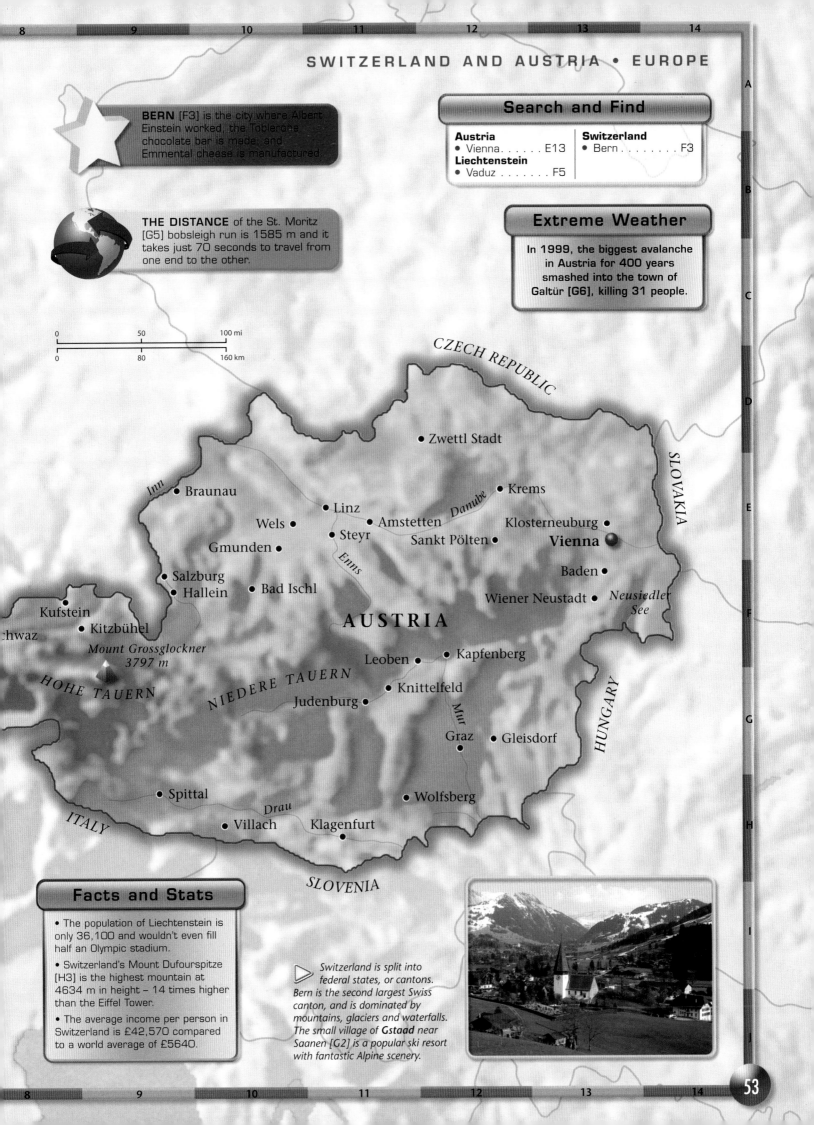

Hungary, Romania and Bulgaria

Bulgaria and Romania became members of the European Union in 2007, with Hungary joining in 2004. These countries will now experience rapid economic growth after decades of communist rule. Romania is the largest of the three and Europe's longest river, the Danube, flows along its southern border to the Black Sea. Hungary's capital, Budapest, has a lively arts and music scene, and is host to a range of cultural and sporting festivals. The countryside is scenic with many lakes, historic towns and villages. Bulgaria also borders the Black Sea, but it is mainly mountainous and rural, and relatively undeveloped.

SLOVAKIA

Miskolc

AUSTRIA

Gyor •   • Esztergom

● **Budapest**

Szombathely

Székesfehérvár •   **HUNGARY**

Lake Balaton

Dunaujvaros   • Kecskemét

SLOVENIA

Kaposvár •

Tisza

Szeged •

Ara

Danube

CROATIA

Pécs •

Timisoa

SERBIA

Facts and Stats

• The Danube [D6/G10] is the longest river at 2860 km in length. The Nile river is twice as long.

• Mount Musala [I10] is the highest mountain at 2925 m, which is nine times higher than the Eiffel Tower.

• The average income per person in Hungary is £8000, compared to a world average of £5640.

On the bank of the Danube river in Budapest [C6] is **Hungary's Parliament building**. Hungarian architect, Imre Steindl, designed the building, although he went blind before the project was completed. More than 40 kg of gold was used in its construction.

Bran Castle in Romania is more commonly known as Dracula's Castle because Bram Stoker based his novel around the building. In 2007, the castle was put up for sale for £40 million.

Did You Know?

One of the few Bulgarian commercial crops is the rose. The petals are used in the perfume industry.

THE DISTANCE from the source to the mouth of the Danube river [D6/G10] is 2888 km – almost all of it is accessible to boats.

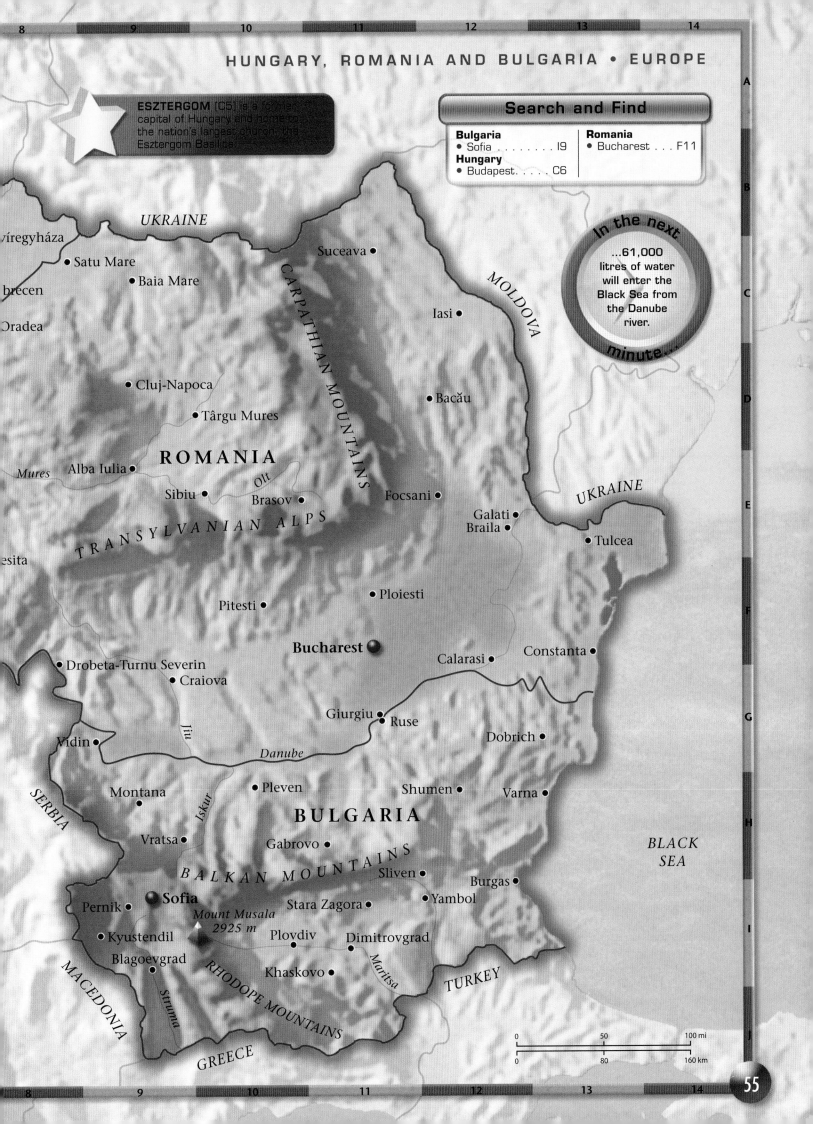

ESZTERGOM [C5] is a former capital of Hungary and home to the nation's largest church, the Esztergom Basilica.

Search and Find

Bulgaria
● Sofia I9

Hungary
● Budapest C6

Romania
● Bucharest . . . F11

In the next
...61,000 litres of water will enter the Black Sea from the Danube river.
minute...

UKRAINE

●víregyháza

● Satu Mare

● Baia Mare

brecen

Oradea

Suceava ●

MOLDOVA

Iasi ●

CARPATHIAN MOUNTAINS

● Cluj-Napoca

● Târgu Mures

Bacău ●

ROMANIA

Mures   ● Alba Iulia ●

Olt

Sibiu ●   ● Brasov ●

Focsani ●

UKRAINE

TRANSYLVANIAN ALPS

Galati ●
Braila ●

● Tulcea

Pitesti ●   ● Ploiesti

Bucharest ●

Calarasi ●   Constanta ●

● Drobeta-Turnu Severin

● Craiova

Jiu

Giurgiu ●
● Ruse

Dobrich ●

Vidin ●

Danube

● Montana

● Pleven

Shumen ●

Varna ●

Iskur

BULGARIA

Vratsa ●

Gabrovo ●

BALKAN MOUNTAINS

Sliven ●

Burgas ●

SERBIA

Pernik ●   **Sofia** ●

Stara Zagora ●

● Yambol

BLACK SEA

● Kyustendil

▲ *Mount Musala 2925 m*

Plovdiv ●

Dimitrovgrad ●

● Blagoevgrad

RHODOPE MOUNTAINS

Khaskovo ●

Maritsa

TURKEY

MACEDONIA

Struma

GREECE

0	50	100 mi
0	80	160 km

Poland, Czech Republic and Slovakia

Poland, Slovakia and the Czech Republic are among the newest members of the European Union. Standards of living are much lower than western Europe and many workers have moved to the United Kingdom and Ireland for better-paid jobs. However, since joining the EU, Slovakia has become a major car producer, and has seen minimal emigration. The Baltic coast of Poland is industrial with steelworks and shipyards, but low-wage rates and money from the EU have attracted new industries. Prague, the capital of the Czech Republic, is situated on the Vltava river and receives more than ten million tourists a year.

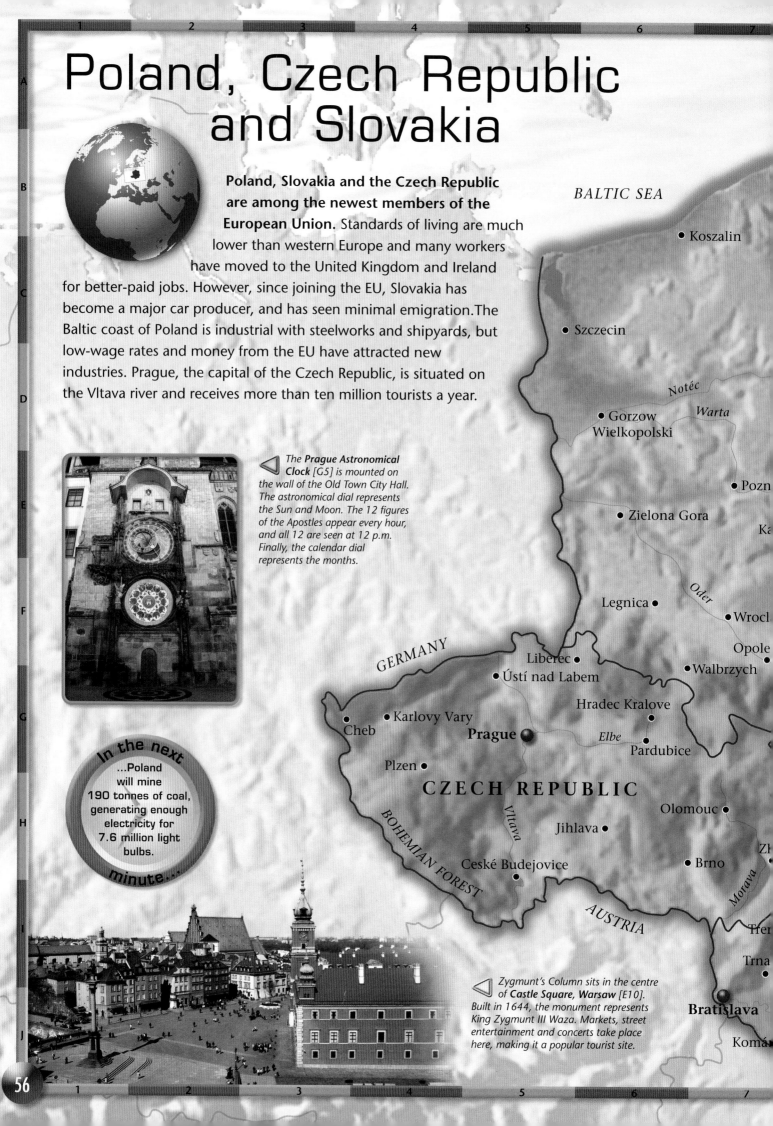

The **Prague Astronomical Clock** [G5] is mounted on the wall of the Old Town City Hall. The astronomical dial represents the Sun and Moon. The 12 figures of the Apostles appear every hour, and all 12 are seen at 12 p.m. Finally, the calendar dial represents the months.

In the next minute... ...Poland will mine 190 tonnes of coal, generating enough electricity for 7.6 million light bulbs.

Zygmunt's Column sits in the centre of **Castle Square, Warsaw** [E10]. Built in 1644, the monument represents King Zygmunt III Waza. Markets, street entertainment and concerts take place here, making it a popular tourist site.

BALTIC SEA

Koszalin

Szczecin

Notéc

Warta

Gorzow Wielkopolski

Pozn

Zielona Gora

Ka

GERMANY

Oder

Legnica

Wrocl

Opole

Walbrzych

Liberec

Ústí nad Labem

Hradec Kralove

Karlovy Vary

Cheb

Prague

Elbe

Pardubice

Plzen

CZECH REPUBLIC

BOHEMIAN FOREST

Vltava

Jihlava

Olomouc

Ceské Budejovice

Brno

Morava

AUSTRIA

Zł

Hr

Trna

Bratislava

Koma

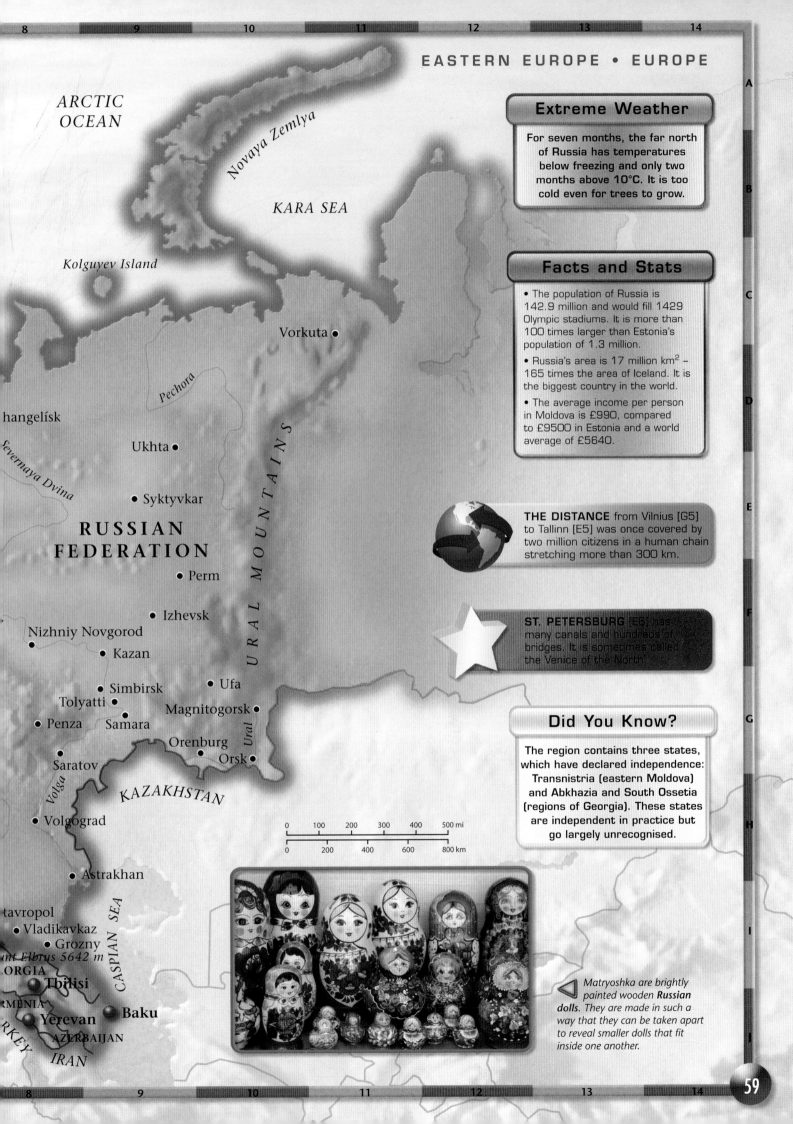

ARCTIC OCEAN

Novaya Zemlya

KARA SEA

Kolguyev Island

Vorkuta •

Pechora

hangelísk

Severnaya Dvina

Ukhta •

• Syktyvkar

RUSSIAN FEDERATION

U R A L   M O U N T A I N S

• Perm

• Izhevsk

Nizhniy Novgorod •

• Kazan

• Simbirsk   • Ufa

Tolyatti

• Penza   Samara   Magnitogorsk •

Ural

Orenburg •

Orsk •

Volga

KAZAKHSTAN

• Saratov

• Volgograd

• Astrakhan

tavropol

• Vladikavkaz

• Grozny

CASPIAN SEA

nt Elbrus 5642 m

ORGIA

• Tbilisi

RMENIA

Yerevan   • Baku

RKEY

AZERBAIJAN

IRAN

Extreme Weather

For seven months, the far north of Russia has temperatures below freezing and only two months above 10°C. It is too cold even for trees to grow.

Facts and Stats

• The population of Russia is 142.9 million and would fill 1429 Olympic stadiums. It is more than 100 times larger than Estonia's population of 1.3 million.

• Russia's area is 17 million km^2 – 165 times the area of Iceland. It is the biggest country in the world.

• The average income per person in Moldova is £990, compared to £9500 in Estonia and a world average of £5640.

THE DISTANCE from Vilnius [G5] to Tallinn [E5] was once covered by two million citizens in a human chain stretching more than 300 km.

ST. PETERSBURG [E6] has many canals and hundreds of bridges. It is sometimes called the Venice of the North.

Did You Know?

The region contains three states, which have declared independence: Transnistria (eastern Moldova) and Abkhazia and South Ossetia (regions of Georgia). These states are independent in practice but go largely unrecognised.

| 0 | 100 | 200 | 300 | 400 | 500 mi |

| 0 | 200 | 400 | 600 | 800 km |

*Matryoshka are brightly painted wooden **Russian dolls**. They are made in such a way that they can be taken apart to reveal smaller dolls that fit inside one another.*

Africa

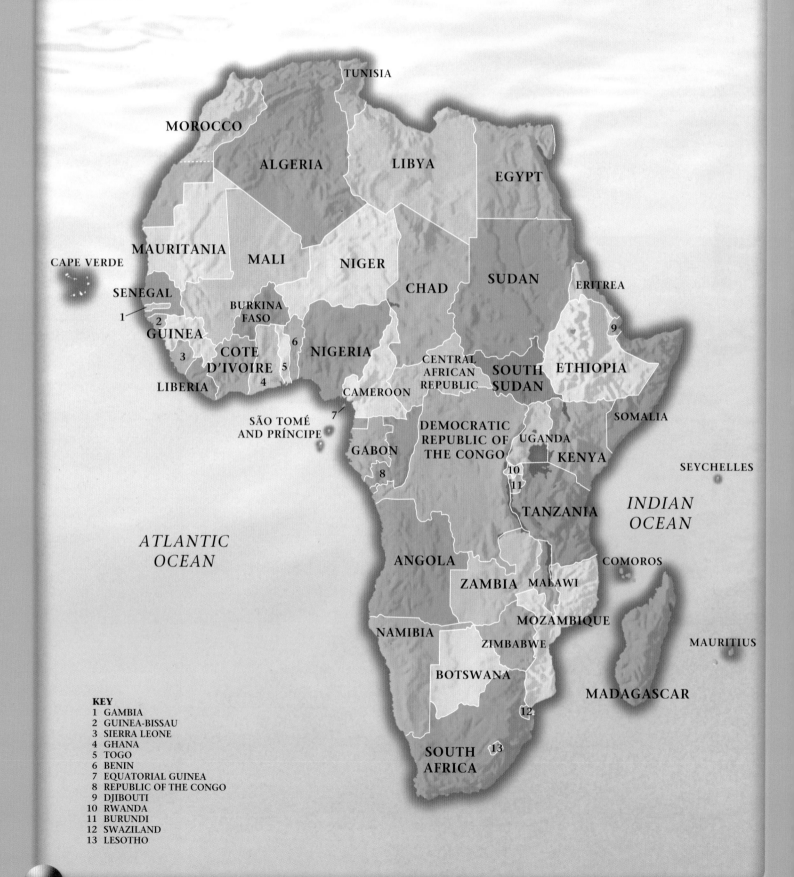

TUNISIA

MOROCCO

ALGERIA

LIBYA

EGYPT

MAURITANIA

CAPE VERDE

MALI

NIGER

SUDAN

ERITREA

SENEGAL

1

2

BURKINA
FASO

CHAD

GUINEA

6

3

COTE
D'IVOIRE

5

NIGERIA

CENTRAL
AFRICAN
REPUBLIC

SOUTH
SUDAN

9

ETHIOPIA

LIBERIA

4

CAMEROON

SÃO TOMÉ
AND PRÍNCIPE

7

SOMALIA

DEMOCRATIC
REPUBLIC OF
THE CONGO

UGANDA

GABON

8

KENYA

SEYCHELLES

10

11

INDIAN
OCEAN

TANZANIA

ATLANTIC
OCEAN

COMOROS

ANGOLA

ZAMBIA

MALAWI

MOZAMBIQUE

NAMIBIA

ZIMBABWE

MAURITIUS

BOTSWANA

12

MADAGASCAR

13

SOUTH
AFRICA

KEY
1 GAMBIA
2 GUINEA-BISSAU
3 SIERRA LEONE
4 GHANA
5 TOGO
6 BENIN
7 EQUATORIAL GUINEA
8 REPUBLIC OF THE CONGO
9 DJIBOUTI
10 RWANDA
11 BURUNDI
12 SWAZILAND
13 LESOTHO

COUNTRY FACTFILE

Country	Life expectancy	Population in thousands	Population growth %	Population as urban %	Literacy %	Area km²	Population density per km²	Capital city	Currency	Languages
Algeria	75	34,080	1.2	66	70	2,381,741	14.3	Algiers	Algerian Dinar	Arabic, Berber, French
Angola	55	20,609	2	59	67	1,246,700	16.5	Luanda	Kwanza	Portuguese, Umbundu
Benin	60	8850	2.9	43	35	112,622	78.6	Porto-Novo,Cotonou	CFA Franc	French, Fon, Yoruba
Botswana	56	2038	1.7	66	81	581,730	3.5	Gaborone	Pula	English, Tswana
Burkina Faso	54	15,225	3.1	26	22	274,122	55.5	Ouagadougou	CFA Franc	French, Mossi
Burundi	59	8039	3.5	11	39	27,834	288.8	Bujumbura	Burundi Franc	Kirundi, French
Cameroon	55	19,406	2.2	58	68	476,077	40.8	Yaoundé	CFA Franc	French, English, Fang
Cape Verde	71	492	1.4	62	77	4033	122	Praia	Cape Verdean Escudo	Portuguese, Crioulo
Central African Republic	50	4400	2.1	42	49	622,436	7.1	Bangui	CFA Franc	French, Sangho
Chad	48	11,176	2	28	26	1,284,000	8.7	N'Djamena	CFA Franc	French, Arabic, Sara
Comoros	63	669	2.7	32	57	1862	359.3	Moroni	Comoran Franc	Comorian, French, Arabic
Congo, Democratic Republic of the	56	66,000	2.6	35	66	2,344,856	28.1	Kinshasa	Congolese Franc	French, Lingala, Swahili
Congo, Republic of the	55	4002	2.8	63	84	342,000	11.7	Brazzaville	CFA Franc	French, Monokutuba, Kongo
Côte d'Ivoire (Ivory Coast)	57	20,080	2.1	51	49	320,783	62.5	Yamoussoukro, Abidjan	CFA Franc	French, Akan
Djibouti	62	818	2.2	85	68	23,200	35.3	Djibouti	Djiboutian Franc	Somali, French, Akan
Egypt	73	77,775	1.9	45	71	997,739	78	Cairo	Egyptian Pound	Arabic
Equatorial Guinea	63	700	2.6	48	87	28,051	25	Malabo	CFA Franc	Spanish, French, Fang
Eritrea	63	5291	2.5	22	59	121,100	43.7	Asmara	Nakfa	Tigrinya, Arabic, Afar
Ethiopia	57	82,102	3.2	18	43	1,127,127	72.8	Addis Ababa	Birr	Amharic, Oromo, Tigrinya
Gabon	52	1505	1.9	86	63	267,667	5.6	Libreville	CFA Franc	French, Fang
Gambia	64	1660	2.4	58	40	10,689	155.3	Banjul	Dalasi	English, Malinke
Ghana	61	24,223	1.8	51	58	238,533	101.5	Accra	Cedi	Hausa, English, Akan
Guinea	59	10,218	2.6	35	36	245,857	41.6	Conakry	Guinean Franc	Fulani, French, Malinke
Guinea-Bissau	49	1521	2	30	42	36,125	42.1	Bissau	CFA Franc	Crioulo, Portuguese, Balante
Kenya	63	38,611	2.5	30	85	582,646	66.3	Nairobi	Kenyan Shilling	Swahili, English, Kikuyu
Lesotho	62	2170	0.3	27	85	30,355	71.5	Maseru	Loti	Sesotho, English
Liberia	57	3990	3.7	60	58	111,370	35.8	Monrovia	US Dollar, Liberian Dollar	Krio, English
Libya	78	6355	2.1	88	83	1,777,060	3.6	Tripoli	Libyan Dinar	Arabic
Madagascar	64	20,696	3	30	69	587,041	35.3	Antananarivo	Madagascar Ariary	Malagasy, French
Malawi	52	14,389	2.8	20	63	118,484	121.4	Lilongwe	Malawian Kwacha	Chichewa, English
Mali	53	14,529	2.6	36	46	1,248,574	11.6	Bamako	CFA Franc	French, Bambara
Mauritania	62	3162	2.3	58	51	1,030,700	3.1	Nouakchott	Ouguiya	Arabic
Mauritius	75	1281	0.7	48	84	2040	627.9	Port Louis	Mauritius Rupee	French Creole, Bhojpuri, English
Morocco	76	31,950	1.1	58	52	446,550	71.5	Rabat	Moroccan Dirham	Arabic, Berber
Mozambique	52	23,300	2.4	38	48	801,590	29.1	Maputo	Metical	Emakhuwa, Portuguese
Namibia	52	2125	0.9	38	85	824,269	2.6	Windhoek	Namibian Dollar	English, Ovambo, Nama
Niger	54	15,731	3.6	21	29	1,186,408	13.3	Niamey	CFA Franc	French, Hausa
Nigeria	52	140,432	1.9	50	68	923,103	152.1	Abuja	Naira	English, Hausa, Yoruba
Rwanda	58	9500	2.8	18	70	26,338	360.7	Kigali	Rwandan Franc	Rwanda, French, English
São Tomé and Príncipe	63	152	2.1	62	85	1001	151.8	São Tomé	Dobra	Portuguese, Crioulo
Senegal	60	12,179	2.6	47	40	196,712	61.9	Dakar	CFA Franc	French, Wolof, Fulani
Seychelles	74	90.9	0.9	59	92	455	199.8	Victoria	Seychelles Rupee	Creole, English
Sierra Leone	57	5870	2.2	38	35	71,740	81.8	Freetown	Leone	English, Krio, Mende
Somalia	50	9300	1.6	37	38	637,657	14.6	Mogadishu	Somali Shilling	Somali, Arabic
South Africa	49	49,900	0.0	62	86	1,224,691	40.7	Pretoria, Cape Town	Rand	Xhosa, English, Zulu, Afrikaans
South Sudan	n/a	8,260	2	22	n/a	619,745	13.3	Juba	South Sudanese Pound	English, Dinka, Arabic
Sudan	63	30,894	2.1	40	60	1,886,070	16.4	Khartoum	Sudanese Dinar	Arabic, Nubian
Swaziland	49	1018	1.2	34	82	17,363	58.6	Mbabane, Lobamba	Lilangeni	Swazi, English
Tanzania	53	44,800	2	26	69	945,037	47.4	Dar es Salaam, Dodoma	Tanzanian Shilling	Swahili, English
Togo	63	6191	2.8	43	61	56,785	109	Lomé	CFA Franc	French, Ewe
Tunisia	76	10,674	1	67	75	163,610	65.2	Tunis	Tunisian Dinar	Arabic, French
Uganda	53	31,785	3.6	14	66	241,040	131.9	Kampala	Ugandan Shilling	Swahili, English, Ganda
Zambia	53	13,047	3.1	44	81	752,614	17.3	Lusaka	Zambian Kwacha	English, Bemba
Zimbabwe	52	12,500	4.3	38	90	390,757	31.9	Harare	Zimbabwean Dollar	English, Shona

North Africa

The Sahara Desert dominates this region at 6000 km in width and 2000 km from north to south. Only a narrow strip of land stands next to the Mediterranean Sea, but the fertile valleys of the Atlas Mountains and the banks of the Nile river have enough water to grow crops.

Algeria, Libya and Tunisia have become wealthy by selling oil and natural gas to Europe. Egypt was the richest country in the world when the pharaohs ruled more than 3000 years ago. Egypt's well-preserved tombs and temples, especially the Great Pyramid of Giza, attract many tourists.

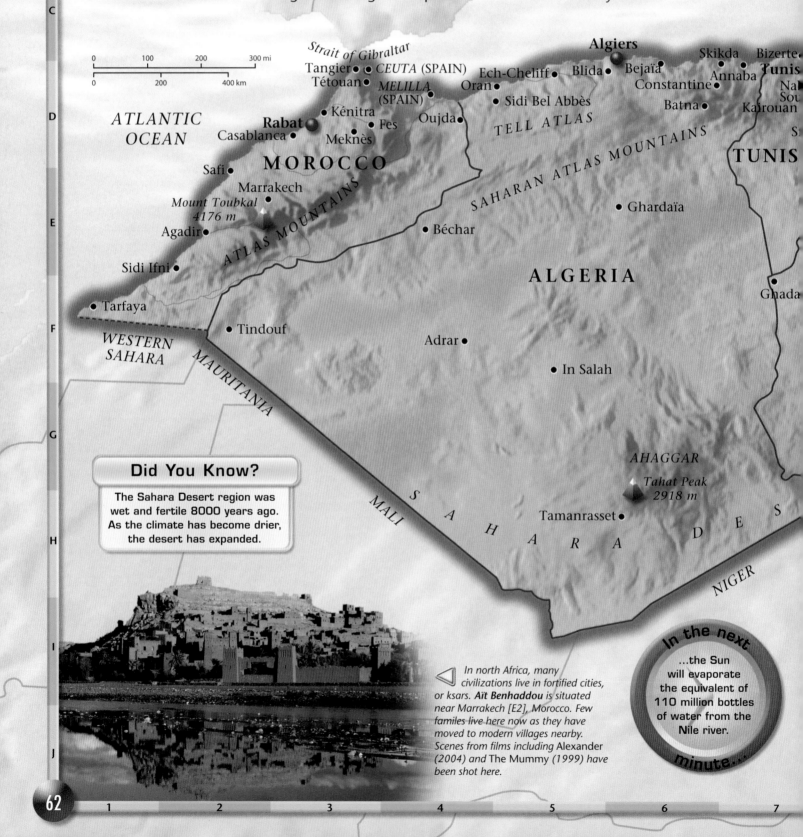

Strait of Gibraltar

Tangier • ● CEUTA (SPAIN)
Tétouan •
MELILLA (SPAIN)

Oran • Ech-Cheliff • Blida • Bejaïa •

Algiers

Skikda • Bizerte •
Annaba • **Tunis**
Constantine • Na
Batna • Sou
Kairouan
S.

Rabat ● Kénitra •
Casablanca • Fes •
Meknès •
Oujda •

MOROCCO

Safi •
Marrakech •
Mount Toubkal
4176 m
Agadir •

Sidi Ifni •

• Tarfaya

WESTERN SAHARA

MAURITANIA

ATLANTIC OCEAN

ATLAS MOUNTAINS

• Tindouf

MALI

Adrar •

• In Salah

Sidi Bel Abbès •

TELL ATLAS

SAHARAN ATLAS MOUNTAINS

• Ghardaïa

• Béchar

ALGERIA

TUNIS

Ghada

AHAGGAR
Tahat Peak
2918 m

Tamanrasset •

S A H A R A   D E S

NIGER

Did You Know?

The Sahara Desert region was wet and fertile 8000 years ago. As the climate has become drier, the desert has expanded.

In north Africa, many civilizations live in fortified cities, or ksars. **Aït Benhaddou** is situated near Marrakech [E2], Morocco. Few families live here now as they have moved to modern villages nearby. Scenes from films including Alexander (2004) and The Mummy (1999) have been shot here.

In the next ...the Sun will evaporate the equivalent of 110 million bottles of water from the Nile river. *minute...*

0   100   200   300 mi
0   200   400 km

Located on the Nile river, Cairo [F13] is the biggest city in Africa. Built in AD 988, **Al-Azhar University** is the second oldest university in the world, after the University of Al Karaouine Fez, Morocco. Al-Azhar Mosque stands alongside the university.

Facts and Stats

• Egypt's population of 77.8 million would fill 778 Olympic stadiums. Libya's population of 6.4 million would only fill 64 stadiums.

• Cairo [F13] is the biggest city with 15.5 million people. This would fill 155 Olympic stadiums, compared to Tripoli which would only fill 14 [E8].

• The average income per person in Libya is £7140, compared to a world average of £5640.

Search and Find

Algeria
• Algiers C6
Egypt
• Cairo. F13
Libya
• Tripoli E8

Morocco
• Rabat D3
Tunisia
• Tunis D7

World Record
The Sahara sand sea in Algeria has the longest sand dunes in the world, with some more than 300 km.

Extreme Weather

The hottest temperature ever recorded was 58°C in Libya's Sahara Desert.

MEDITERRANEAN SEA

Tripoli
Zawiyah
Misurata
Gulf of Sidra
Surt
Darnah
Benghazi
Tubruq
Ajdabiya
Alexandria
Tanta
Port Said
Suez Canal
Cairo
Giza
Suez
Sinai Peninsula
Gulf of Suez
ISRAEL
QATTARA DEPRESSION
GREAT SAND SEA
Nile
Gulf of Aqaba
oha
LIBYA
LIBYAN DESERT
WESTERN DESERT
Sharm al Sheikh
El Minya
Al Ghardaqah
Asyut
RED SEA
FEZZAN
EGYPT
Qena
Luxor
T
Aswan
GILF KEBIR PLATEAU
Lake Nasser
CHAD
SUDAN

THE DISTANCE separating Morocco from Spain, Europe, at the Strait of Gibraltar's [C3] narrowest point is only 13 km.

EGYPT has huge pyramids, built more than 3000 years ago. Each one held the body of a king.

Desert tribe people, such as the Berbers and Tuaregs, travel by camel from oasis to oasis across the Sahara Desert to trade cloth, salt and spices.

West Africa

Stretching from the heart of the Sahara Desert to the tropical forests of southern Nigeria, this region is one of the poorest in the world. In the north, Mali and Niger are plagued by drought and famine. The southern countries of Sierra Leone, Liberia, Côte d'Ivoire and Nigeria suffer with armed unrest, government corruption and civil wars. Oil provides 65 percent of Nigeria's income, but this fails to lift the rapidly growing population out of poverty.

CANARY ISLANDS (SPAIN)

Las Palmas de Gran Canaria

MOROCCO

El Aaiún

WESTERN SAHARA

ALGERIA

Dakhla

Zouérat

S A H A R

Nouadhibou

MAURITANIA

MALI

Mindelo

CAPE VERDE

Nouakchott

Senegal

Tombouctou

Praia

St. Louis · Kaédi

Touba

Dakar · Thiès

SENEGAL

Kayes

Mopti

Djenné

Banjul · GAMBIA

Ségou

ATLANTIC OCEAN

Bissau · GUINEA-BISSAU

Bamako

Ouagadou

BURKIN

GUINEA

Sikasso

Conakry

Kankan

Bobo Dioulasso

Freetown · SIERRA LEONE

COTE D'IVOIRE

Tama

Bo

Man · Bouaké

Daloa

Kumasi

Monrovia · Harbel
Buchanan

Yamoussoukro

GHAN

LIBERIA

Abidjan

Accr

Sekondi-Tako

Cape Palmas

GULF

| 0 | 100 | 200 | 300 | 400 mi |
| 0 | 200 | 400 | 600 km |

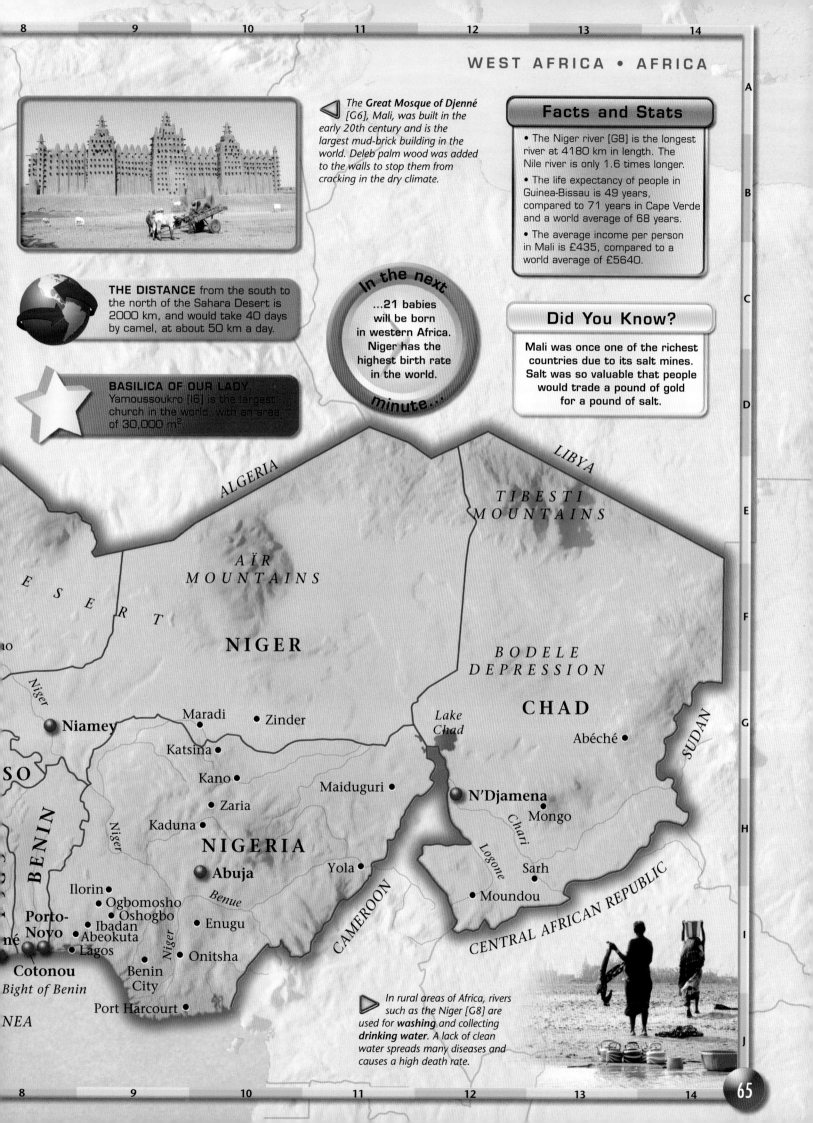

The **Great Mosque of Djenné** [G6], Mali, was built in the early 20th century and is the largest mud-brick building in the world. Deleb palm wood was added to the walls to stop them from cracking in the dry climate.

Facts and Stats

• The Niger river [G8] is the longest river at 4180 km in length. The Nile river is only 1.6 times longer.

• The life expectancy of people in Guinea-Bissau is 49 years, compared to 71 years in Cape Verde and a world average of 68 years.

• The average income per person in Mali is £435, compared to a world average of £5640.

THE DISTANCE from the south to the north of the Sahara Desert is 2000 km, and would take 40 days by camel, at about 50 km a day.

In the next ...21 babies will be born in western Africa. Niger has the highest birth rate in the world. minute...

BASILICA OF OUR LADY, Yamoussoukro [I6] is the largest church in the world, with an area of 30,000 m².

Did You Know?

Mali was once one of the richest countries due to its salt mines. Salt was so valuable that people would trade a pound of gold for a pound of salt.

ALGERIA

LIBYA

TIBESTI MOUNTAINS

AÏR MOUNTAINS

DESERT

NIGER

BODELE DEPRESSION

CHAD

Niger

● **Niamey**

● Maradi   ● Zinder

Katsina ●

Lake Chad

Abéché ●

Kano ●

● Zaria

Maiduguri ●

● **N'Djamena**

Mongo ●

Kaduna ●

Niger

NIGERIA

Chari

SUDAN

● **Abuja**

Yola ●

Logone

Sarh ●

Ilorin ●

Benue

CAMEROON

● Moundou

● Ogbomosho

BENIN

Porto-Novo

● Oshogbo

● Enugu

● Ibadan

Abeokuta

Niger

CENTRAL AFRICAN REPUBLIC

● Lagos

● Onitsha

Cotonou

Benin City

Bight of Benin

SO

NEA

Port Harcourt ●

In rural areas of Africa, rivers such as the Niger [G8] are used for **washing** and collecting **drinking water**. A lack of clean water spreads many diseases and causes a high death rate.

East Africa

Due to the high altitude of Kenya, Tanzania and Uganda, the climate is suited to growing crops. These countries have strong economies based on exporting crops, such as tea and coffee, which are grown on large plantations run by European companies. Kenya also has a strong tourist industry as people visit to see animals in their natural habitat. The countries of Ethiopia, Somalia and Sudan are poorer as they have harsher climates and a history of civil war. The droughts that have repeatedly affected this southern fringe of the Sahara Desert have caused millions of deaths as well as the destruction of crops and animals.

Lesser flamingos are the smallest of the flamingo family. They are numerous throughout Africa and are always found in large groups called 'pats'. The colour of flamingos comes from their food – unhealthy birds are pale in colour.

Facts and Stats

- Mount Kilimanjaro [H9] is the highest mountain at 5895 m. It is 18 times higher than the Eiffel Tower.
- Sudan's area is 1.9 million km². This is 18 times the area of Iceland.
- Ethiopia has a population of 82.1 million. This would fill 821 Olympic stadiums. Djibouti's population is 818,000 and would only fill 8 Olympic stadiums.

Extreme Weather

The Danakil Valley [D10], Ethiopia, has the hottest average daily temperature of 55°C.

Did You Know?

Somaliland declared itself independent from Somalia in 1991 but although it has been a separate country for two decades, no other nation has recognized its independence.

LIBYA

LIBYAN DESERT Wadi Ha

EGYPT

CHAD

Japal Marrah 3089 m

• El Fasher

El Obeid

• Nyala

DARFUR   SUDAN

CENTRAL AFRICAN REPUBLIC

BAHR AL-GHAZAL

• Wau

SOUTH SUDA

• Yambi

DEMOCRATIC REPUBLIC OF THE CONGO

Ar

Lak

Lak Albe

Lake Edward

RWAND

Kigali

Lake Kivu

BURUND

Bujumbura

Kigoma •

Lake Tanganyi

0	100	200	300	400	500 mi
0	200	400	600	800 km	

The *Maasai people* of Kenya and Tanzania wear toga-like garments called shukkas, which can be bought at roadside shops. The official colour of the Maasai tribe is red, and is always worn as clothing or jewellery.

8 9 10 11 12 13 14

A

B

C

D

E

F

G

H

I

J

*NUBIAN
DESERT*

RED SEA

Port Sudan

rowe

bara

Kassala Keren Massawa *DAHLAK
ISLANDS*

Omdurman **Asmara**

Khartoum ERITREA

Wad Medani Aksum *Ras Dashen
4533 m* Asseb

Kosti **DJIBOUTI**

Gonder *Lake
Tana* **Djibouti**

lakal Debre Markos Berbera

Addis Ababa Dire Dawa Hargeisa

Gore Harer Nazret *SOMALILAND*

nciel Jima *OGADEN
PLATEAU* Eyl

ETHIOPIA *Shebele*

uba

ANDA *Lake
Turkana* *Jubba*

*Mount Elgon
4322 m* **KENYA** Baidoa **SOMALIA**

Kampala **Mogadishu**

Kisumu Nanyuki Marka

saka Nakuru *Mount Kenya
5200 m* Baraawe

ke Thika Garissa

toria **Nairobi** Kismaayo *Tana*

nza *Lake
Natron*

Arusha *Galana* **INDIAN
OCEAN**

*Lake
Eyasi* Malindi

yanga *Mount Kilimanjaro
5895 m* Mombasa

Tabora

ANZANIA Tanga *Pemba Island*

Dodoma Zanzibar *Zanzibar Island*

Rungwa Bagamoyo

Kilosa **Dar es Salaam**

Iringa *Mafia Island*

Mbeya *Rufiji* Kilwa

*Lake
Malawi*

MALAWI Songea Lindi Mtwara

Ruvuma

MOZAMBIQUE

DANAKIL VALLEY

Blue Nile *Atbara* *Blue Nile*

GREAT RIFT VALLEY

GULF OF ADEN

*Cape
Caseyr*

> **Seaweed** is farmed in coastal areas throughout Africa and Asia. It can be used as food or fertilizer and also in medicines.

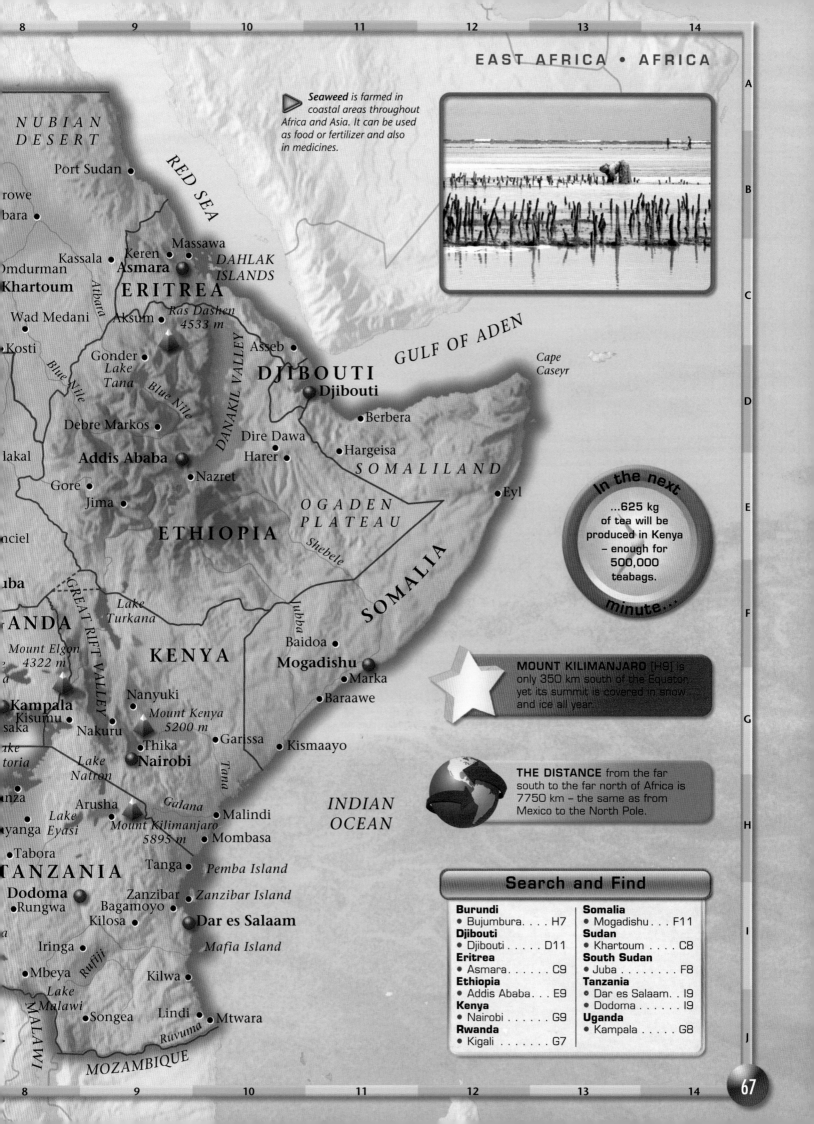

In the next
...625 kg of tea will be produced in Kenya – enough for 500,000 teabags.
minute...

MOUNT KILIMANJARO [H9] is only 350 km south of the Equator, yet its summit is covered in snow and ice all year.

THE DISTANCE from the far south to the far north of Africa is 7750 km – the same as from Mexico to the North Pole.

Search and Find

8 9 10 11 12 13 14

67

Central and southern Africa

This region stretches from the tropical rainforests of Cameroon to the rich agricultural lands of South Africa. Only those countries with mineral wealth have prospered. Political unrest is widespread, bringing great poverty to Mozambique, the Central African Republic and Zimbabwe. Once an exporter of food and tobacco, Zimbabwe is now reliant on international aid. Farming, commerce, and gold and diamond mining have brought prosperity to many South Africans.

Victoria Falls [G8] on the Zambezi river tumbles more than 128 m into the gorge below, creating the largest sheet of falling water in the world. The local people called the waterfall 'the smoke that thunders'.

Facts and Stats

- The longest river is the Congo [C7]. At 4700 km in length, the Nile river is only 1.5 times longer.

- Mont Ngaliema (Mount Stanley) [C9] is the highest mountain at 5109 m in height – 16 times higher than the Eiffel Tower.

- The life expectancy of people in Swaziland is 49 years, compared to 75 years in Mauritius and a world average of 68 years.

Did You Know?

The Namib Desert [H6] is the oldest desert in the world. It covers 270,000 km² – more than twice the area of Iceland. Some parts have fewer than 2 cm of rain a year.

*The **quiver tree** is a species of aloe found in southern Africa, especially throughout Namibia. Native people use the branches and bark of the tree to make containers, or quivers, for their arrows.*

NIGERIA
Garoua
Garba
CH
CEN
AFRICAN
Mount Cameroon 4071 m
Bamenda
Bouar Bambari
CAMEROON
Berbérati
Malabo
Douala
Bangui
Bioko Island
Yaoundé
EQUATORIAL GUINEA
SÃO TOMÉ AND PRÍNCIPE
Príncipe
São Tomé
São Tomé
C
Libreville
Mband
GABON
REPUBLIC OF THE CONGO
DEMOC OF T
Port-Gentil
Lake Mai-Ndombe
Bandundu
Brazzaville
Kasai
Loubomo
Kinshasa
Kikwi
Pointe-Noire
Matadi
Tsh
Kwango
Kwilu
Luanda
Cuanza
Saurimo
Luer
ANGOLA
Lobito
Benguela
Huambo
Namibe
Lubango
Cubango
Cuito
Kin
Cunene
Cape Fria
ETOSHA PAN
Grootfontein
NAMIBIA
Windhoek
KALAH DESE
Swakopmund
Walvis Bay
NAMIB DESERT
Rehoboth
Keetmanshoo
Lüderitz
Alexander Bay
Kenhardt
Carnarvor
Calvinia
Beaufort W
Great Karoo
Word
Cape Town
Cape of Good Hope
Mossel
False Bay

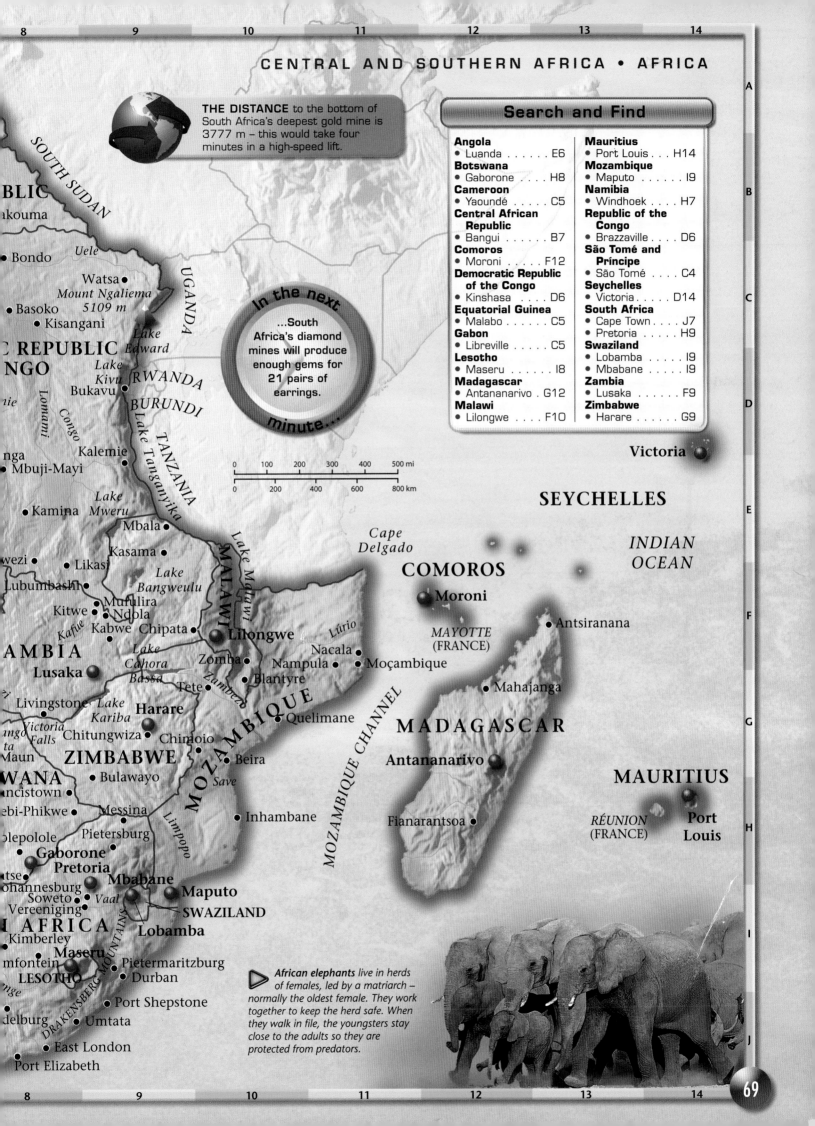

THE DISTANCE to the bottom of South Africa's deepest gold mine is 3777 m – this would take four minutes in a high-speed lift.

In the next minute... ...South Africa's diamond mines will produce enough gems for 21 pairs of earrings.

Search and Find

Angola
• Luanda E6

Botswana
• Gaborone H8

Cameroon
• Yaoundé C5

Central African Republic
• Bangui B7

Comoros
• Moroni F12

Democratic Republic of the Congo
• Kinshasa D6

Equatorial Guinea
• Malabo C5

Gabon
• Libreville C5

Lesotho
• Maseru I8

Madagascar
• Antananarivo . G12

Malawi
• Lilongwe F10

Mauritius
• Port Louis . . . H14

Mozambique
• Maputo I9

Namibia
• Windhoek H7

Republic of the Congo
• Brazzaville D6

São Tomé and Príncipe
• São Tomé C4

Seychelles
• Victoria D14

South Africa
• Cape Town . . . J7
• Pretoria H9

Swaziland
• Lobamba I9
• Mbabane I9

Zambia
• Lusaka F9

Zimbabwe
• Harare G9

SOUTH SUDAN

Bondo

Watsa

Uele

akouma

Basoko

Mount Ngaliema 5109 m

Kisangani

UGANDA

Lake Edward

Lake Kivu

Bukavu

RWANDA

BURUNDI

C REPUBLIC NGO

Lomami

Congo

Kalemie

Mbuji-Mayi

nga

TANZANIA

Lake Tanganyika

Kamina

Lake Mweru

Mbala

Kasama

Likasi

Lubumbashi

Lake Bangweulu

Mufulira

Kitwe

Ndola

Kafue

Kabwe

Chipata

Lusaka

Lake Cahora Bassa

Zomba

Tete

Blantyre

Livingstone

Lake Kariba

Harare

Chitungwiza

Chimoio

ZIMBABWE

Bulawayo

Victoria Falls

Maun

ncistown

ebi-Phikwe

Messina

Pietersburg

MALAWI

Lake Malawi

Lilongwe

Lúrio

Nacala

Nampula

Moçambique

Quelimane

MOZAMBIQUE

Zambezi

Save

Beira

Inhambane

Limpopo

Cape Delgado

MAYOTTE (FRANCE)

COMOROS

Moroni

Antsiranana

Mahajanga

MADAGASCAR

Antananarivo

Fianarantsoa

MOZAMBIQUE CHANNEL

SEYCHELLES

Victoria

INDIAN OCEAN

MAURITIUS

RÉUNION (FRANCE)

Port Louis

blepolole

Gaborone

Pretoria

ohannesburg

Soweto

Vereeniging

Vaal

Mbabane

Maputo

SWAZILAND

Lobamba

AFRICA

Kimberley

Maseru

mfontein

Pietermaritzburg

LESOTHO

Durban

DRAKENSBERG MOUNTAINS

delburg

Umtata

Port Shepstone

East London

Port Elizabeth

0 100 200 300 400 500 mi
0 200 400 600 800 km

African elephants live in herds of females, led by a matriarch – normally the oldest female. They work together to keep the herd safe. When they walk in file, the youngsters stay close to the adults so they are protected from predators.

Asia

ARCTIC OCEAN

RUSSIAN FEDERATION

KAZAKHSTAN

MONGOLIA

UZBEKISTAN

KYRGYZSTAN

NORTH
KOREA

TURKEY

TURKMENISTAN

TAJIKISTAN

JAPAN

1

SYRIA

CHINA

SOUTH
KOREA

2

IRAQ

AFGHANISTAN

3 4

IRAN

5

PAKISTAN

NEPAL

9

6
7

8

TAIWAN

SAUDI
ARABIA

BANGLADESH

INDIA

BURMA
(MYANMAR)

LAOS

PACIFIC
OCEAN

OMAN

THAILAND

VIETNAM

YEMEN

CAMBODIA

PHILIPPINES

SRI
LANKA

10

MALAYSIA

12

11

INDONESIA

INDIAN
OCEAN

EAST
TIMOR

KEY
1 CYPRUS
2 LEBANON
3 ISRAEL
4 JORDAN
5 KUWAIT
6 BAHRAIN
7 QATAR
8 UNITED ARAB EMIRATES
9 BHUTAN
10 BRUNEI
11 SINGAPORE
12 MALDIVES

COUNTRY FACTFILE

Country	Life expectancy	Population in thousands	Population growth %	Population as urban %	Literacy %	Area km²	Population density per km²	Capital city	Currency	Languages
Afghanistan	49	23,994	2.4	23	28	645,807	37.1	Kabul	Afghani	Dari, Pashto
Bahrain	78	1235	2.8	92	89	716	1724.9	Manama	Bahraini Dinar	Arabic, Urdu, English
Bangladesh	70	142,319	1.6	28	48	147,570	964.4	Dhaka	Taka	Bangla, English
Bhutan	68	696	1.3	36	47	46,500	15	Thimphu	Ngultrum	Dzongkha, Nepali
Brunei	76	423	1.7	76	93	5765	73.4	Bandar Seri Begawan	Bruneian Dollar	Malay
Burma (Myanmar)	65	52,171	1.1	34	90	676,577	77.1	Naypyidaw	Kyat	Burmese, Shan
Cambodia	63	13,396	1.7	22	74	181,035	74	Phnom Penh	Riel	Khmer
China	75	1,340,000	0.5	51	91	9,559,686	140.2	Beijing	Yuan	Chinese (Guoyo), Wu, Yuëh
*Cyprus	78	1121	1.6	70	98	9251	121.2	Nicosia	Euro	Greek, Turkish, English
East Timor	68	1067	2	28	59	14,874	71.7	Dili	US Dollar	Tetum, Portuguese
India	67	1,210,000	1.3	30	61	3,287,263	368.1	New Delhi	Indian Rupee	Hindi, English, Telegu, Bengali
Indonesia	72	237,641	1.1	52	90	1,904,413	124.8	Jakarta	Indonesian Rupiah	Bhasa Indonesia, Javanese, Sudanese
Iran	70	74,733	1.2	71	77	1,641,918	45.5	Tehran	Iranian Rial	Farsi (Persian), Azeri
Iraq	71	33,331	2.4	76	74	434,128	76.8	Baghdad	New Iraqi Dinar	Arabic, Kurdish
Israel	81	7695	1.6	92	98	20,400	377.2	Jerusalem	Israeli Shekel	Hebrew, Arabic
Japan	84	128,057	0.0	78	99	377,819	338.9	Tokyo	Yen	Japanese
Jordan	79	5103	2.3	79	89.9	89,342	57.1	Amman	Jordanian Dinar	Arabic
Kazakhstan	70	16,675	0.4	59	99	2,717,300	6.1	Astana	Tenge	Kazakh, Russian
Korea, North	69	24,052	0.4	61	99	122,762	195.9	Pyongyang	North Korean Won	Korean
Korea, South	79	48,219	0.2	83	98	99,461	484.6	Seoul	South Korean Won	Korean
Kuwait	77	2496	2	98	93	17,818	140	Kuwait City	Kuwaiti Dinar	Arabic, Farsi, English
Kyrgyzstan	69	5418	1.4	35	99	198,500	27.1	Bishkek	Som	Kyrgyz, Russian
Laos	53	6128	1.7	33	73	236,800	25.9	Vientiane	Kip	Lao
Lebanon	75	4220	0.2	90	87	10,201	413.7	Beirut	Lebanese Pound	Arabic
Malaysia	74	28,334	1.6	72	89	329,847	85.9	Kuala Lumpur, Putrajaya	Ringgit	Bahasa Melayu (Malay), Chinese, English
Maldives	75	315	0.0	40	94	298	1057	Male	Rufiyaa	Dhivehi (Maldivian)
Mongolia	69	2648	1.5	62	98	1,564,100	1.7	Ulaanbaatar	Tugrik	Khalkha Mongol
Nepal	67	26,621	1.6	19	49	147,181	180.9	Kathmandu	Nepalese Rupee	Nepali, Maithali
Oman	74	2773	2	81	81	309,500	9	Muscat	Omani Rial	Arabic, Baluchi
Pakistan	66	192,289	1.6	38	50	796,095	241.5	Islamabad	Pakistani Rupee	Urdu, Punjabi, Sindhi
Philippines	72	92,338	1.9	65	93	300,076	307.7	Manila	Philippine Peso	Filipino (Tagalog), Cebuano, English
Qatar	78	1699	1	96	89	11,427	148.7	Doha	Qatari Rial	Arabic, Hindi, Malayalam
Russian Federation	66	142,905	−0.5	78	99	17,075,400	8.4	Moscow	Rouble	Russian, Tatar, Ukrainian
Saudi Arabia	74	27,137	1.5	86	79	2,149,690	12.6	Riyadh	Saudi Riyal	Arabic, Malayalam, Tagalog
Singapore	84	5077	0.8	100	95	697	7212.6	Singapore	Singapore Dollar	Chinese, Malay, English
Sri Lanka	76	20,653	0.9	23	91	65,610	314.8	Colombo, Kotte	Sri Lankan Rupee	Sinhala, Tamil
Syria	75	21,377	2.9	56	80	185,180	115.4	Damascus	Syrian Pound	Arabic
Taiwan	78	23,225	0.2	75	97	36,179	641.9	Taipei	Taiwan dollar	Chinese (Mandarin), Min
Tajikistan	66	7374	1.8	28	98	143,100	51.5	Dushanbe	Somoni	Tajik, Uzbek
Thailand	74	65,479	0.6	35	93	514,000	130.6	Bangkok	Baht	Thai, Chinese
Turkey	73	74,724	1.2	75	88	780,580	95.9	Ankara	Turkish Lira	Turkish, Kurdish
Turkmenistan	69	6550	1.1	50	99	488,100	11.6	Ashgabat	Turkmen Manat	Turkmen, Uzbek
United Arab Emirates	77	7500	3.3	90	78	83,600	89.7	Abu Dhabi	Emirati Dirham	Arabic, Hindu, Urdu
Uzbekistan	73	29,123	0.9	39	99.	444,103	65.6	Tashkent	Uzbek Soum	Uzbek, Russian
Vietnam	72	85,847	1.1	30	90	329,315	260.7	Hanoi	Dong	Vietnamese
Yemen	64	22,492	2.6	32	50	527,970	42.6	Sanaa	Yemeni Rial	Arabic

*NB: Cyprus is part of Europe, but the mapping can be found in the Asia section.

The Near East

A poor, mountainous region, Turkey has a beautiful coastline and thriving tourist industry. The country is currently being transformed by the Great Anatolian project – reservoirs will be built along the Tigris and Euphrates rivers, to irrigate 16,000 km² of land. Although geographically closer to Asia, Turkey is internationally recognized as part of Europe. Israel was created in 1948. Land was taken from the Palestinians resulting in conflict with Syria, Jordan and Lebanon. Sheep and goats are the main livestock. Where irrigation is possible, vegetables and fruit are grown, much of which is exported to Europe.

BULGARIA

GREECE

Edirne

Bosporus Strait

Tekirdag • Istanbul •
Sea of Marmara
Izmit •

Bursa •
Saka

Balikesir •
Eskisehir •

Kütahy
A N A T
P L A

Manisa •
Izmir •
Usak •

Ephesus •
Nazilli •

Aydin •
Denizli •
Isp

Bodrum •
T A

Antalya •

The **Temple Mount** in Jerusalem [I9] is an important religious site. The Dome of the Rock is a Muslim shrine. The Western Wall dates back to 500 BC and is used by Jews for prayer.

THE DISTANCE from Europe to Asia across the Bosporus Strait [B6] is only 700 m and takes one minute by car across a bridge.

Did You Know?

Cyprus is the third largest island in the Mediterranean. The northern area of the island is Turkish Cypriot and the southern area is Greek Cypriot. Although geographically closer to Asia, Cyprus joined the EU in 2004.

Search and Find

Cyprus
• Nicosia F8

Israel
• Jerusalem I9

Jordan
• Amman H10

Lebanon
• Beirut G9

Syria
• Damascus . . . H10

Turkey
• Ankara C8

Facts and Stats

• Turkey's area of 780,580 km² is 7.5 times the area of Iceland.

• Mount Ararat [D14] is the highest mountain at 5137 m –16 times higher than the Eiffel Tower.

• The life expectancy of people in Israel is 81 years, compared to 75 years in Syria and a world average of 68 years.

Pamukkale, which means 'cotton castle' in Turkish, was formed from the water of a very hot spring. The water contains a lot of chalk, which results in the limestone cliffs that can be seen today.

8 9 10 11 12 13 14

0 50 100 150 200 mi
0 100 200 300 km

The **Dead Sea** [I9] is the second saltiest body of water in the world and is called 'dead' because fish and other organisms cannot survive in it. Salty deposits cover the beaches and cliffs, and it is almost impossible to sink in the water because of the high salt content.

A
B
C
D
E
F
G
H
I
J

BLACK SEA

GEORGIA
ARMENIA

Zonguldak
• Karabük

Samsun •

Ordu •   Trabzon •

• Çorum   PONTIC MOUNTAINS

Kars •

Ankara
• Kirikkale

Kelkit

Erzurum •

Mount Ararat
5137 m

Sivas •   Erzincan •

I A N
A U

TURKEY

Lake
Tuz

Kizilirmak   • Kayseri

Murat

Lake
Van   • Van

• Konya

Malatya •

Elazig •

IRAN

U S   M O U N T A I N S

Adiyaman •

Diyarbakir •   • Batman

Firat

Tarsus •   Adana •
• Osmaniye   • Gaziantep

Khabur   • Al Qamishli

Mersin •

Antakya •

• Al Bab
• Aleppo

Al Hasakah •

CYPRUS

Ar Raqqah •

Euphrates

Nicosia

Lake
Assad

Dayr az Zawr •

SYRIA

aphos
• Limassol

Latakia •

Baniyas •   • Hamah

Tartus •

• Hims

Abu Kamal •

Tripoli •

SYRIAN
DESERT

LEBANON

IRAQ

EDITERRANEAN
SEA

Beirut

Sidon •

Tyre •   **Damascus**
• Al Kiswah

Acre •   • Al Qunaytirah

Haifa •
Nazareth •   Sea of
Galilee   • Dar'a

Hadera •
Netanya •   WEST   • Irbid
Ramallah •   BANK
Tel Aviv •   • Az-Zarqa
Jerusalem   Dead   **Amman**
Gaza •   Sea
• Bethlehem   • Ma'daba
GAZA STRIP
Beersheba •   • Al-Karak

ISRAEL

NEGEV
DESERT   Ma'an •

EGYPT

JORDAN

Elat •   • Aqaba

Gulf of
Aqaba

SAUDI ARABIA

Wadi al Hasa

In the next

...Turkey will produce enough Turkish delight confectionery to create a pillar 305 m in height.

minute...

The ruins of Ephesus [D5] are a major tourist attraction. Built in 135 AD, the restored **Library of Celsus** is a monumental tomb for Celsus Polemaeanus, the governor of Asia. His grave is across the entrance, under the ground floor.

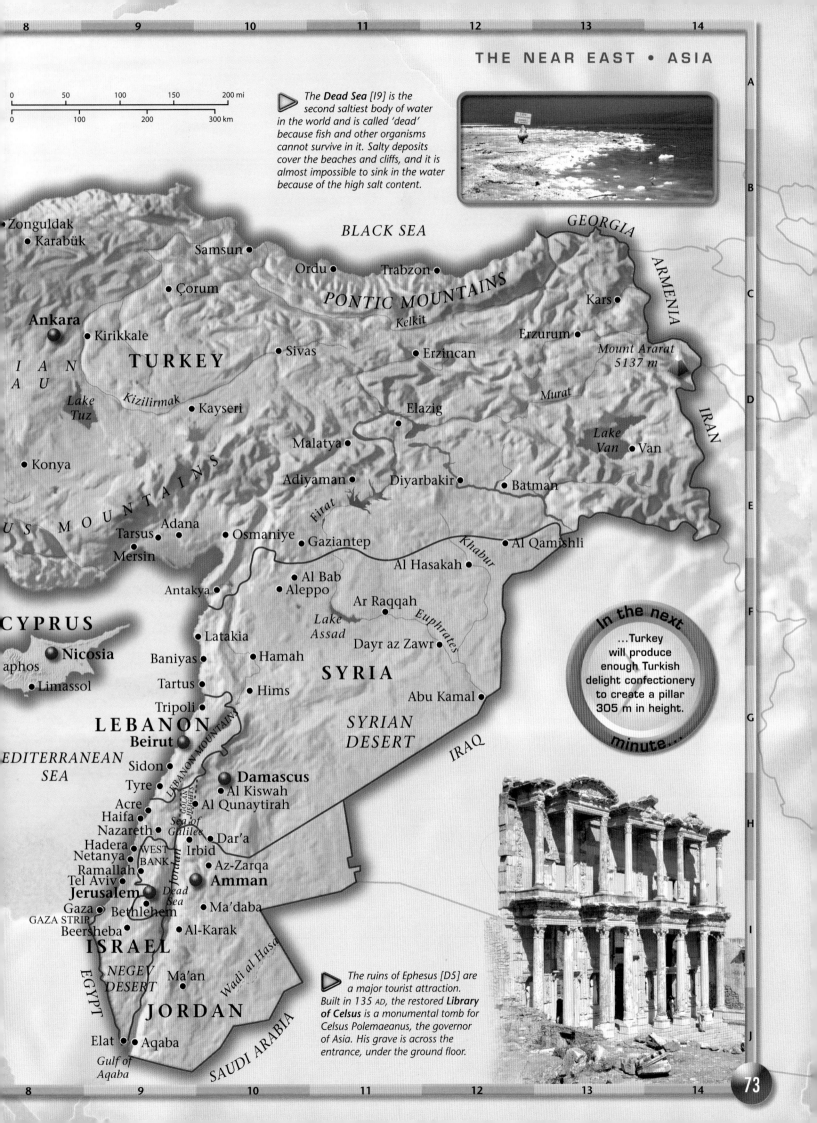

8 9 10 11 12 13 14

The Middle East

Vast oil and gas reserves have made several countries in the Middle East some of the wealthiest in the world. However, before oil was discovered, this was a poor region of desert tribes and coastal fishing. The area between the Euphrates and Tigris rivers was once home to the great civilization of Mesopotamia. Recent wars have damaged the economies of Iran and Iraq, but other countries such as Bahrain are investing in tourism and other forms of industry. The city of Dubai now has the largest indoor ski slope in the world.

For thousands of years, Iran has been the centre of the hand-woven **Persian carpet** industry. Although machinery is widely used today, traditional methods are still used in some areas. A medium-sized rug can take a skilled worker up to a year to complete.

Extreme Weather

Midday temperatures can reach 50°C in the desert areas, but snow is common in the mountains of Iran and Iraq.

Did You Know?

The United Arab Emirates obtains more than 80 percent of its water supply by desalinating sea water.

Millions of Muslims have made a pilgrimage, or Hajj, to Mecca [G5]. The holiest place in Islam is the **Kaaba**. Non-Muslims cannot enter Mecca.

ARMEN

TURKEY

T

Mosul● ●Arbil

Kirkuk ●

I R A Q

Bakht.

SYRIA

Baghdad ●

S Y R I A N
D E S E R T

Tigris

Karbala ●

Euphrates

Najaf ●

JORDAN

An Nasiriyah

EGYPT

Al Jawf ● ● Sakakah

N A F U D
D E S E R T

Buraydah ●

H
I
J
A
Z

Shaqra ●

Riyadl

● Medina

● Yanbu

RED SEA

Jiddah ●
● Mecca
● Taif

S A U I

As-Sulayyil ●

A S I R

● Abha

● Jizan
● Harad

● Sanaa
● Al-Hudaydah

● Ta'izz

Sha

● Aden

GU

CASPIAN SEA

TURKMENISTAN

AZERBAIJAN

asht •
• Babol   • Gorgan
Karaj • • Tehran   • Mashhad

ELBURZ MOUNTAINS

• Qom
• Hamadan
Kashan •

IRAN

• Esfahan

• Yazd

AFGHANISTAN

ZAGROS MOUNTAINS

• Ahvaz

sra •
• Abadan   Kerman •   Zahedan •

WAIT
Kuwait
City   • Shiraz

PAKISTAN

• Bushehr

PERSIAN GULF

Bandar-e •   • Bandar 'Abbas
Lengeh

Al Qatif •
BAHRAIN   Strait of Hormuz   • Jask
-Dammam • • **Manama**
QATAR   Sharjah •   **GULF OF OMAN**
Al-Hufuf • • **Doha**   Dubai •
Abu Dhabi •   • Suhar

UNITED ARAB   Jabal ash Sham   • Matrah
EMIRATES   3035 m   • **Muscat**

RABIA   Nizwa •   • Sur   **ARABIAN SEA**

EMPTY QUARTER   **OMAN**

• Khaluf

• Salalah

YEMEN

• Al Mukalla

*SOCOTRA
(YEMEN)*

ADEN

THE DISTANCE from Yemen to Africa is only 30 km across the Red Sea and takes four hours by canoe.

Facts and Stats

• The average income per person in Qatar is £45,600, compared to a world average of £5640.

• Saudi Arabia has an area of 2.2 million km² and is 21 times the area of Iceland.

• The longest river is the Euphrates [C7]. At 2800 km in length, it is nearly 2.5 times shorter than the Nile river.

In the next ...Saudi Arabia will produce 850,000 litres of oil – enough for a car to travel 10 million km. **minute...**

0   100   200   300   400 mi
0   200   400   600 km

Built in the 1970s, **Kuwait's water towers [D8]** are more than 145 m in height. One tower provides electricity, and the other two towers store water – the middle tower holds more than 4 million litres of water. The main tower also has a viewing platform and revolving restaurant.

Indian subcontinent

With ice-covered mountains, tropical lowlands and hot deserts, this region is one of contrasts. Afghanistan is a war-torn, semi-desert nation that is in the process of rebuilding amidst ongoing conflicts. India has one of the most rapidly growing economies in the world. A highly educated, English-speaking workforce has resulted in many European and American companies establishing various support operations in India. The 'Bollywood' film studios are a worldwide success and cities are rapidly expanding. However, out of India's 1.1 billion population, two-thirds remain poor, rural farmers. Pakistan, Bangladesh and the Himalayan states of Nepal and Bhutan remain relatively undeveloped.

The **Taj Mahal** in Agra [D9], India, was built for Mumtaz Mahal, the wife of Emperor Shah Jahan. When she died in 1629, the Emperor ordered the most beautiful tomb in the world to be built. It took 20,000 workers about 20 years to build. The Emperor and his wife are buried beneath the 60-m-high white dome.

Search and Find

Afghanistan
- Kabul B7

Bangladesh
- Dhaka E11

Bhutan
- Thimphu D11

India
- New Delhi D9

Nepal
- Kathmandu . . D10

Pakistan
- Islamabad B8

Sri Lanka
- Colombo J9
- Kotte J9

Did You Know?

Great Britain ruled India until 1947. This is why English is widely spoken and cricket is the national sport.

THE DISTANCE from the Everest base camp to the summit is 10 km. In 2000, it was climbed in less than 17 hours.

World Record

In 1985, Mawsynram [E12] recorded the world's highest yearly rainfall – over 26,000 mm.

Many Hindus go to a 'mandir', or **temple**, to say prayers and to make offerings of food to the gods. The temples are beautifully decorated with carvings of gods and spirits.

TURKMENISTAN

Sheberghan •

Mazar-e Sh

• Herat

AFGHANISTA

Kab

• Farah

IRAN

Helmand

RIGESTAN
DESERT

• Qandaha

Quetta •

PAKISTA

Larkana • • Suk

• Gwadar

Indus

Hyderabad •

Karachi •

• Mirpur K

RANN O
KACHCH

Gulf of
Kachchh

Ahmada

Jamnagar •

*ARABIAN
SEA*

Bhavnaga
Su

Gulf of
Khambha

Mumba
(Bombay

INDIAN OCEAN

SIGIRIYA, or Lion's Mouth, was the fortress of Sri Lankan King Kashyapa (AD 477–495). Only the two giant paws of the lion remain.

Facts and Stats

• The longest river in the region is the Brahmaputra [D12]. At 2900 km in length, it is almost half the length of the Nile river.

• The highest mountain in the world is Mount Everest [D11] at 8848 m in height – 28 times higher than the Eiffel Tower.

• The life expectancy of people in Afghanistan is 49 years, compared to 76 years in Sri Lanka and a world average of 68 years.

Extreme Weather

The heaviest recorded hailstones, weighing up to one kg killed 92 people in Bangladesh on 14 April 1986.

TAJIKISTAN

K2 8611 m

CHINA

HIMALAYAS

Mardan
Islamabad
awar
alpindi
Srinagar
alabad • Gujranwala
Lahore • Amritsar
tan • Sabiwel
Sutlej • Ludhiana
awalpur
Chandigarh

Meerut
Delhi
New Delhi

NEPAL

Ganges

Kathmandu

Thimphu
BHUTAN

Jaipur • Agra
hpur • Ajmer
Yamuna
Lucknow
Kanpur
Varanasi
Mount Everest 8848 m
Biratnagar
Jorhat

Rangpur
Brahmaputra
Guwahati

NAGA HILLS

•Udaipur
Lalitpur
Allahabad •
Patna
Rajshahi
Sylhet • Mawsynram
Imphal

Bhopal
odara
Narmada
Indore

INDIA

Dhanbad •
BANGLADESH
Dhaka
Agartala

Jamshedpur •
Khulna

Nagpur •
Raipur •
Kolkata
(Calcutta)
Chittagong

BURMA (MYANMAR)

Cuttack •

Godavari

EASTERN GHATS

BAY OF BENGAL

•Solapur
hapur
Hyderabad
Krishna
Vishakhapatnam

Vijayawada

Kurnool

The **Ganges river** flows through the city of Varanasi [E10] and is believed to be sacred. Many Hindus make pilgrimages to pray and bathe in the holy water.

Nellore
galore
Bengaluru
(Bangalore)
Chennai (Madras)
•Mysore
Puducherry
Kozhikode (Calicut)
• Coimbatore
Tiruchchirappalli

ANDAMAN ISLANDS (INDIA)

Kochi Madurai
Cochin)
Palk Strait
Jaffna

0   100   200   300   400 mi
0   200   400   600 km

iruvananthapuram
ivandrum)
Trincomalee

SRI LANKA

NICOBAR ISLANDS (INDIA)

Colombo
Kandy
Kotte
Galle

In the next ...more than 50 babies will be born in India – that's 66,000 every day. minute...

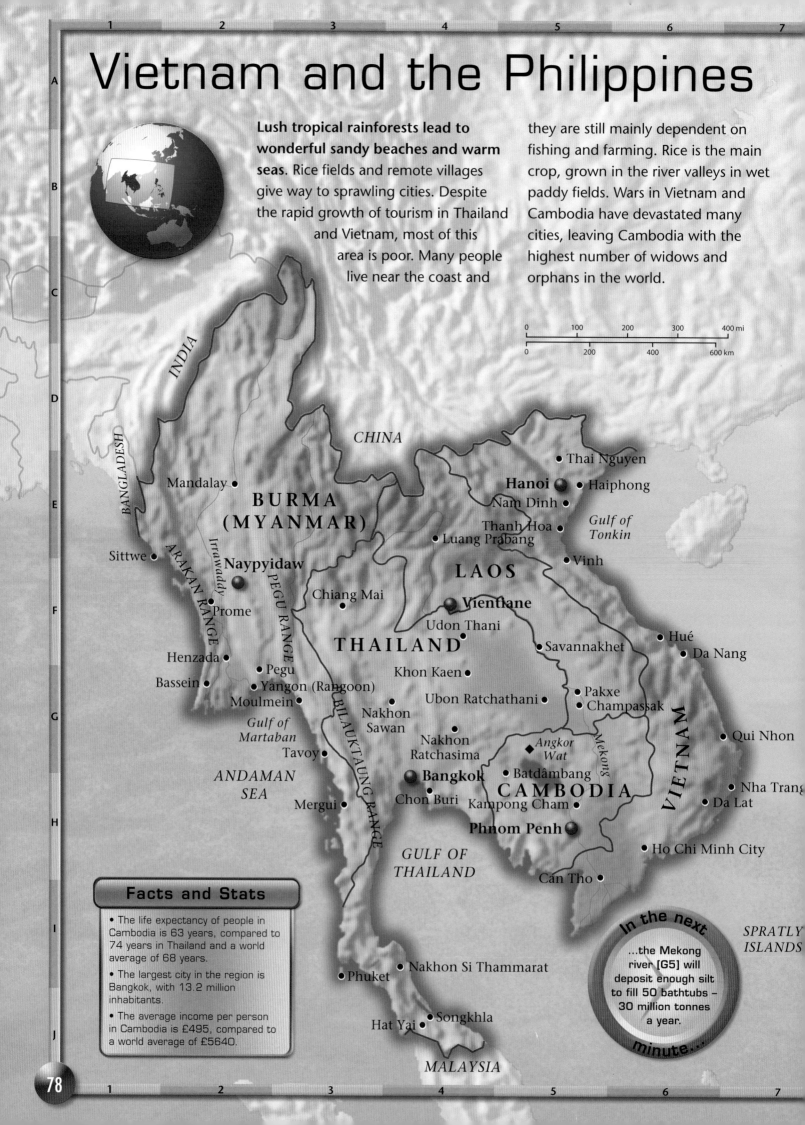

Vietnam and the Philippines

Lush tropical rainforests lead to wonderful sandy beaches and warm seas. Rice fields and remote villages give way to sprawling cities. Despite the rapid growth of tourism in Thailand and Vietnam, most of this area is poor. Many people live near the coast and they are still mainly dependent on fishing and farming. Rice is the main crop, grown in the river valleys in wet paddy fields. Wars in Vietnam and Cambodia have devastated many cities, leaving Cambodia with the highest number of widows and orphans in the world.

0 100 200 300 400 mi
0 200 400 600 km

INDIA

CHINA

● Thai Nguyen

BANGLADESH

Mandalay ●

BURMA (MYANMAR)

Hanoi ● ● Haiphong
Nam Dinh ●

Gulf of Tonkin

Sittwe ●

Irrawaddy

ARAKAN RANGE

Naypyidaw

Thanh Hoa ●
● Luang Prabang

● Vinh

LAOS

Prome ●

PEGU RANGE

Chiang Mai ●

Vientiane

Udon Thani ●

● Hué
● Da Nang

Henzada ●

THAILAND

Savannakhet ●

Khon Kaen ●

Pegu ●
Bassein ●
Yangon (Rangoon) ●

Ubon Ratchathani ●

● Pakxe
● Champassak

Moulmein ●

Gulf of Martaban

BILAUKTAUNG RANGE

Nakhon Sawan ●

VIETNAM

Tavoy ●

Nakhon Ratchasima ●

Mekong

● Qui Nhon

ANGKOR Wat ◆

ANDAMAN SEA

Bangkok

● Batdâmbang

● Nha Trang

Mergui ●

Chon Buri ●

CAMBODIA

● Da Lat

Kampong Cham ●

Phnom Penh ●

● Ho Chi Minh City

GULF OF THAILAND

Can Tho ●

● Nakhon Si Thammarat

● Phuket

SPRATLY ISLANDS

In the next ...the Mekong river [G5] will deposit enough silt to fill 50 bathtubs – 30 million tonnes a year. **minute...**

● Songkhla

Hat Yai ●

MALAYSIA

VIETNAM AND THE PHILIPPINES • ASIA

*Many young men in Thailand temporarily become **Buddhist monks** to learn more about their faith. They shave their heads and beards and wear robes to show commitment to the holy life.*

Search and Find

Cambodia	**Philippines**
● Phnom Penh . . H5	● Manila F10
Laos	**Thailand**
● Vientiane F4	● Bangkok H4
Burma (Myanmar)	**Vietnam**
● Naypyidaw F2	● Hanoi E5

THE DISTANCE from Yangon [G2] to Bangkok [H4] is 640 km and would take an elephant three days of non-stop walking.

*The canals in Bangkok [H4] are used for **floating markets** where fresh produce, such as fruit, vegetables and flowers, is sold from boats.*

Luzon Strait

BABUYAN
ISLANDS

Laoag ●

● Tuguegarao

Luzon

PACIFIC
OCEAN

PHILIPPINES

● Cabanatuan

Angeles ●

● Quezon City

Manila ●

Batangas ●

Mindoro

SOUTH
CHINA
SEA

Mindoro Strait

● Calbayog
Samar

● Ormoc
Leyte

Bacolod
Panay ●

Iloilo ●

● Cebu

Negros

Butuan ●

Cagayan de Oro ●

Palawan Passage

● Puerto Princesa

Palawan

Mindanao

Pagadian ●

Davao ●

*Moro
Gulf*

General
Santos ●

*SULU
SEA*

Zamboanga ●

*CELEBES
SEA*

Balabac Strait

*SULU
ARCHIPELAGO*

Did You Know?

The ruins of the ancient city of Angkor Wat [G5], complete with Hindu temples and royal palaces, were discovered in the Cambodian rainforest 150 years ago.

Extreme Weather

In July, the monsoon rains bring the city of Yangon [G2] as much rain as London gets in a year.

*Many tropical countries suffer from rainy seasons called monsoons, which result in serious flooding. In some parts of Asia, **houses are built on stilts** over bodies of water to protect them against water damage.*

Indonesia, Malaysia and Singapore

Situated on the Equator, this region has a hot, wet climate. Malaysia is part of the Asian mainland and the large island of Borneo. It is developing rapidly with car and shipbuilding industries. Singapore is the richest country in this region, based on its technology industry, banking and high educational standards. A safe, law-abiding nation, laws against all types of crime, even dropping litter, are strictly enforced. Indonesia consists of over 13,000 islands. Natural disasters, poor communications and corruption have restricted economic growth. Although East Timor became independent from Indonesia in 2002, it remains impoverished.

THAILAND

George Town
Kuala Terengganu
Ipoh • *MALAY*
PENINSULA
Medan •
Kelang • **Kuala Lumpur**   *Natuna Island*
Putrajaya   M A L A Y S I A
Strait of Malacca   Johor Baharu
Singapore
Pekanbaru •   **SINGAPORE**
Sumatra
Padang •
Bangka
Jambi •
Belitung
Palembang •

Kota Kinabalu •   • Sandakan
Bandar Seri Begawan
BRUNEI   *SABAH*

CELEBES SEA

SARAWAK
• Kuching   Manado •

Pontianak • *Kapuas*   *MOLU SEA*

KALIMANTAN   • Palu
Balikpapan •   *Sulawesi*
Borneo   *Makassar Strait*
Barito
Banjarmasin •

I N D O N E S I A

• Makasar

Tanjungkarang •
Telukbetung
Jakarta   *JAVA SEA*
Bandung • *Java*   • Semarang   *FLORES SEA*
Surakarta •   • Surabaya
Malang •   *Komodo Flores*
Bali • Mataram
Lombok   *Sumbawa*   • Ende
Sumba   Kupang • *Ti*

◁ More than 450 m in height, the **Petronas Towers** in Kuala Lumpur [E2] contain 88 floors of offices, a shopping mall, a concert hall and parking for 4500 cars.

Extreme Weather

At the Equator, the climate is the same throughout the year – hot and very wet. Singapore's temperature averages at 27°C.

In the next minute... ...five new cars will be made in this region – that's 2.6 million a year.

Tea has been grown throughout Indonesia for more than 200 years, especially in Java and Sumatra. These small islands now produce 7 percent of the world's tea exports. The shoots are picked by hand, packed and exported.

Did You Know?

The 2004 tsunami in southeast Asia was caused by an undersea earthquake. The waves travelled at speeds of up to 800 km/h – 230,000 people were killed and five million were made homeless.

Search and Find

Brunei
- Bandar Seri Begawan E5

East Timor
- Dili H7

Indonesia
- Jakarta H3

Malaysia
- Kuala Lumpur . . E2
- Putrajaya E2

Singapore
- Singapore F2

THE DISTANCE from Singapore to Malaysia is only 1056 m and the Joho–Singapore Causeway can be crossed by car in one minute.

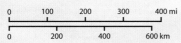

```
0    100   200   300   400 mi
0      200     400      600 km
```

Imahera

• Sorong

SERAM SEA

Seram

• Ambon

Jayapura •

New Guinea

DA SEA

Tanimbar Island

ARU ISLANDS

ARAFURA SEA

au

ST TIMOR

The **Batak people** live in Sumatra, Indonesia. Easily recognizable, their houses are built on stilts and have high, thatched roofs. Often ornaments and paintings are placed on the outside to ward away evil spirits.

Facts and Stats

- The average income per person in Singapore is £26,740 compared to £310 in East Timor and a world average of £5640.

- The life expectancy of people in Singapore is 84 years, compared to 74 years in Malaysia and a world average of 68 years.

- Indonesia's area of 1.9 million km^2 is 18 times the area of Iceland.

Japan

Japan consists of four main islands – Kyushu, Hokkaido, Honshu and Shikoku. More than 70 percent of the country is covered with forested volcanic mountains such as Mount Fuji. Most of Japan's population lives on the flatlands along the coast, resulting in a very high population density. People live in high-rise flats or small houses, but frequent earthquakes can cause immense damage. Agriculture, industry, and urban development are concentrated on the main island of Honshu in the area between Osaka and Tokyo. Japan is one of the richest nations in the world, with well-known brands such as Toyota, Honda, Nissan, Sony, Panasonic and JVC.

▷ *The Golden Pavilion, Kyoto [G8], was originally built in the 14th century for a samurai general. The temple has been destroyed many times, and was most recently rebuilt in the 1950s. The pavilion, except the basement floor, is covered in pure gold leaf.*

World Record
The Seikan tunnel is the longest railway in the world at 54 km in length.

SEA OF JAPAN

MOUNT FUJI [G9] is an active volcano, but last erupted in 1707. More than 200,000 people walk to its snow-capped summit each year.

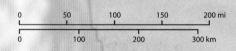

THE DISTANCE from Tokyo [G10] to Osaka [H8] is 515 km. It only takes 2.5 hours by high-speed train, travelling at 206 km/h.

▷ *Sumo wrestling is a popular sport in Japan. Competitors have a body weight of up to 270 kg and their aim is to push their opponent out of the ring. Sumo is more than 2000 years old, and has strict rules and ceremonies.*

Oki Island

Matsue • Yonago • Tot

Korea Strait

Tsushima Hiroshima Okayama • Ko

Shimonoseki Kure • Takamatsu•

Kitakyushu • Hofu Wakay

Fukuoka • Matsuyama • Tokushima

Sasebo • Oita • Kochi

Kumamoto • Saiki • *Shikoku*

Nagasaki •

Amakusa Island Nobeoka • *Bungo Channel*

Koshiki Island *Kyushu*

 Miyazaki

Miyakonojo

Kagoshima

Yaku Island *Tanega Island*

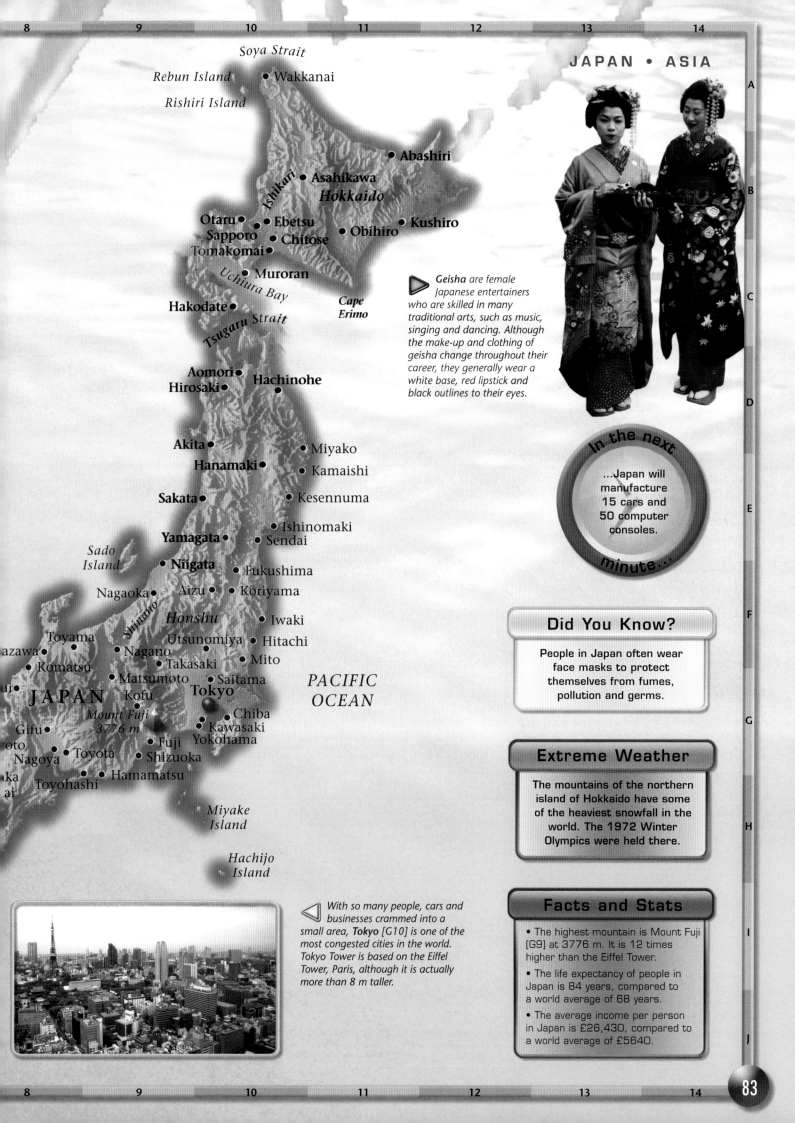

JAPAN • ASIA

Soya Strait

Rebun Island • Wakkanai

Rishiri Island

• Abashiri

Ishikari • Asahikawa

Hokkaido

Otaru• • Ebetsu •Kushiro
Sapporo • Obihiro
Tomakomai• • Chitose

• Muroran

Uchiura Bay

Hakodate •

Cape Erimo

Tsugaru Strait

Aomori•
Hirosaki• **Hachinohe**

Akita• • Miyako
Hanamaki• • Kamaishi

Sakata• • Kesennuma

• Ishinomaki
Yamagata• • Sendai

Sado Island
• **Niigata** • Fukushima

Nagaoka• Aizu• • Koriyama

Shinano
Honshu • Iwaki

Toyama Utsunomiya• • Hitachi
azawa• Nagano • Mito
• Komatsu • Takasaki
Matsumoto• • Saitama
JAPAN Kofu **Tokyo**
• Chiba
Mount Fuji • Kawasaki
Gifu• 3776 m Yokohama
voto • • Fuji
Nagoya • Toyota • Shizuoka
ka • Hamamatsu
ai Toyohashi

Miyake Island

PACIFIC OCEAN

Hachijo Island

Geisha are female Japanese entertainers who are skilled in many traditional arts, such as music, singing and dancing. Although the make-up and clothing of geisha change throughout their career, they generally wear a white base, red lipstick and black outlines to their eyes.

In the next

...Japan will manufacture 15 cars and 50 computer consoles.

minute...

Did You Know?

People in Japan often wear face masks to protect themselves from fumes, pollution and germs.

Extreme Weather

The mountains of the northern island of Hokkaido have some of the heaviest snowfall in the world. The 1972 Winter Olympics were held there.

With so many people, cars and businesses crammed into a small area, **Tokyo [G10]** is one of the most congested cities in the world. Tokyo Tower is based on the Eiffel Tower, Paris, although it is actually more than 8 m taller.

Facts and Stats

• The highest mountain is Mount Fuji [G9] at 3776 m. It is 12 times higher than the Eiffel Tower.

• The life expectancy of people in Japan is 84 years, compared to a world average of 68 years.

• The average income per person in Japan is £26,430, compared to a world average of £5640.

China and Korea

One-fifth of the world's population lives in China, despite each family being limited to just one child. Once a poor, rural nation, China has the fastest-growing economy in the world. Each year, millions of farm workers move to the cities to work in factories. A new power station has to be built every week, making China the biggest user of coal and oil in the world. In contrast, Mongolia has a small, mainly rural population. North Korea is a Communist state with a low standard of living, but South Korea is much richer due to its shipbuilding, electronic and car industries.

In 210–209 BC, thousands of **terracotta soldiers** were buried with the first emperor of China, Qin Shi Huangdi, as it was believed to make him powerful in heaven. The tomb was discovered in 1974 near Xi'an [F10].

Search and Find

China
- Beijing E11

Mongolia
- Ulaanbaatar . . . C9

North Korea
- Pyongyang . . . D12

South Korea
- Seoul E13

Taiwan
- Taipei H13

LHASA [H7] in the Himalayas is the capital of Tibet and home to many Buddhist monasteries and ancient palaces.

THE DISTANCE from one end of The Great Wall of China to the other is 3460 km – nearly half the length of the Nile river.

Facts and Stats

- China has a population of 1340 million, which would fill 13,400 Olympic stadiums. Mongolia's population of 2.6 million would only fill 26 stadiums.
- China's area of 9.6 million km^2 is 93 times the area of Iceland.
- The Chang Jiang (Yangtze) [G10] is the longest river at 6300 km in length. The Nile river is nearly twice as long.

One of China's largest cities, **Shanghai** [F12] has a population of 14.2 million. The skyline is dominated by high-rise office buildings and the city is rapidly becoming one of the most important financial centres in the world. The Oriental Pearl Tower is the fifth highest tower in the world at 468 m.

Ulaang·

ALTAI MOUNTA·

Uliast·

KAZAKHSTAN

Tacheng·

Yining·

Urumqi·

Turpan·

Bosten Hu

Korla·

KYRGYZSTAN

TARIM BASIN

·Kashi

S I N K I A N G

TAJIKISTAN

·Shache

TAKLIMAKAN

DESERT

ALTUN SHAN

AFGHANISTAN

·Hotan

Golmud·

PAKISTAN

K U N L U N   S H A N

T I B E T

INDIA

·Gar

Amdo·

PLATEAU

HIMALAYAS

·Lhasa

NEPAL

·Gyangzê

Mount Everest
8850 m

IN·

BHUTAN

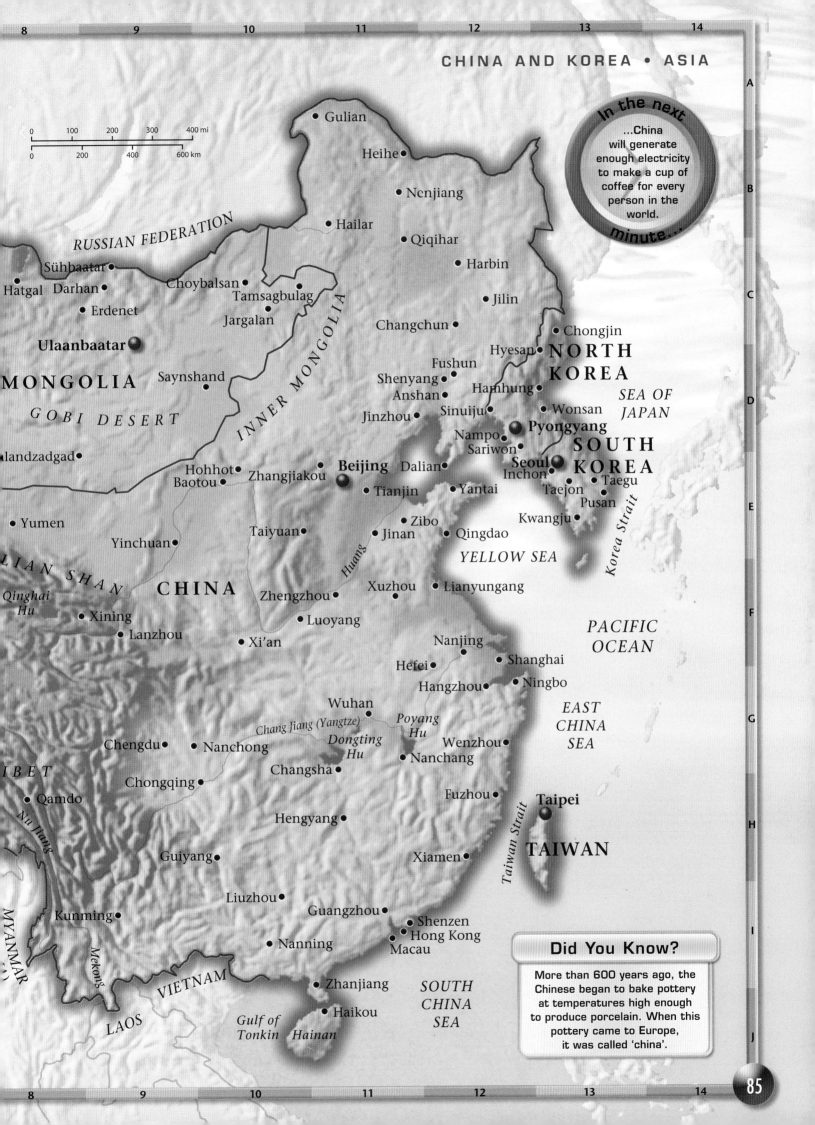

In the next minute...
...China will generate enough electricity to make a cup of coffee for every person in the world.

0 100 200 300 400 mi
0   200   400   600 km

Gulian

Heihe

Nenjiang

RUSSIAN FEDERATION

Hailar

Qiqihar

Harbin

Sühbaatar

Jilin

Hatgal Darhan

Choybalsan

Tamsagbulag

Changchun

Chongjin

Erdenet

Jargalan

NORTH KOREA

Hyesan

Fushun

Ulaanbaatar

Shenyang

Hamhung

INNER MONGOLIA

Anshan

Wonsan

MONGOLIA

Saynshand

Jinzhou

Sinuiju

Pyongyang

SEA OF JAPAN

GOBI DESERT

Nampo

Sariwon

SOUTH KOREA

landzadgad

Seoul

Hohhot

Zhangjiakou

Beijing

Dalian

Inchon

Taegu

Baotou

Tianjin

Yantai

Taejon

Pusan

Yumen

Zibo

Kwangju

Korea Strait

Yinchuan

Taiyuan

Jinan

Qingdao

YELLOW SEA

LIAN SHAN

CHINA

Zhengzhou

Xuzhou

Lianyungang

Qinghai Hu

Xining

Luoyang

PACIFIC OCEAN

Lanzhou

Xi'an

Nanjing

Hefei

Shanghai

Hangzhou

Ningbo

Chang Jiang (Yangtze)

Poyang Hu

EAST CHINA SEA

Wuhan

Dongting Hu

Chengdu

Nanchong

Wenzhou

TIBET

Chongqing

Changsha

Nanchang

Qamdo

Hengyang

Fuzhou

Taipei

Nu Jiang

Guiyang

Xiamen

TAIWAN

Kunming

Liuzhou

Guangzhou

Taiwan Strait

MYANMAR

Mekong

Nanning

Shenzen

Hong Kong

Macau

LAOS

VIETNAM

Zhanjiang

SOUTH CHINA SEA

Gulf of Tonkin

Haikou

Hainan

Did You Know?

More than 600 years ago, the Chinese began to bake pottery at temperatures high enough to produce porcelain. When this pottery came to Europe, it was called 'china'.

East Russia

The Russian Federation is the largest country in the world. However, eastern Russia contains large areas that are unpopulated. Vast areas north of the Arctic Circle suffer freezing conditions that make farming impossible. To the south, much is covered by forest or grassland. Towns are found only where there are natural resources, such as coal, oil, gas, iron and uranium. Kazakhstan is rapidly becoming wealthy due to selling oil, gas and metals to Europe and China, but Turkmenistan, Uzbekistan, Tajikistan and Kyrgyzstan remain underdeveloped.

Extreme Weather

In January 1926, Oymyakon [F10] recorded the lowest temperature for any permanently inhabited location on Earth at −71.2°C.

In the next minute...

...11,000 Russians will be playing chess, making it the nation's most popular sport.

SEVERNAYA ZEMLYA

ARCTIC OCEAN

KARA SEA

SIBERIA

Vorkuta

Noril'sk

RUSSIA

Yenisey

Tunguska

Surgut

Serov

Nizhnevartovsk

Ob

Angara

Lena

Yekaterinburg

Krasnoyarsk

Ust'Ilimsk

Kurgan

Tomsk

Kansk

Chelyabinsk

Kemerovo

Bratsk

YABL MOU

Omsk

Novosibirsk

Semey

Novokuznetsk

Abakan

Usol'ye-Sibirskoye

Lake Baikal

Kokshetau

Barnaul

Orenburg

Pavlodar

Angarsk

Chita

Astana

Irkutsk

Ulan-Ud

Aqtobe

Oskemen

MONGOLIA

Ural

Qaraghandy

Lake Balkhash

Atyrau

Zhezkazgan

KAZAKHSTAN

CHINA

CASPIAN SEA

Ustyurt Plateau

Aral Sea

Qyzylorda

Taldyqorgan

Aktau

Almaty

UZBEKISTAN

Tashkent

Bishkek

KYRGYZSTAN

TURKMENISTAN

Samarkand

Amu Darya

Balkanabat

Dushanbe

Ashgabat

TAJIKISTAN

IRAN

AFGHANISTAN

PAKISTAN

Search and Find

Kazakhstan	Tajikistan
● Astana H3	● Dushanbe J3
Kyrgyzstan	**Turkmenistan**
● Bishkek I4	● Ashgabat J3
Russian Federation	**Uzbekistan**
● Moscow [see page 45]	● Tashkent. I3

▷ *Lake Baikal* *[H7] is the oldest and deepest lake in the world at 1637 m in depth. It holds more than 20 percent of the world's fresh water.*

Facts and Stats

• Turkmenistan's population of 6.6 million would fill 66 stadiums.

• The life expectancy in Russia is 66 years, compared to a world average of 68 years.

• The average income per person in Russia is £6490, compared to £495 in Tajikistan and a world average of £5640.

THE DISTANCE from Moscow in European Russia to the far east of Russia takes six days and four hours to travel by train at 62 km/h.

Did You Know?

Russia has 9 time zones. When it is 12 p.m. in Moscow, it is 3 p.m. in Novosibirsk [H5] and 7 p.m. in Vladivostok [I9].

LAPTEV SEA

EAST SIBERIAN SEA

CHUKCHI SEA

Lena

VERKHOYANSKIY MOUNTAINS

CHERSKIY MOUNTAINS

Kolyma

Yakutsk•

Oymyakon•

EDERATION

BERING SEA

Magadan•

SEA OF OKHOTSK

| 0 | 250 | 500 | 750 | 1000 mi |
| 0 | 400 | 800 | 1200 | 1600 km |

OV Y Y AINS

Amur

Petropavlovsk-Kamchatskiy•

VLADIVOSTOK [I9] is home to the Russian navy's Pacific fleet. Until 1991, foreigners were not allowed into the city in case they were spies.

CHINA

Blagoveshchensk•

• Komsomol'sk-na-Amure

PACIFIC OCEAN

Khabarovsk•

SIKHOTE-ALIN MOUNTAINS

• Yuzhno-Sakhalinsk

Vladivostok•

NORTH KOREA

▷ *The Aral Sea [I3] has shrunk by 90 percent since 1960. The remaining water has become very salty, killing off so many fish that the commercial fishing industry stopped and many boats have been abandoned.*

Oceania

PACIFIC
OCEAN

PALAU
MICRONESIA
MARSHALL
ISLANDS

PAPUA
NEW GUINEA
NAURU
SOLOMON
ISLANDS
TUVALU
KIRIBATI

VANUATU
SAMOA
COOK ISLANDS
TONGA NIUE
FIJI

INDIAN
OCEAN

PACIFIC
OCEAN

AUSTRALIA

NEW
ZEALAND

SOUTHERN OCEAN

COUNTRY FACTFILE

Country	Life expectancy	Population in thousands	Population growth %	Population as urban %	Literacy %	Area km²	Population density per km²	Capital city	Currency	Languages
Australia	82	22,618	1.1	90	99	7,703,429	2.9	Canberra	Australian Dollar	English
Cook Islands	75	17.8	-3.0	75	95	237	75.1	Avarua	New Zealand Dollar	Cook Island Maori, English
Fiji	72	860	0.8	52	94	18,272	47.1	Suva	Fijian Dollar	English, Fijian
Kiribati	65	99	1.2	44	90	717	138.1	Bairiki	Australian Dollar	I-Kiribati, English
Marshall Islands	72	56	2	72	94	181	309.4	Majuro	US Dollar	Marshallese, English
Micronesia	72	103	-0.3	26	89	701	146.9	Palikir	US Dollar	English, Chuukese, Pohnpeain
Nauru	66	9.3	0.0	N/A	90	21	442.9	Yaren	Australian Dollar	Nauruan
New Zealand	81	4405	0.9	87	99	270,534	16.3	Wellington	New Zealand Dollar	English, Maori
Niue	75	1.6	-0.03	38	95	259	6.2	Alofi	New Zealand Dollar	Niuean, English
Palau	72	19.9	0.4	83	92	458	43.4	Ngerulmud-Melekeok	US Dollar	Palauan, English
Papua New Guinea	66	7060	2	17	17	462,840	15.3	Port Moresby	Kina	Tok Pisin (Pidgin English), English
Samoa	73	186	0.6	34	99	2831	65.7	Apia	Tala	Samoan
Solomon Islands	74	516	2.2	18	54	28,370	18.2	Honiara	Solmon Islands Dollar	Melanesian languages
Tonga	75	103	0.2	43	99	748	137.7	Nuku'alofa	Pa'anga	Tongan
Tuvalu	65	11	0.7	50	95	24	458.3	Vaiaku (Funafuti)	Australian Dollar	Melanesian languages
Vanuatu	65	243	1.3	26	74	12,190	19.9	Port-Vila	Vatu	Bislama, English, French

* Both the Cook Islands and Niue are self-governing states, but in free association with New Zealand, which is responsible for the aspects of foreign relations and defence that these countries agree to.

Australia

Much of Australia's inland is desert, known as the outback. Most people live in the eastern fertile land between Adelaide and Brisbane, and the capital, Canberra, is in the mountains of the Great Dividing Range. Many lakes in Australia vary in extent and some dry out in drought. Aboriginal people have lived in Australia for more than 40,000 years, but in 1787, British settlers began to arrive and immigration has continued ever since. Aboriginals now make up just 2 percent of the population. Rich in gold, iron ore and coal, Australia is one of the wealthiest nations in the world.

Extreme Weather

To fight the effects of long periods of drought, Toowoomba [F13] may use recycled sewage in the water supply.

Did You Know?

The Great Barrier Reef [D12] stretches for more than 2000 km off the coast of Queensland.

SYDNEY [H12] is the largest city and has two of the most famous sights in the world – the Opera House and Sydney Harbour Bridge.

THE DISTANCE from the east coast to the west coast is 3000 km – the same as from London to Boston, USA.

Facts and Stats

• Australia's area of 7.7 million km² is 75 times the area of Iceland.

• The Murray–Darling [H11] is the longest river. At 3750 km, it is more than half the length of the Nile river.

• Mount Kosciuszko [H11] is the highest mountain at 2229 m in height – seven times higher than the Eiffel Tower.

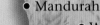
The widest bridge in the world, **Sydney Harbour Bridge** [H12] is almost 50 m in width. At 503 m in length, the bridge has two railway tracks, eight lanes for cars, a bicycle path and a pedestrian path. About 160,000 vehicles cross the bridge each day.

INDIAN
OCEAN

Me
Isl
Bathurst
Island
Darwi

Joseph
Bonaparte
Gulf

Drysdale

• Wyndham

KIMBERLEY
PLATEAU

Broome •   • Derby
                Fitzroy

• Halls Creek

GREAT SANDY
DESERT

• Port Hedland
Dampier •

De Grey

• Onslow
• Exmouth

Ashburton

WESTERN AUSTRALIA

Ay
Ro
(Ul

• Carnarvon   GIBSON DESERT

• Denham   Murchison

• Meekatharra

• Laverton

GREAT VICTORIA DESERT

• Geraldton

• Kalgoorlie

Balladonia •
• Perth   • Norseman
• Freemantle
• Mandurah   Great Austra

Bunbury •   • Wagin

Augusta •   • Esperance

• Albany   SOUTHERN OCEAN

AUSTRALIA • OCEANIA

HEM LAND

Groote
Eylandt

Gulf of
Carpentaria

Roper

erine

*Cape
York
Peninsula*

WELLESLEY
ISLANDS

Kangaroos can reach
speeds of up to 50 km/h.
They can be a danger on the
roads, causing damage to
vehicles in accidents as they
weigh up to 90 kg. Therefore
'kangaroo crossing' signs are
found throughout Australia.

B

• Cooktown

Mitchell

• Normanton   Atherton •   • Port Doulgas
• Burketown   Cairns
                                • Innisfail

C

Flinders

• Tennant Creek   • Townsville
                    Bowen •

GREAT BARRIER REEF

*PACIFIC
OCEAN*

NAMI
SERT

• Mount Isa   *Norman*

Georgina

• Mackay

RN TERRITORY

QUEENSLAND

D

GREAT DIVIDING RANGE

• Alice Springs

NNELL RANGES

• Rockhampton
  • Gladstone

E

Diamantina   *Thomson*   *Barcoo*

• Bundaberg   *Fraser
Island*

AUSTRALIA

Marla •

• Charleville

Warrego

• Sunshine Coast
Toowoomba •   • Brisbane
            • Gold Coast

F

ober Pedy •

OUTH AUSTRALIA   • Marree

• Bourke

• Grafton
• Coffs Harbour
• Port Macquarie

Tarcoola •

• Tamworth

NEW SOUTH WALES

Ceduna •

Darling

• Dubbo

G

Port Augusta •
Whyalla •   • Port Pirie

• Newcastle
• Gosford
• Sydney
• Wollongong

GREAT DIVIDING RANGE

Port Lincoln •   • Adelaide

• Mildura

Murray

Wagga Wagga •

• Canberra
AUSTRALIAN
CAPITAL
TERRITORY

H

*Kangaroo
Island*

VICTORIA   *Mount Kosciuszko
2229 m*

Bendigo •

*TASMAN
SEA*

Mount Gambier •   Ballarat •   • Melbourne
            Geelong •   Sale •

...38
kangaroos
will be born in
Australia. There are
three times more
kangaroos than
humans.

I

King Island   *Bass Strait*   *Flinders Island*
                        Cape Barren Island

100   200   300   400   500 mi

Burnie •   • Devonport
          • Launceston

200   400   600   800 km

Queenstown •

TASMANIA

• Hobart

South East Cape

New Zealand and the Pacific Islands

New Zealand consists of two main islands and has a population of four million. The country generates a wealthy economy, mainly by selling its farm produce worldwide. English is the national language due to the many immigrants who started commercial farms and industries. The area of the Pacific Ocean east of Australia contains thousands of tropical islands including the Solomon Islands, Fiji, Vanuatu, Samoa, Kiribati, Tonga, Micronesia, Palau, the Marshall Islands, Papua New Guinea, Nauru and Tuvalu. Many people are leaving the Pacific Islands for education and work in Australia, New Zealand and the USA.

Bora-Bora is a small island in French Polynesia [I14] with a population of only 8000 people. The biggest industry is tourism as people are attracted to the stunning clear waters and tranquil atmosphere. Resorts with bungalows on stilts are a common feature.

In the next minute... ...New Zealand's wine growers will make more than 230 bottles of wine for export.

THE DISTANCE from the top to the bottom of the Nevis Highwire, New Zealand's highest bungee jump, is 135 m.

OTAGO PENINSULA [I7] is home to albatrosses, penguins, seals, whales and dolphins.

Facts and Stats

- The life expectancy of people in New Zealand is 81 years, compared to a world average of 68 years.
- There are 24 doctors per 10,000 people compared to a world average of 17 doctors.
- Mount Cook [H7] is the highest mountain at 3754 m – 12 times higher than the Eiffel Tower.

*The Maori were the first settlers in New Zealand, as they sailed from Polynesia 1000 years ago. **Maori tikis** are large carvings that are believed to protect sacred sites against evil.*

TASMAN SEA

Cape Foulwin

Westpo

Greymouth

Sot

Mount Cook 3754 m

SOUTHERN ALPS

Timaru

Waitaki

Oam

Otas Penins

Dunedir

Clutha

Cape Providence

Foveaux Strait

Invercargill

Codfish Island

Ruapuke Island

Stewart Island

NEW ZEALAND AND THE PACIFIC ISLANDS • OCEANIA

North Cape

Whangarei •

Great Barrier Island

Hauraki Gulf

Auckland •
• Manukau

Waikato

Bay of Plenty

Hamilton •   • Tauranga

East Cape

Rotorua •

North Island

Lake Taupo

New Plymouth •

Mount Ruapehu 2797 m

• Gisborne

Poverty Bay

Cape Egmont

Wanganui

Hawke Bay

NEW ZEALAND

Napier •
Hastings •

Wanganui •

• Palmerston North

Cape Farewell

Cook Strait

Lower Hutt •
Wellington •

Nelson •
Blenheim •

Cape Palliser

and

• Christchurch

SOUTH PACIFIC OCEAN

terbury
Bight

Rotorua [C10] is well-known for geothermal activity including geysers and mud pools. Each day, soap is put into the opening of **Lady Knox Geyser** to make it erupt. The jets of water can reach up to 20 m in height.

Search and Find

Cook Islands	. . . I13	**Palau**	. . . . . . H10
Fiji	. . . . . . I12	**Papua New Guinea**	
Kiribati	. . . . . . H12		. . . . I11
Marshall Islands		**Samoa**	. . . . I13
	. . . . H12	**Solomon Islands**	
Micronesia	. . . H12		. . . . I12
Nauru	. . . . . . H12	**Tonga**	. . . . I13
New Zealand		**Tuvalu**	. . . . I12
• Wellington	. . . . F9	**Vanuatu**	. . . . . . I12
Niue	. . . . I13		

Extreme Weather

The mountains of South Island have hurricane winds of more than 250 km/h.

Scale:
0   50   100   150 mi
0   100   200 km

Did You Know?

The sea level is rising due to global warming. Two South Pacific islands in Kiribati, Tebua Tarawa and Abanuea, have already disappeared.

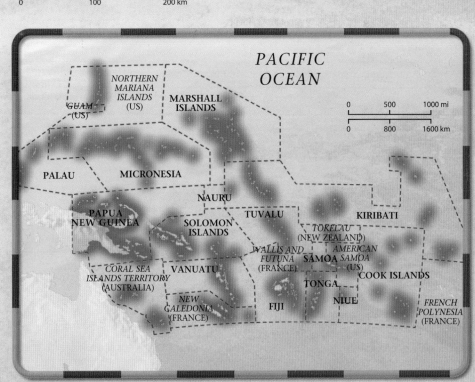

PACIFIC OCEAN

NORTHERN MARIANA ISLANDS (US)

GUAM (US)

MARSHALL ISLANDS

Scale:
0   500   1000 mi
0   800   1600 km

PALAU

MICRONESIA

NAURU

PAPUA NEW GUINEA

SOLOMON ISLANDS

TUVALU

KIRIBATI

TOKELAU (NEW ZEALAND)

WALLIS AND FUTUNA (FRANCE)

SAMOA

AMERICAN SAMOA (US)

CORAL SEA ISLANDS TERRITORY (AUSTRALIA)

VANUATU

COOK ISLANDS

NEW CALEDONIA (FRANCE)

FIJI

TONGA

NIUE

FRENCH POLYNESIA (FRANCE)

Countries of the world

Gazetteer

The gazetteer helps you to find towns and features on the maps. For example, **New York City** *Town* New York, USA 21 F12 shows that New York City is a town in the state of New York, USA. The town is on page 21 and can be found in square F12 by using the grid, or graticule. The letters run on the left and right, and the numbers run along the top and bottom. Trace where F and 21 meet to find New York City.

KEY: DRC – Democratic Republic of the Congo, UAE – United Arab Emirates, CAR – Central African Republic, RS – Research station

Aachen *Town* Germany 50 F6
Aalst *Town* Belgium 50 E5
Abadan *Town* Iran 75 D8
Abakan *Town* Russian Fed. 86 H5
Abéché *Town* Chad 65 G13
Aberdeen *Town* Scotland, UK 41 D9
Aberdeen *Town* S Dakota, USA 25 F13
Aberystwyth *Town* Wales, UK 41 H8
Abha *Town* Saudi Arabia 74 H6
Abidjan *Capital* Côte d'Ivoire 64 I6
Abilene *Town* Texas, USA 27 G12
Abkhazia *State* Georgia 58 I7
Abu Dhabi *Capital* UAE 75 F10
Abuja *Capital* Nigeria 65 H10
Abu Kamal *Town* Syria 73 G12
Acapulco *Town* Mexico 31 I9
Acarigua *Town* Venezuela 35 F9
Accra *Capital* Ghana 64 I7
Aconcagua, Cerro *Mountain* Argentina 36 G7
Adana *Town* Turkey 73 E9
Ad-Dammam *Town* Saudi Arabia 75 E8
Addis Ababa *Capital* Ethiopia 67 E9
Adelaide *Town* Australia 91 H9
Aden, Gulf of 67 C12, 74 J7
Aden *Town* Yemen 74 J7
Adirondack Mountains USA 21 E11
Adiyaman *Town* Turkey 73 E11
Adrar *Town* Algeria 62 F4
Adriatic Sea 49 E8
Afghanistan *Country* 76
Agadir *Town* Morocco 62 E2
Agen *Town* France 46 G7
Agra *Town* India 77 D9
Agrigento *Town* Sicily, Italy 48 H6
Aguascalientes *Town* Mexico 31 G8
Ahaggar *Mountain range* Algeria 62 G6
Ahmadabad *Town* India 76 E7
Ahvaz *Town* Iran 75 D8
Aïr Mountains Niger 65 F10
Aix-en-Provence *Town* France 47 H10
Aizu *Town* Japan 83 F10
Ajaccio *Town* France 47 J12
Akita *Town* Japan 83 D10
Akron *Town* Ohio, USA 21 G8
Aktau *Town* Kazakhstan 86 I2
Alabama *River* Alabama, USA 23 F8

Alabama *State* USA 23
Åland Island Finland 43 G9
Alaska, Gulf of 25 C11, 28 F4
Alaska *State* USA 25
Albacete *Town* Spain 45 F10
Alba Iulia *Town* Romania 55 E9
Albania *Country* 49
Albany *River* Ontario, Canada 29 H10
Albany *State capital* New York, USA 21 E12
Albany *Town* Australia 90 H5
Albany *Town* Georgia, USA 23 F9
Albert, Lake DRC/Uganda 66 F7
Alberta *Province* Canada 28
Albuquerque *Town* New Mexico, USA 27 F9
Alcoy *Town* Spain 45 G11
Aleppo *Town* Syria 73 F10
Alessandria *Town* Italy 48 C5
Aleutian Islands Alaska, USA 25 C9
Alexandria *Town* Egypt 63 E12
Alexandria *Town* Louisiana, USA 22 G5
Alexandroúpolis *Town* Greece 49 F13
Algeciras *Town* Spain 44 I7
Algeria *Country* 62
Algiers *Capital* Algeria 62 C6
Al Hasakah *Town* Syria 73 F12
Al-Hudaydah *Town* Yemen 74 I6
Al-Hufuf *Town* Saudi Arabia 75 F8
Alicante *Town* Spain 45 G11
Alice Springs *Town* Australia 91 E8
Al Jawf *Town* Saudi Arabia 74 D5
Al-Karak *Town* Jordan 73 I9
Alkmaar *Town* Netherlands 50 C6
Allahabad *Town* India 77 E9
Allegheny *River* Pennsylvania, USA 21 G9
Allentown *Town* Pennsylvania, USA 21 G11
Almaty *Town* Kazakhstan 86 I4
Almería *Town* Spain 45 H9
Al Mukalla *Town* Yemen 75 I8
Alps *Mountain range* France/Italy/ Switzerland 47 G10
Al Qamishli *Town* Syria 73 E12
Al Qunaytirah *Town* Syria 73 H9
Altai Mountains Mongolia/Russian Fed. 84 D7
Altamaha *River* Georgia, USA 23 F10

Altamira *Town* Brazil 37 B9
Altun Shan *Mountain range* China 84 F6
Amarillo *Town* Texas, USA 27 F11
Amazon *River* Brazil 36 B7, 37 B9
Amazon Basin Brazil 36 B7
Ambato *Town* Ecuador 36 B5
Ambon *Town* Indonesia 81 G8
American Samoa *Dep. territory* USA 93 I13
Amiens *Town* France 47 B9
Amman *Capital* Jordan 73 H10
Amritsar *Town* India 77 C8
Amsterdam *Capital* Netherlands 50 D6
Amu Dar'ya *River* Uzbekistan 86 J3
Amundsen Gulf 17 D9
Amundsen-Scott (US) *RS* Antarctica 16 F4
Amundsen Sea 16 F1
Amur *River* China/Russian Fed. 87 H8
Anaheim *Town* California, USA 26 F5
Anápolis *Town* Brazil 37 D9
Anatolian Plateau Turkey 72 D7
Anchorage *Town* Alaska, USA 25 C11
Ancona *Town* Italy 48 D7
Andaman Islands India 77 H12
Andaman Sea 78 H2
Anderson *Town* Indiana, USA 20 H7
Andes *Mountain range* 36 F7
Andorra *Country* 45
Andorra la Vella *Capital* Andorra 45 C12
Andreanof Islands Alaska, USA 25 C9
Angarsk *Town* Russian Fed. 86 H6
Angeles *Town* Philippines 79 F10
Angers *Town* France 46 C7
Angola *Country* 68
Angoulême *Town* France 46 E7
Anguilla *Dep. territory* UK 35 D12
Ankara *Capital* Turkey 73 C8
Annaba *Town* Algeria 62 D7
Annapolis *State capital* Maryland, USA 21 H11
Ann Arbor *Town* Michigan, USA 20 F7
An Nasiriyah *Town* Iraq 74 D7

Anshan *Town* China 85 D12
Antakya *Town* Turkey 73 F10
Antalya *Town* Turkey 72 E7
Antananarivo *Capital* Madagascar 69 G12
Antarctica 16
Antarctic Peninsula Antarctica 16 E2
Antibes *Town* France 47 H11
Anticosti Island Quebec, Canada 29 H13
Antigua and Barbuda *Country* 35
Antofagasta *Town* Chile 36 E6
Antsiranana *Town* Madagascar 69 F13
Antwerp *Town* Belgium 50 E5
Aomori *Town* Japan 83 D10
Aosta *Town* Italy 48 B4
Apeldoorn *Town* Netherlands 50 D7
Appalachian Mountains USA 21 H10, 23 C10
Appleton *Town* Wisconsin, USA 20 F5
Aqaba *Town* Jordan 73 J9
Aqtobe *Town* Russian Fed. 86 H2
Arabian Sea 75 F12, 76 E6
Aracaju *Town* Brazil 37 C11
Arad *Town* Romania 54 D7
Arafura Sea 81 H9
Araguaína *Town* Brazil 37 C10
Arakan Range *Mountain range* Burma (Myanmar) 78 F2
Aral Sea Kazakhstan/Uzbekistan 86 I3
Ararat, Mount Turkey 73 D14
Arbil *Town* Iraq 74 B7
Arctic Ocean 17, 28, 43, 59, 86
Arequipa *Town* Peru 36 D6
Arezzo *Town* Italy 48 D6
Argentina *Country* 36
Århus *Town* Denmark 42 I6
Arica *Town* Chile 36 D6
Arizona *State* USA 26
Arkansas *State* USA 22
Arkhangelísk *Town* Russian Fed. 59 D8
Arles *Town* France 47 H9
Arlington *Town* Texas, USA 27 G13
Armenia *Country* 59
Armenia *Town* Colombia 35 H8
Arnhem *Town* Netherlands 50 D6
Arnhem Land Australia 91 B8
Ar Raqqah *Town* Syria 73 F11

Arua *Town* Uganda 66 F7
Aruba *Dep. territory* Netherlands 35 E9
Aru Islands Indonesia 81 G9
Arusha *Town* Tanzania 67 H9
Asahikawa *Town* Japan 83 B10
Ashgabat *Capital* Turkmenistan 86 J3
Asmara *Capital* Eritrea 67 C9
Assad, Lake Syria 73 F11
Assen *Town* Netherlands 50 C7
As-Sulayyil *Town* Saudi Arabia 74 G7
Astana *Capital* Kazakhstan 86 H3
Astrakhan *Town* Russian Fed. 59 H8
Asunción *Capital* Paraguay 37 E8
Aswan *Town* Egypt 63 H13
Asyut *Town* Egypt 63 G13
Atacama Desert Chile 36 E7
Atbara *Town* Sudan 67 B8
Athens *Capital* Greece 49 H12
Atlanta *State capital* Georgia, USA 23 E9
Atlantic City *Town* New Jersey, USA 21 G12
Atlantic Ocean 21, 23, 29, 37, 40, 42, 43, 44, 62, 64
Atlas Mountains Morocco 62 E3
Atyrau *Town* Kazakhstan 86 I2
Auckland *Town* New Zealand 93 C9
Augsburg *Town* Germany 51 I9
Augusta *Town* Georgia, USA 23 E10
Augusta *State capital* Maine, USA 21 D13
Aurora *Town* Illinois, USA 20 G6
Austin *State capital* Texas, USA 27 H13
Australia *Country* 90
Australian Capital Territory *State* Australia 91
Austria *Country* 40
Auxerre *Town* France 47 D9
Aveiro *Town* Portugal 44 E5
Avignon *Town* France 47 G9
Ávila *Town* Spain 45 E8
Axel Heiberg Island Nunavut, Canada 29 C9
Ayacucho *Town* Peru 36 D6
Aydin *Town* Turkey 72 D6
Azerbaijan *Country* 59
Azov, Sea of 58 I7
Az-Zarqa *Town* Jordan 73 H10
Az-Zawiyah *Town* Libya 73 H10

Bacău *Town* Romania 55 D12
Bacolod *Town* Philippines 79 G11
Badajoz *Town* Spain 44 F6
Baden-Baden *Town* Germany 50 H7
Baffin Bay Canada 17 G9, 29 D10
Baffin Island Canada 17 G8, 29 E10

Baghdad *Capital* Iraq 74 C7
Bahamas *Country* 35
Bahawalpur *Town* Pakistan 77 C8
Bahía Blanca *Town* Argentina 37 G8
Bahrain *Country* 75
Baikal, Lake Russian Fed. 86 H7
Bakersfield *Town* California, USA 26 E5
Bakhtaran *Town* Iran 74 C7
Baku *Capital* Azerbaijan 59 J9
Balaton, Lake Hungary 54 D5
Balearic Islands Spain 45
Bali *Island* Indonesia 80 H5
Balikesir *Town* Turkey 72 C6
Balikpapan *Town* Indonesia 80 F5
Balkanabat *Town* Turkmenistan 86 J2
Balkan Mountains Bulgaria 55 H10
Balkhash, Lake Kazakhstan 86 I4
Ballarat *Town* Australia 91 I10
Baltic Sea 43 H9, 56 B6, 58 F5
Baltimore *Town* Maryland, USA 21 H11
Bamako *Capital* Mali 64 G5
Bambari *Town* CAR 68 B7
Bamberg *Town* Germany 51 G9
Bamenda *Town* Cameroon 68 B5
Bandar 'Abbas *Town* Iran 75 E10
Bandar Seri Begawan *Capital* Brunei 80 E5
Banda Sea 81 G8
Bandundu *Town* DRC 68 D7
Bandung *Town* Indonesia 80 H3
Bangalore *See Bengaluru*
Bangkok *Capital* Thailand 78 H4
Bangladesh *Country* 77
Bangor *Town* Maine, USA 21 C13
Bangui *Capital* CAR 68 B7
Baniyas *Town* Syria 73 F10
Banja Luka *Town* Bosnia and Herz. 49 C8
Banjarmasin *Town* Indonesia 80 G5
Banjul *Capital* Gambia 64 G3
Banská Bystrica *Town* Slovakia 57 I8
Baotou *Town* China 85 E10
Bar *Town* Montenegro 49 E9
Barbados *Country* 35
Barcelona *Town* Spain 45 D13
Barcelona *Town* Venezuela 35 F11
Barents Sea 17 G13, 58 B7
Bari *Town* Italy 49 F8
Barinas *Town* Venezuela 35 F9
Barnaul *Town* Russian Fed. 86 H5
Barquisimeto *Town* Venezuela 35 F9
Barrancabermeja *Town* Colombia 35 G8
Barranquilla *Town* Colombia 35 F8
Basel *Town* Switzerland 52 E3
Basra *Town* Iraq 75 D8

Bassein *Town* Burma (Myanmar) 78 G2
Basseterre *Capital* St. Kitts and Nevis 35 D12
Bass Strait Australia 91 I11
Batangas *Town* Philippines 79 F10
Batdâmbang *Town* Cambodia 78 G5
Batman *Town* Turkey 73 E12
Batna *Town* Algeria 62 D6
Baton Rouge *State capital* Louisiana, USA 22 G6
Bayamo *Town* Cuba 35 C8
Bayreuth *Town* Germany 51 G10
Beaufort Sea 17 C9, 28 D6
Beaumont *Town* Texas, USA 27 H14
Béchar *Town* Algeria 62 E4
Beersheba *Town* Israel 73 I9
Beijing *Capital* China 85 E11
Beira *Town* Mozambique 69 G10
Beirut *Capital* Lebanon 73 G9
Beja *Town* Portugal 44 G5
Belarus *Country* 58
Belém *Town* Brazil 37 B10
Belfast *Capital* Northern Ireland, UK 40 F7
Belgium *Country* 50
Belgrade *Capital* Serbia 49 C10
Belgrano II (Argentina) *RS* Antarctica 16 E3
Belize *Country* 34
Belize City *Town* Belize 34 C5
Bellingham *Town* Washington, USA 24 C4
Belmopan *Capital* Belize 34 C5
Belo Horizonte *Town* Brazil 37 E10
Bendigo *Town* Australia 91 H11
Benevento *Town* Italy 48 F7
Bengal, Bay of 77 F11
Bengaluru (Bangalore) *Town* India 77 H8
Benghazi *Town* Libya 63 E10
Benguela *Town* Angola 68 F6
Benidorm *Town* Spain 45 G11
Benin *Country* 65
Benin City *Town* Nigeria 65 I9
Ben Nevis *Mountain* Scotland, UK 41 D8
Benue *River* Nigeria 65 I10
Berbera *Town* Somalia 67 D11
Bergamo *Town* Italy 48 B5
Bergen *Town* Norway 42 F5
Bergerac *Town* France 46 F7
Bering Sea 25 B9, 87 G13
Berlin *Capital* Germany 51 D11
Bern *Capital* Switzerland 52 F3
Besançon *Town* France 47 E10
Bethlehem *Town* Israel 73 I9
Béziers *Town* France 47 H8
Bhavnagar *Town* India 76 E7

Bhopal *Town* India 77 E8
Bhutan *Country* 77
Bialystok *Town* Poland 57 D11
Biel *Town* Switzerland 52 F3
Bielefeld *Town* Germany 51 D8
Bielsko-Biala *Town* Poland 57 H8
Bighorn Mountains Wyoming, USA 25 G9
Bihac *Town* Bosnia and Herz. 49 C8
Bilauktaung Range Thailand 78 G3
Bilbao *Town* Spain 45 B9
Billings *Town* Montana, USA 25 F9
Biloxi *Town* Mississippi, USA 22 G7
Biratnagar *Town* Nepal 77 D11
Birmingham *Town* Alabama, USA 23 E8
Birmingham *Town* England, UK 41 H9
Biscay, Bay of 45 A9, 46 E5
Bishkek *Capital* Kyrgyzstan 86 I4
Bismarck *State capital* N Dakota, USA 25 F12
Bissau *Capital* Guinea-Bissau 64 G3
Bitola *Town* Macedonia 49 F11
Bizerte *Town* Tunisia 62 C7
Black Forest Germany 50 I7
Blackpool *Town* England, UK 41 F8
Black Sea 55 H14, 58 I6, 73 B11
Blagoevgrad *Town* Bulgaria 55 I9
Blagoveshchensk *Town* Russian Fed. 87 H8
Blantyre *Town* Malawi 69 G10
Blida *Town* Algeria 62 D6
Bloemfontein *Town* South Africa 69 I8
Bloomington *Town* Indiana, USA 20 I6
Bloomington *Town* Minnesota, USA 20 E3
Blue Nile *River* Ethiopia/Sudan 67 D8
Bo *Town* Sierra Leone 64 I4
Boa Vista *Town* Brazil 37 A8
Bobo Dioulasso *Town* Burkina Faso 64 H6
Bodrum *Town* Turkey 72 E5
Bogotá *Capital* Colombia 35 H8
Bohemian Forest Czech Republic/ Germany 51 H11, 56 H4
Boise *State capital* Idaho, USA 24 G5
Bolivia *Country* 36
Bologna *Town* Italy 48 C6
Bolzano *Town* Italy 48 B6
Bombay *See Mumbai*
Bonaire *Dep. territory* Netherlands 35 F10
Bonifacio, Strait of 47 J12
Bonn *Town* Germany 50 F7
Borås *Town* Sweden 42 H7

Bordeaux *Town* France 46 F6

Borgholm *Town* Sweden 43 I8

Borneo *Island* Indonesia 80 G4

Bornholm *Dep. territory* Denmark 42 J7

Bosnia and Herzegovina *Country* 49

Boston *State capital* Massachusetts, USA 21 E13

Botswana *Country* 69

Bouar *Town* CAR 68 B6

Boulder *Town* Colorado, USA 27 C10

Boulogne *Town* France 47 A9

Bourges *Town* France 47 D9

Bourke *Town* Australia 91 F11

Bournemouth *Town* England, UK 41 I9

Bozeman *Town* Montana, USA 25 F8

Brahmaputra *River* Asia 77 E12

Braila *Town* Romania 55 E12

Brandenburg *Town* Germany 51 D11

Brasília *Capital* Brazil 37 D10

Brasov *Town* Romania 55 E10

Bratislava *Capital* Slovakia 56 J7

Bratsk *Town* Russian Fed. 86 G6

Braunschweig *Town* Germany 51 D10

Brazil *Country* 37

Brazzaville *Capital* Republic of the Congo 68 D6

Breda *Town* Netherlands 50 D5

Bremen *Town* Germany 51 C9

Bremerhaven *Town* Germany 51 C8

Brescia *Town* Italy 48 B5

Brest *Town* France 46 B5

Bridgeport *Town* Connecticut, USA 21 F12

Bridgetown *Capital* Barbados 35 E12

Brig *Town* Switzerland 52 G3

Brighton *Town* England, UK 41 I10

Brindisi *Town* Italy 49 F9

Brisbane *Town* Australia 91 F13

Bristol *Town* England, UK 41 H9

British Columbia *Province* Canada 28

Brive *Town* France 47 F8

Brno *Town* Czech Republic 56 H6

Broome *Town* Australia 90 C5

Brownsville *Town* Texas, USA 27 J13

Bruges *Town* Belgium 50 E4

Brunei *Country* 80

Brussels *Capital* Belgium 50 E5

Bryansk *Town* Russian Fed. 58 G6

Bucaramanga *Town* Colombia 35 G8

Bucharest *Capital* Romania 55 F11

Budapest *Capital* Hungary 54 C6

Buenaventura *Town* Colombia 34 H7

Buenos Aires *Capital* Argentina 37 G8

Buffalo *Town* New York, USA 21 F9

Bug *River* Poland 57 D10

Bujumbura *Capital* Burundi 66 H7

Bukavu *Town* DRC 69 D9

Bulawayo *Town* Zimbabwe 69 G9

Bulgaria *Country* 55

Buraydah *Town* Saudi Arabia 74 E7

Burgas *Town* Bulgaria 55 H12

Burgos *Town* Spain 45 C8

Burketown *Town* Australia 91 C10

Burkina Faso *Country* 64

Burlington *Town* Vermont, USA 21 D12

Burma (Myanmar) *Country* 78

Burns *Town* Oregon, USA 24 G4

Burnsville *Town* Minnesota, USA 20 E3

Bursa *Town* Turkey 72 C6

Burundi *Country* 66

Butuan *Town* Philippines 79 G12

Bydgoszcz *Town* Poland 57 D8

Bytom *Town* Poland 57 G8

Cabanatuan *Town* Philippines 79 E10

Cáceres *Town* Spain 44 F6

Cádiz *Town* Spain 44 I7

Caen *Town* France 47 B8

Cagayan de Oro *Town* Philippines 79 G11

Cagliari *Town* Sardinia, Italy 48 G4

Cairns *Town* Australia 91 C11

Cairo *Capital* Egypt 63 F13

Calais *Town* France 47 A9

Calama *Town* Chile 36 E7

Calarasi *Town* Romania 55 F12

Calbayog *Town* Philippines 79 F11

Calcutta *See* Kolkata

Calgary *Town* Alberta, Canada 28 H7

Cali *Town* Colombia 34 H7

Calicut *See* Kozhikode

California, Gulf of 30 D5

California *State* USA 26

Callao *Town* Peru 36 D5

Caltanissetta *Town* Sicily, Italy 48 H7

Camagüey *Town* Cuba 35 C8

Cambodia *Country* 78

Cambrian Mountains Wales, UK 41 H8

Cambridge *Town* England, UK 41 H10

Cameroon *Country* 68

Campeche, Bay of Mexico 31 H11

Campina Grande *Town* Brazil 37 C12

Campinas *Town* Brazil 37 E10

Campobasso *Town* Italy 48 E7

Campo Grande *Town* Brazil 37 E9

Canada *Country* 28

Canary Islands Spain 64 B4

Canberra *Capital* Australia 91 H12

Cancún *Town* Mexico 31 G14

Cannes *Town* France 47 H11

Cantabrian Mountains Spain 44 B7

Can Tho *Town* Vietnam 78 H5

Canton *Town* Ohio, USA 21 G9

Cape Horn Chile 37 J8

Cape Town *Capital* South Africa 68 J7

Cape Verde Country 64

Cap-Haïtien *Town* Haiti 35 C9

Caracas *Capital* Venezuela 35 F10

Cárdenas *Town* Cuba 34 B7

Cardiff *Capital* Wales, UK 41 H8

Caribbean Sea 35 E9

Carlisle *Town* England, UK 41 F9

Carlsbad *Town* New Mexico, USA 27 G10

Carnarvon *Town* Australia 90 E3

Carpathian Mountains Poland/ Romania/Slovakia 55 D11

Carrara *Town* Italy 48 C5

Carson City *State capital* Nevada, USA 26 C5

Cartagena *Town* Colombia 35 F8

Cartagena *Town* Spain 45 H11

Casablanca *Town* Morocco 62 D3

Casey (Australia) *RS* Antarctica 16 G7

Casper *Town* Wyoming, USA 25 H9

Caspian Sea 59 I9, 75 B8, 86 I2

Cassai (Kasai) *River* Angola/DRC 68 E7

Castellón de la Plana *Town* Spain 45 E11

Castries *Capital* St. Lucia 35 E12

Catania *Town* Sicily, Italy 48 H7

Catanzaro *Town* Italy 49 G8

Cayman Islands *Dep. territory* UK 34 C7

Cebu *Town* Philippines 79 G11

Cedar City *Town* Utah, USA 26 D7

Cedar Rapids *Town* Iowa, USA 20 G4

Celebes Sea 79 H11, 80 E6

Celje *Town* Slovenia 49 B8

Central African Republic (CAR) *Country* 68

Ceske Budejovice *Town* Czech Republic 56 H5

Ceuta *Town* Spain 44 J7, 62 D3

Chad, Lake Chad 65 G12

Chad *Country* 65

Châlons-en-Champagne *Town* France 47 C10

Chalon-sur-Saône *Town* France 47 E10

Chambéry *Town* France 47 F10

Champaign *Town* Illinois, USA 20 H6

Chandigarh *Town* India 77 C8

Chang Cheng (China) *RS* Antarctica 16 D1

Changchun *Town* China 85 C12

Chang Jiang (Yangtze) *River* China 85 G10

Changsha *Town* China 85 G11

Channel Islands *Dep. territory* UK 41 J9

Charleroi *Town* Belgium 50 F5

Charleston *State capital* West Virginia, USA 21 I9

Charleston *Town* S Carolina, USA 23 E11

Charleville Mézières *Town* France 47 B10

Charlotte *Town* N Carolina, USA 23 C10

Charlottetown *Province capital* Prince Edward Islands, Canada 29 I13

Châteauroux *Town* France 47 D8

Chattanooga *Town* Tennessee, USA 23 D8

Cheb *Town* Czech Republic 56 G3

Chelm *Town* Poland 57 F11

Chelyabinsk *Town* Russian Fed. 86 G3

Chemnitz *Town* Germany 51 F11

Chengdu *Town* China 85 G9

Chennai (Madras) *Town* India 77 H9

Chester *Town* England, UK 41 G9

Chetumal *Town* Mexico 31 H13

Cheyenne *State capital* Wyoming, USA 25 I10

Chiang Mai *Town* Thailand 78 F3

Chiba *Town* Japan 83 G10

Chicago *Town* Illinois, USA 20 G6

Chichén Itzá Mexico 31 G13

Chiclayo *Town* Peru 36 C5

Chicoutimi *Town* Quebec, Canada 29 I12

Chihuahua *Town* Mexico 30 D7

Chile *Country* 36

Chillan *Town* Chile 36 G6

Chilpancingo *Town* Mexico 31 I9

Chimbote *Town* Peru 36 C5

Chimoio *Town* Mozambique 69 G10

China *Country* 85

Chinandega *Town* Nicaragua 34 E5

Chioggia *Town* Italy 48 C6

Chipata *Town* Zambia 69 F9

Chirripó Grande, Cerro *Mountain* Costa Rica 34 F5

Chisinau *Capital* Moldova 58 H6

Chita *Town* Russian Fed. 86 H7

Chitose *Town* Japan 83 B10

Chittagong *Town* Bangladesh 77 F12

Chitungwiza *Town* Zimbabwe 69 G9

Chon Buri *Town* Thailand 78 H4

Chongjin *Town* North Korea 85 C13

Chongqing *Town* China 85 H10

Choybalsan *Town* Mongolia 85 C10

Christchurch *Town* New Zealand 93 G8

Chukchi Sea 17 C11, 25 A10, 87 E13

Churchill *Town* Manitoba, Canada 29 G9

Cienfuegos *Town* Cuba 34 B7

Cincinnati *Town* Ohio, USA 21 H7

Ciudad Bolívar *Town* Venezuela 35 G11

Ciudad del Este *Town* Paraguay 37 F9

Ciudad Guayana *Town* Venezuela 35 G11

Ciudad Juárez *Town* Mexico 30 C7

Ciudad Madero *Town* Mexico 31 F10

Ciudad Obregón *Town* Mexico 30 D6

Ciudad Real *Town* Spain 45 F8

Ciudid Victoria *Town* Mexico 31 F9

Civitavecchia *Town* Italy 48 E6

Clarksville *Town* Tennessee, USA 22 C7

Clearwater *Town* Florida, USA 23 H10

Clermont-Ferrand *Town* France 47 E9

Cleveland *Town* Ohio, USA 21 G8

Clovis *Town* New Mexico, USA 27 F11

Cluj-Napoca *Town* Romania 55 D9

Coast Ranges California/Oregon, USA 24 F2, 26 B4

Coatzacoalcos *Town* Mexico 31 H11

Cochin *See* Kochi

Cognac *Town* France 46 E7

Coimbatore *Town* India 77 I8

Coimbra *Town* Portugal 44 E5

Colchester *Town* England, UK 41 H10

Colima *Town* Mexico 31 H8

Cologne *Town* Germany 50 E7

Colombia *Country* 35

Colombo *Capital* Sri Lanka 77 J9

Colón *Town* Panama 34 F7

Colorado *River* Mexico/USA 27 D8

Colorado *State* USA 27

Colorado Springs *Town* Colorado, USA 27 D10

Columbia *State capital* S Carolina, USA 23 D10

Columbia *Town* Missouri, USA 22 B5

Columbus *State capital* Ohio, USA 21 H8

Columbus *Town* Georgia, USA 23 F9

Como *Town* Italy 48 B5

Comodoro Rivadavia *Town* Argentina 36 H7

Comoros *Country* 69

Conakry *Capital* Guinea 64 H4

Concepción *Town* Chile 36 G6

Concord *State capital* New Hampshire, USA 21 E13

Congo *River* Western Central Africa 68 C7, 69 D8

Congo, Democratic Republic of the (DRC) *Country* 68

Congo, Republic of the *Country* 68

Connecticut *State* USA 21

Constanta *Town* Romania 55 F13

Constantine *Town* Algeria 62 D6

Coober Pedy *Town* Australia 91 F8

Cook, Mount New Zealand 92 G7

Cook Islands *Dep. territory* New Zealand 93 I13

Cook Strait New Zealand 93 F9

Cooktown *Town* Australia 91 B11

Copenhagen *Capital* Denmark 42 I7

Coquimbo *Town* Chile 36 F6

Coral Sea Islands Territory *Dep. territory* Australia 93 I11

Cordillera Central *Mountain range* Colombia/Panama 34 F6, 35 H8

Córdoba *Town* Argentina 36 F7

Córdoba *Town* Spain 45 G8

Corfu *Island* Greece 49 G10

Cork *Town* Republic of Ireland 40 H6

Corpus Christi *Town* Texas, USA 27 I13

Corrientes *Town* Argentina 37 F8

Corsica *Island* France 47 I12

Çorum *Town* Turkey 73 C9

Corvallis *Town* Oregon, USA 24 F3

Cosenza *Town* Italy 49 G8

Costa Rica *Country* 34

Côte d'Ivoire *Country* 64

Cotonou *Capital* Benin 65 I8

Cottbus *Town* Germany 51 E12

Council Bluffs *Town* Iowa, USA 20 H2

Coventry *Town* England, UK 41 H9

Craiova *Town* Romania 55 G9

Cremona *Town* Italy 48 C5

Crete, Sea of Greece 49 I12

Crete *Island* Greece 49 J12

Crimea Ukraine 58 I7

Croatia *Country* 49

Crotone *Town* Italy 49 G8

Cuba *Country* 34

Cúcuta *Town* Colombia 35 G8

Cuernavaca *Town* Mexico 31 H9

Cuito *River* Angola 68 G7

Culiacán *Town* Mexico 30 E6

Cumaná *Town* Venezuela 35 F11

Curaçao *Dep. territory* Netherlands 35 E10

Curitiba *Town* Brazil 37 F9

Cusco *Town* Peru 36 D6

Cuttack *Town* India 77 F10

Cuxhaven *Town* Germany 51 B9

Cyprus *Country* 73

Czech Republic *Country* 56

Czestochowa *Town* Poland 57 F8

Dakar *Capital* Senegal 64 F3

Dalandzadgad *Town* Mongolia 85 D8

Da Lat *Town* Vietnam 78 H6

Dalian *Town* China 85 E12

Dallas *Town* Texas, USA 27 G13

Damascus *Capital* Syria 73 H10

Dampier *Town* Australia 90 D4

Da Nang *Town* Vietnam 78 F6

Danube *River* Europe 51 I8, 40 E12, 54 D5, 55 G10, 57 J8

Danzig, Gulf of 57 B8

Dar'a *Town* Syria 73 H10

Dar es Salaam *Capital* Tanzania 67 I9

Darfur Sudan 66 D6

Darhan *Town* Mongolia 85 C9

Darien, Gulf of 34 F7

Darling *River* Australia 91 G10

Darmstadt *Town* Germany 51 G8

Darnah *Town* Libya 63 E10

Darwin *Town* Australia 90 B7

Davao *Town* Philippines 79 H12

Davenport *Town* Iowa, USA 20 G5

David *Town* Panama 34 F6

Davis (Australia) *RS* Antarctica 16 E7

Dayr az Zawr *Town* Syria 73 F12

Dayton *Town* Ohio, USA 21 H8

Daytona Beach *Town* Florida, USA 23 G11

Dead Sea Jordan 73 I9

Death Valley California, USA 26 E6

Debrecen *Town* Hungary 55 C8

Decatur *Town* Illinois, USA 20 H6

Delaware *State* USA 21

Delft *Town* Netherlands 50 D5

Delhi *Town* India 77 D9

Del Rio *Town* Texas, USA 27 I11

Democratic Republic of the Congo (DRC) *See* Congo, Republic of the

Den Helder *Town* Netherlands 50 C6

Denizli *Town* Turkey 72 D6

Denmark *Country* 42

Denver *State capital* Colorado, USA 27 C10

Derby *Town* England, UK 41 G9

Des Moines *State capital* Iowa, USA 20 G3

Dessau *Town* Germany 51 E11

Detroit *Town* Michigan, USA 20 F8

Devon Island Nunavut, Canada 29 D9

Dhaka *Capital* Bangladesh 77 E11

Dhanbad *Town* India 77 E10

Dieppe *Town* France 47 B8

Dijon *Town* France 47 D10

Dili *Capital* East Timor 80 H7

Dimitrovgrad *Town* Bulgaria 55 I11

Dire Dawa *Town* Ethiopia 67 D10

Diyarbakir *Town* Turkey 73 E12

Djibouti *Capital* Djibouti 67 D11

Djibouti *Country* 67

Dnieper *River* Ukraine 58 H6

Dniester *River* Ukraine 58 H6

Dnipropetrovsik *Town* Ukraine 58 H7

Dobrich *Town* Bulgaria 55 G13

Dodge City *Town* Kansas, USA 27 E12

Dodoma *Capital* Tanzania 67 I9

Doha *Capital* Qatar 75 F9

Dominica *Country* 35

Dominican Republic *Country* 35

Don *River* Russian Fed. 59 H8

Donetsk *Town* Ukraine 58 H7

Dordogne *River* France 46 F7

Dordrecht *Town* Netherlands 50 D5

Dortmund *Town* Germany 50 E7

Douala *Town* Cameroon 68 B5

Douglas *Town* Arizona, USA 27 G8

Dover *State capital* Delaware, USA 21 G12

Dover *Town* England, UK 41 I11

Drakensberg Mountains South Africa 69 J8

Drama *Town* Greece 49 F12

Drammen *Town* Norway 42 G6

Dresden *Town* Germany 51 F12

Drobeta-Turnu Severin *Town* Romania 55 F8

Drogheda *Town* Republic of Ireland 40 F7

Dubai *Town* UAE 75 F10

Dublin *Capital* Republic of Ireland 40 G7

Dubrovnik *Town* Croatia 49 E9

Duisburg *Town* Germany 50 E7

Duluth *Town* Minnesota, USA 20 D3

Dumont d'Urville (France) *RS* Antarctica 16 H5

Dunaujvaros *Town* Hungary 54 D6

Dundee *Town* Scotland, UK 41 D9

Dunedin *Town* New Zealand 92 I7
Dunkerque *Town* France 47 A9
Durango *Town* Colorado, USA 27 E9
Durango *Town* Mexico 30 F7
Durban *Town* South Africa 69 I9
Durham *Town* N Carolina, USA
 23 C11
Durrës *Town* Albania 49 F9
Dushanbe *Capital* Tajikistan 86 J3
Düsseldorf *Town* Germany 50 E7

East Cape New Zealand 93 C11
East China Sea Pacific Ocean
 85 G13
Eastern Ghats *Mountain range*
 India 77 G9
East London *Town* South Africa
 69 J8
East Siberian Sea Arctic Ocean
 17 C13, 87 E11
East Timor *Country* 81
Eau Claire *Town* Wisconsin, USA
 20 E4
Ebetsu *Town* Japan 83 B10
Ebro *River* Spain 45 C10
Ecuador *Country* 36
Edinburgh *Capital* Scotland, UK
 41 E8
Edirne *Town* Turkey 72 B5
Edmonton *Province capital* Alberta,
 Canada 28 H7
Edward, Lake DRC/Uganda 66 G7,
 69 C9
Edwards Plateau Texas, USA 27 H12
Egypt *Country* 63
Eindhoven *Town* Netherlands 50 E6
El Aaiún *Capital* Western Sahara
 64 C5
Elat *Town* Israel 73 J9
Elazig *Town* Turkey 73 D11
Elbasan *Town* Albania 49 F10
Elbe *River* Czech Republic/ Germany
 51 E11, 56 G6
Elblag *Town* Poland 57 B8
Elbrus, Mount Russian Fed. 59 I8
Elche *Town* Spain 45 G11
El Fasher *Town* Sudan 66 C6
Elgin *Town* Illinois, USA 20 G6
Ellesmere Island Canada 17 F10,
 29 C9
Ellsworth Land Antarctica 16 F2
El Minya *Town* Egypt 63 F13
El Obeid *Town* Sudan 66 D7
El Paso *Town* Texas, USA 27 G9
El Progreso *Town* Honduras 34 D5
El Salvador *Country* 34
Emmen *Town* Netherlands 50 C7
Empty Quarter *Desert* Saudi Arabia
 75 H9
Ende *Town* Indonesia 80 H6

England *Country* UK 41
English Channel France/UK 41 I9,
 46 A6
Enid *Town* Oklahoma, USA 27 E13
Enschede *Town* Netherlands 50 D7
Ensenada *Town* Mexico 30 B4
Enugu *Town* Nigeria 65 I10
Equatorial Guinea *Country* 68
Erdenet *Town* Mongolia 85 C9
Erfurt *Town* Germany 51 F10
Erie, Lake USA 21 F9
Erie *Town* Pennsylvania, USA 21 F9
Eritrea *Country* 67
Erzincan *Town* Turkey 73 D11
Erzurum *Town* Turkey 73 C13
Esbjerg *Town* Denmark 42 I5
Escuintla *Town* Guatemala 34 D4
Esfahan *Town* Iran 75 C9
Eskisehir *Town* Turkey 72 C7
Esmeraldas *Town* Ecuador 36 A5
Esperance *Town* Australia 90 H6
Esperanza (Argentina) *RS*
 Antarctica 16 D1
Espoo *Town* Finland 43 G10
Essen *Town* Germany 50 E7
Estonia *Country* 58
Ethiopia *Country* 67
Etna, Mount Italy 48 H7
Eugene *Town* Oregon, USA 24 F3
Euphrates *River* Iraq/Syria/Turkey 73
 F12, 74 C8
Evansville *Town* Indiana, USA 20 J6
Everest, Mount China/Nepal
 77 D11, 84 H6
Everett *Town* Washington, USA
 24 D4
Everglades, The Florida, USA 23 J11
Évora *Town* Portugal 44 G5
Exeter *Town* England, UK 41 I8

Fairbanks *Town* Alaska, USA 25 B11
Faisalabad *Town* Pakistan 77 C8
Falkland Islands *Dep. territory* UK
 37 J8
Fargo *Town* N Dakota, USA 25 F13
Fayetteville *Town* N Carolina, USA
 23 C11
Feira de Santana *Town* Brazil
 37 D11
Ferrara *Town* Italy 48 C6
Fes *Town* Morocco 62 D3
Feuilles *River* Quebec, Canada
 29 G11
Fianarantsoa *Town* Madagascar
 69 H12
Fiji *Country* 93 I12
Finland, Gulf of 58 E5
Finland *Country* 43
Firat *River* Turkey 73 E11
Fitzroy *River* Australia 90 C6

Flagstaff *Town* Arizona, USA 27 F8
Flensburg *Town* Germany 51 A9
Flint *Town* Michigan, USA 20 F7
Florence *Town* Italy 48 D6
Flores Sea 80 H6
Florianópolio *Town* Brazil 37 F9
Florida *State* USA 23
Florida Keys *Island group* Florida,
 USA 23 J11
Focsani *Town* Romania 55 E12
Foggia *Town* Italy 49 E8
Fontainebleau *Town* France 47 C9
Forli *Town* Italy 48 C6
Fort Albany *Town* Ontario, Canada
 29 H10
Fortaleza *Town* Brazil 37 B11
Fort Collins *Town* Colorado, USA
 27 C10
Fort Lauderdale *Town* Florida, USA
 23 I12
Fort Myers *Town* Florida, USA 23 I11
Fort Smith *Town* Arkansas, USA
 22 D4
Fort Wayne *Town* Indiana, USA
 20 G7
Fort Worth *Town* Texas, USA 27 G13
Foveaux Strait New Zealand 92 J5
Fox Islands Alaska, USA 25 C9
France *Country* 46
Francistown *Town* Botswana 69 H8
Frankfurt am Main *Town* Germany
 51 G8
Frankfurt an der Oder *Town*
 Germany 51 D12
Fraser Island Australia 91 E13
Fredericton *Province capital* New
 Brunswick, Canada 29 I13
Fredrikstad *Town* Norway 42 G6
Freemantle *Town* Australia 90 G4
Freetown *Capital* Sierra Leone
 64 H4
Freiburg im Breisgau *Town*
 Germany 50 I7
French Guiana *Dep. territory* France
 35 H14
French Polynesia *Dep. territory*
 France 93 I14
Fresno *Town* California, USA 26 D5
Fuji, Mount Japan 83 G9
Fuji *Town* Japan 83 G9
Fukui *Town* Japan 83 G8
Fukuoka *Town* Japan 82 H5
Fukushima *Town* Japan 83 F10
Fulda *Town* Germany 51 F9
Fürth *Town* Germany 51 H9
Fushun *Town* China 85 D12
Fuzhou *Town* China 85 H12

Gabon *Country* 68
Gaborone *Capital* Botswana 69 H8

Gabrovo *Town* Bulgaria 55 H11
Gainesville *Town* Florida, USA
 23 G10
Gallup *Town* New Mexico, USA
 27 E9
Galveston *Town* Texas, USA 27 I14
Galway *Town* Republic of Ireland
 40 G6
Gambia *Country* 64
Gander *Town* Newfoundland and
 Labrador, Canada 29 H14
Ganges *River* India 77 D9
Gao *Town* Mali 65 F8
Gar *Town* China 84 G5
Garland *Town* Texas, USA 27 G13
Garonne *River* France 46 F7
Garoua *Town* Cameroon 68 A6
Gary *Town* Indiana, USA 20 G6
Gaspé *Town* Quebec, Canada
 29 H13
Gävle *Town* Sweden 43 G8
Gaza *Town* Israel 73 I9
Gaza Strip *Disputed region*
 Near East 73 I9
Gaziantep *Town* Turkey 73 E10
Gdansk *Town* Poland 57 B8
Gdynia *Town* Poland 57 B8
Geelong *Town* Australia 91 I11
General Santos *Town* Philippines 79
 H12
Geneva, Lake Switzerland 52 G1
Geneva *Town* Switzerland 52 G1
Genk *Town* Belgium 50 E6
Genoa *Town* Italy 48 C5
Georgetown *Capital* Guyana
 35 G13
George Town *Town* Malaysia
 80 E2
Georgia *Country* 59
Georgia *State* USA 23
Gera *Town* Germany 51 F10
Germany *Country* 50
Ghana *Country* 64
Ghardaïa *Town* Algeria 62 E6
Ghent *Town* Belgium 50 E5
Gibraltar *Dep. territory* UK 44 I7
Gibraltar, Strait of Morocco/Spain
 44 I7, 62 C3
Gibson Desert Australia 90 E5
Giessen *Town* Germany 51 F8
Gifu *Town* Japan 83 G8
Gijón *Town* Spain 44 B7
Gillette *Town* Wyoming, USA 25 G10
Girona *Town* Spain 45 C13
Gisborne *Town* New Zealand
 93 D11
Giurgiu *Town* Romania 55 G11
Glasgow *Town* Scotland, UK
 41 E8
Gliwice *Town* Poland 57 G8

Gloucester *Town* England, UK 41 H9

Gobi Desert Mongolia 85 D9

Godavari *River* India 77 F9

Godoy Cruz *Town* Argentina 36 G7

Goiânia *Town* Brazil 37 D9

Golan Heights *Mountain range* Syria 73 H9

Golmud *Town* China 84 F7

Gómez Palacio *Town* Mexico 31 E8

Gonaïves *Town* Haiti 35 C9

Gonder *Town* Ethiopia 67 D9

Gore *Town* Ethiopia 67 E9

Gorgan *Town* Iran 75 B9

Görlitz *Town* Germany 51 F12

Gorzow Wielkopolski *Town* Poland 56 D6

Gosford *Town* Australia 91 G12

Göteborg *Town* Sweden 42 H6

Gotland *Island* Sweden 43 H8

Göttingen *Town* Germany 51 E9

Gouda *Town* Netherlands 50 D6

Governador Valadares *Town* Brazil 37 E10

Grafton *Town* Australia 91 F13

Grampian Mountains Scotland, UK 41 D8

Granada *Town* Spain 45 H9

Gran Chaco Argentina 36 F7

Grand Canyon Arizona, USA 26 E7

Grand Forks *Town* N Dakota, USA 25 E13

Grand Rapids *Town* Michigan, USA 20 F7

Graz *Town* Austria 40 G12

Great Australian Bight Australia 90 G7

Great Barrier Island New Zealand 93 B9

Great Barrier Reef Australia 91 C12

Great Basin Nevada, USA 26 D6

Great Dividing Range Australia 91 D12

Great Falls *Town* Montana, USA 25 E8

Great Karoo South Africa 68 J7

Great Rift Valley Kenya 67 F9

Great Sandy Desert Australia 90 D6

Great Victoria Desert Australia 90 G5

Greece *Country* 49

Greeley *Town* Colorado, USA 27 C10

Green Bay *Town* Wisconsin, USA 20 E5

Greenland Sea 17 H11, 43 G12

Greensboro *Town* N Carolina, USA 23 C11

Greenville *Town* Mississippi, USA 22 E6

Greenville *Town* S Carolina, USA 23 D10

Greifswald *Town* Germany 51 B12

Grenada *Country* 35

Grenoble *Town* France 47 F10

Greymouth *Town* New Zealand 92 G7

Groningen *Town* Netherlands 50 C7

Grootfontein *Town* Namibia 68 G7

Grosseto *Town* Italy 48 D6

Grozny *Town* Russian Fed. 59 I8

Guadalajara *Town* Mexico 31 G8

Guadalajara *Town* Spain 45 E9

Guadeloupe *Dep. territory* France 35 D12

Guam *Dep. territory* USA 93 H11

Guanabacoa *Town* Cuba 34 B7

Guanare *Town* Venezuela 35 F9

Guangzhou *Town* China 85 I11

Guantánamo *Town* Cuba 35 C8

Guatemala *Country* 34

Guatemala City *Capital* Guatemala 34 D4

Guayaquil *Town* Ecuador 36 B5

Guaymas *Town* Mexico 30 D5

Guernsey *Island* Channel Islands, UK 41 J9

Guiana Highlands *Mountain range* Guyana/Venezuela 35 G12

Guinea, Gulf of 64 J7

Guinea *Country* 64

Guinea-Bissau *Country* 64

Guiyang *Town* China 85 H10

Gujranwala *Town* Pakistan 77 C8

Guwahati *Town* India 77 E12

Guyana *Country* 35

Gwadar *Town* Pakistan 76 D5

Gyor *Town* Hungary 54 C5

Haarlem *Town* Netherlands 50 D6

Hachinohe *Town* Japan 83 D10

Hadera *Town* Israel 73 H9

Haifa *Town* Israel 73 H9

Haikou *Town* China 85 J11

Hailar *Town* China 85 B11

Haiphong *Town* Vietnam 78 E5

Haiti *Country* 35

Hakodate *Town* Japan 83 C10

Halifax *Province capital* Nova Scotia, Canada 29 I13

Halle *Town* Germany 51 E10

Halley (UK) *RS* Antarctica 16 D3

Halmstad *Town* Sweden 42 I7

Hamadan *Town* Iran 75 C8

Hamah *Town* Syria 73 F10

Hamamatsu *Town* Japan 83 G9

Hamar *Town* Norway 42 G6

Hamburg *Town* Germany 51 C9

Hamhung *Town* North Korea 85 D13

Hamilton *Town* New Zealand 93 C9

Hamilton *Town* Ontario, Canada 29 J11

Hamm *Town* Germany 51 E8

Hanamaki *Town* Japan 83 E10

Hangzhou *Town* China 85 G12

Hannover *Town* Germany 51 D9

Hanoi *Capital* Vietnam 78 E5

Harare *Capital* Zimbabwe 69 G9

Harbel *Town* Liberia 64 I5

Harbin *Town* China 85 C12

Harer *Town* Ethiopia 67 E10

Hargeisa *Town* Somalia 67 D11

Harrisburg *State capital* Pennsylvania, USA 21 G11

Hartford *State capital* Connecticut, USA 21 F12

Hasselt *Town* Belgium 50 E6

Hastings *Town* New Zealand 93 E10

Hat Yai *Town* Thailand 78 J4

Haugesund *Town* Norway 42 G5

Havana *Capital* Cuba 34 B7

Hawaii *State* USA 26

Hefei *Town* China 85 F12

Heidelberg *Town* Germany 51 G8

Heilbronn *Town* Germany 51 H8

Helena *State capital* Montana, USA 24 E7

Helsingborg *Town* Sweden 42 I7

Helsinki *Capital* Finland 43 G10

Hengyang *Town* China 85 H11

Henzada *Town* Burrma (Myanmar) 78 F2

Herat *Town* Afghanistan 76 A6

Hermosillo *Town* Mexico 30 D5

Hilversum *Town* Netherlands 50 D6

Himalayas *Asia* 77 D10, 84 H6

Hims *Town* Syria 73 G10

Hirosaki *Town* Japan 83 D10

Hiroshima *Town* Japan 82 H6

Hitachi *Town* Japan 83 F10

Hobart *Town* Australia 91 J11

Ho Chi Minh City *Town* Vietnam 78 H6

Hofu *Town* Japan 82 H6

Hohhot *Town* China 85 E10

Hokkaido *Island* Japan 83 B11

Holguín *Town* Cuba 35 C8

Homyel *Town* Belarus 58 G6

Honduras *Country* 34

Hong Kong *Town* China 85 I11

Honolulu *State capital* Hawaii, USA 26 H3

Honshu *Island* Japan 83 F9

Hormuz, Strait of Iran/Oman 75 E10

Houston *Town* Texas, USA 27 H14

Hradec Kralove *Town* Czech Republic 56 G6

Hrodna *Town* Belarus 58 G5

Huacho *Town* Peru 36 C5

Huambo *Town* Angola 68 F6

Huancayo *Town* Peru 36 D6

Huang *River* China 85 F11

Hudson Bay Canada 29 G10

Hué *Town* Vietnam 78 F6

Huelva *Town* Spain 44 H6

Hull *Town* England, UK 41 F10

Hungary *Country* 54

Huntington *Town* West Virginia, USA 21 I9

Huntsville *Town* Alabama, USA 23 D8

Huron, Lake USA 20 E8

Hyderabad *Town* India 77 G8

Hyderabad *Town* Pakistan 76 D7

Hyesan *Town* North Korea 85 D13

Iasi *Town* Romania 55 C12

Ibadan *Town* Nigeria 65 I9

Ibagué *Town* Colombia 35 H8

Ibarra *Town* Ecuador 36 A5

Ibiza Balearic Islands, Spain 45 F12

Ibiza *Town* Ibiza, Spain 45 F12

Ica *Town* Peru 36 D5

Iceland *Country* 43

Idaho *State* USA 24

Idaho Falls *Town* Idaho, USA 24 G7

Illinois *River* Illinois, USA 20 H5

Illinois *State* USA 20

Iloilo *Town* Philippines 79 G11

Ilorin *Town* Nigeria 65 I9

Imperatriz *Town* Brazil 37 B10

Imphal *Town* India 77 E12

Inchon *Town* South Korea 85 E13

Independence *Town* Missouri, USA 22 B4

India *Country* 77

Indiana *State* USA 20

Indianapolis *State capital* Indiana, USA 20 H7

Indian Ocean 67, 69, 76, 90

Indonesia *Country* 80

Indore *Town* India 77 E8

Indus *River* Pakistan 76 D7

Ingolstadt *Town* Germany 51 H10

Inhambane *Town* Mozambique 69 H10

Innsbruck *Town* Austria 52 F7

In Salah *Town* Algeria 62 F5

Invercargill *Town* New Zealand 92 J6

Inverness *Town* Scotland, UK 41 C8

Ioánnina *Town* Greece 49 G10

Ionian Sea 49 H9

Iowa *State* USA 20

Ipoh *Town* Malaysia 80 E2

Ipswich *Town* England, UK 41 H10

Iqaluit *Province capital* Nunavut, Canada 29 F11

Iquique *Town* Chile 36 E6

Iquitos *Town* Peru 36 B6

Iráklion *Town* Crete, Greece 49 I12

Iran *Country* 75
Iraq *Country* 74
Irbid *Town* Jordan 73 H9
Ireland, Republic of *Country* 40
Iringa *Town* Tanzania 67 I9
Irish Sea 40 F7
Irkutsk *Town* Russian Fed. 86 H6
Irrawaddy *River* Burma (Myanmar) 78 F2
Ishinomaki *Town* Japan 83 E10
Islamabad *Capital* Pakistan 77 B8
Isle of Man *Dep. territory* UK 41 F8
Isparta *Town* Turkey 72 E7
Israel *Country* 73
Istanbul *Town* Turkey 72 B6
Itabuna *Town* Brazil 37 D11
Italy *Country* 48
Iwaki *Town* Japan 83 F10
Izhevsk *Town* Russian Fed. 59 F9
Izmir *Town* Turkey 72 D5
Izmit *Town* Turkey 72 C7

Jackson *State capital* Mississippi, USA 22 F6
Jacksonville *Town* Florida, USA 23 G10
Jaén *Town* Spain 45 H8
Jaffna *Town* Sri Lanka 77 I9
Jaipur *Town* India 77 D8
Jakarta *Capital* Indonesia 80 H3
Jamaica *Country* 35
Jambi *Town* Indonesia 80 F2
Jamnagar *Town* India 76 E7
Jamshedpur *Town* India 77 E10
Janesville *Town* Wisconsin, USA 20 G5
Japan, Sea of 82 F7, 85 D13
Japan *Country* 82
Java *Island* Indonesia 80 H4
Java Sea 80 H4
Jayapura *Town* Indonesia 81 F11
Jefferson City *State capital* Missouri, USA 22 B5
Jena *Town* Germany 51 F10
Jersey *Island* Channel Islands, UK 41 J9
Jerusalem *Capital* Israel 73 I9
Jiddah *Town* Saudi Arabia 74 G5
Jihlava *Town* Czech Republic 56 H6
Jilin *Town* China 85 C12
Jima *Town* Ethiopia 67 E9
Jinan *Town* China 85 E11
Jinzhou *Town* China 85 D11
João Pessoa *Town* Brazil 37 C12
Jodhpur *Town* India 77 D8
Johannesburg *Town* South Africa 69 J9
John o'Groats *Town* Scotland, UK 41 C9
Johor Baharu *Town* Malaysia 80 F2
Joliet *Town* Illinois, USA 20 G6

Jönköping *Town* Sweden 42 H7
Jordan *Country* 73
Jordan *River* Jordan 73 H9
Jorhat *Town* India 77 D12
Joseph Bonaparte Gulf 90 B7
Juazeiro *Town* Brazil 37 C11
Juazeiro do Norte *Town* Brazil 37 C11
Juba *Capital* South Sudan 67 F8
Judenburg *Town* Austria 40 G11
Juliaca *Town* Peru 36 D6
Juneau *State capital* Alaska, USA 25 C11
Jyväskylä *Town* Finland 43 F10

K2 *Mountain* China/Pakistan 77 B9
Kabul *Capital* Afghanistan 76 B7
Kabwe *Town* Zambia 69 F9
Kachchh, Rann of *India* 76 E7
Kaduna *Town* Nigeria 65 H10
Kagoshima *Town* Japan 82 I5
Kairouan *Town* Tunisia 62 D7
Kaiserslautern *Town* Germany 50 G7
Kalahari Desert *Namibia* 68 H7
Kalamata *Town* Peleponnese, Greece 49 I11
Kalamazoo *Town* Michigan, USA 20 G7
Kalemie *Town* DRC 69 E9
Kalgoorlie *Town* Australia 90 G5
Kaliningrad *Town* Russian Fed. 58 G5
Kalisz *Town* Poland 56 E7
Kamina *Town* DRC 69 E8
Kamloops *Town* British Columbia, Canada 28 H6
Kampala *Capital* Uganda 67 G8
Kampong Cham *Town* Cambodia 78 H5
Kananga *Town* DRC 69 E8
Kanazawa *Town* Japan 83 F8
Kandy *Town* Sri Lanka 77 J9
Kankan *Town* Guinea 64 H5
Kano *Town* Nigeria 65 G10
Kanpur *Town* India 77 D9
Kansas *River* Kansas, USA 27 D13
Kansas *State* USA 27
Kansas City *Town* Missouri, USA 22 B4
Kansk *Town* Russian Fed. 86 G6
Kaposvár *Town* Hungary 54 D5
Karabük *Town* Turkey 73 B8
Karachi *Town* Pakistan 76 D6
Kara Sea 17 G14, 59 B10, 86 D4
Karbala *Town* Iraq 74 C7
Kardhitsa *Town* Greece 49 G11
Karlovac *Town* Croatia 49 C8
Karlovy Vary *Town* Czech Republic 56 G4
Karlskrona *Town* Sweden 42 I7

Karlsruhe *Town* Germany 50 H7
Karlstad *Town* Sweden 42 G7
Kars *Town* Turkey 73 C13
Kasai (Cassai) *River* Angola/DRC 68 D7
Kashi *Town* China 84 E4
Kassala *Town* Sudan 67 C9
Kassel *Town* Germany 51 E9
Katherine *Town* Australia 91 B8
Kathmandu *Capital* Nepal 77 D10
Katowice *Town* Poland 57 G8
Katsina *Town* Nigeria 65 G10
Kattegat *Sea* 42 H6
Kaunas *Town* Lithuania 58 G5
Kaválla *Town* Greece 49 F12
Kawasaki *Town* Japan 83 G10
Kayseri *Town* Turkey 73 D9
Kazakhstan *Country* 86
Kazan *Town* Russian Fed. 59 F9
Kecskemét *Town* Hungary 54 D6
Kelang *Town* Malaysia 80 E2
Kemerovo *Town* Russian Fed. 86 G5
Kemi *Town* Finland 43 D9
Kénitra *Town* Morocco 62 D3
Kentucky *State* USA 23
Kenya *Country* 67
Kerman *Town* Iran 75 D10
Kesennuma *Town* Japan 83 E10
Kettering *Town* Ohio, USA 21 H8
Key West *Town* Florida, USA 23 J11
Khabarovsk *Town* Russian Fed. 87 H9
Kharkiv *Town* Ukraine 58 H7
Khartoum *Capital* Sudan 67 C8
Khaskovo *Town* Bulgaria I11
Khon Kaen *Town* Thailand 78 G4
Khulna *Town* Bangladesh 77 F11
Kiel *Town* Germany 51 B10
Kiev *Capital* Ukraine 58 G6
Kigali *Capital* Rwanda 66 G7
Kigoma *Town* Tanzania 66 H7
Kikwit *Town* DRC 68 D7
Kilimanjaro, Mount *Tanzania* 67 H9
Kimberley *Town* South Africa 69 I8
Kimberley Plateau *Australia* 90 C6
Kingston *Capital* Jamaica 35 D8
Kingstown *Capital* St. Vincent 35 E12
Kinshasa *Capital* DRC 68 D6
Kiribati *Country* 93 I13
Kirikkale *Town* Turkey 73 C9
Kirkuk *Town* Iraq 74 B7
Kirov *Town* Russian Fed. 58 G6
Kiruna *Town* Sweden 43 C8
Kisangani *Town* DRC 69 C8
Kismaayo *Town* Somalia 67 G10
Kisumu *Town* Kenya 67 G8
Kitakyushu *Town* Japan 82 H5
Kitchener *Town* Ontario, Canada 29 J11

Kitwe *Town* Zambia 69 F9
Kivu, Lake *DRC/Rwanda* 66 H7, 69 D9
Klagenfurt *Town* Austria 40 H11
Klamath Falls *Town* Oregon, USA 24 G3
Knoxville *Town* Tennessee, USA 23 C9
Kobe *Town* Japan 82 H7
Koblenz *Town* Germany 50 F7
Kochi (Cochin) *Town* India 77 I8
Kochi *Town* Japan 82 H7
Kodiak *Town* Alaska, USA 25 C10
Kofu *Town* Japan 83 G9
Kokshetau *Town* Kazakhstan 86 H3
Kolhapur *Town* India 76 G7
Kolkata (Calcutta) *Town* India 77 F11
Kolwezi *Town* DRC 69 E8
Komatsu *Town* Japan 83 F8
Komsomol'sk-na-Amure *Town* Russian Fed. 87 H9
Konya *Town* Turkey 73 E8
Koper *Town* Slovenia 48 B7
Korçë *Town* Albania 49 F10
Korea, North *Country* 85
Korea, South *Country* 85
Korea Strait *Japan/South Korea* 82 H4, 85 E13
Koriyama *Town* Japan 83 F10
Korla *Town* China 84 E6
Kortrijk *Town* Belgium 50 E4
Kosice *Town* Slovakia 57 I10
Kosovo *Country* 49
Kosovska Mitrovica *Town* Serbia 49 D10
Koszalin *Town* Poland 56 B6
Kotka *Town* Finland 43 G10
Kotte *Capital* Sri Lanka 77 J9
Kotto *River* CAR 68 B7

Kozáni *Town* Greece 49 F11
Kozhikode (Calicut) *Town* India 77 H8
Kragujevac *Town* Serbia 49 D10
Kraków *Town* Poland 57 G9
Krasnodar *Town* Russian Fed. 58 I7
Krasnoyarsk *Town* Russian Fed. 86 G5
Krefeld *Town* Germany 50 E7
Kristiansand *Town* Norway 42 H5
Krusevac *Town* Serbia 49 D11
Kryvyy Rih *Town* Ukraine 58 H6
Kuala Lumpur *Capital* Malaysia 80 E2
Kuala Terengganu *Town* Malaysia 80 E2
Kuching *Town* Malaysia 80 F4
Kugluktuk *Town* Nunavut, Canada 28 E7
Kumamoto *Town* Japan 82 I5

Kumanovo *Town* Macedonia 49 E11
Kumasi *Town* Ghana 64 I7
Kunlun Shan *Mountain range* China 84 F6
Kunming *Town* China 85 I9
Kuopio *Town* Finland 43 E10
Kupang *Town* Indonesia 80 H7
Kure *Town* Japan 82 H6
Kushiro *Town* Japan 83 B11
Kütahya *Town* Turkey 72 D7
Kuwait *Country* 75
Kuwait City *Capital* Kuwait 75 D8
Kwangju *Town* South Korea 85 E13
Kwango *River* DRC 68 E6
Kwilu *River* DRC 68 D7
Kyoto *Town* Japan 83 G8
Kyrgyzstan *Country* 86
Kyushu *Island* Japan 82 I5
Kyustendil *Town* Bulgaria 55 I9

Labrador Sea 29 F12
La Ceiba *Town* Honduras 34 D5
La Coruña *Town* Spain 44 B5
La Crosse *Town* Wisconsin, USA 20 F4
Ladoga, Lake *Russian Fed.* 58 E6
Lafayette *Town* Louisiana, USA 22 H5
Lagos *Town* Nigeria 65 I8
Lagos *Town* Portugal 44 H5
Lahore *Town* Pakistan 77 C8
Lahti *Town* Finland 43 F10
Lake Charles *Town* Louisiana, USA 22 H5
Lakewood *Town* Colorado, USA 27 D10
Lalitpur *Town* India 77 E9
Lamía *Town* Greece 49 G11
Lansing *State capital* Michigan, USA 20 F7
Lanzhou *Town* China 85 F9
Laoag *Town* Philippines 79 D10
Laos *Country* 78
La Paz *Capital* Bolivia 36 D7
La Paz *Town* Mexico 30 F5
La Plata *Town* Argentina 37 G8
Laptev Sea 17 D13, 87 D8
Laredo *Town* Texas, USA 27 I12
Larissa *Town* Greece 49 G11
Larkana *Town* Pakistan 76 C7
La Rochelle *Town* France 46 E6
La Romana *Town* Dominican Republic 35 D10
Las Cruces *Town* New Mexico, USA 27 G9
La Serena *Town* Chile 36 F6
La Spezia *Town* Italy 48 C5
Las Vegas *Town* Nevada, USA 26 E6
Latina *Town* Italy 48 E6

Latvia *Country* 58
Launceston *Town* Australia 91 J11
Lausanne *Town* Switzerland 52 G1
Laval *Town* France 46 C7
Lawton *Town* Oklahoma, USA 27 F12
Lebanon *Country* 73
Lecce *Town* Italy 49 F9
Leeds *Town* England, UK 41 F9
Leeuwarden *Town* Netherlands 50 C7
Legnica *Town* Poland 56 F6
Le Havre *Town* France 47 B8
Leicester *Town* England, UK 41 G9
Leiden *Town* Netherlands 50 D6
Leipzig *Town* Germany 51 F11
Le Mans *Town* France 47 C8
Lena *River* Russian Fed. 86 G7
León *Town* Mexico 31 G8
León *Town* Nicaragua 34 E5
León *Town* Spain 44 C7
Lerwick *Town* Scotland, UK 41 A9
Leskovac *Town* Serbia 49 D11
Lesotho *Country* 69
Lethbridge *Town* Alberta, Canada 28 I7
Leuven *Town* Belgium 50 E5
Lewis *Island* Scotland, UK 40 C7
Lewiston *Town* Idaho, USA 24 E5
Lewiston *Town* Maine, USA 21 D13
Lexington *Town* Kentucky, USA 23 B8
Lhasa *Town* China 84 H7
Lianyungang *Town* China 85 F12
Liberec *Town* Czech Republic 56 F5
Liberia *Country* 64
Libreville *Capital* Gabon 68 C5
Libya *Country* 63
Libyan Desert *Egypt/Libya/Sudan* 63 G11, 66 A6
Liechtenstein *Country* 52
Liège *Town* Belgium 50 F6
Liepaja *Town* Latvia 58 F5
Likasi *Town* DRC 69 F8
Lille *Town* France 47 A10
Lillehammer *Town* Norway 42 F6
Lilongwe *Capital* Malawi 69 F10
Lima *Capital* Peru 36 D5
Limassol *Town* Cyprus 73 G8
Limerick *Town* Republic of Ireland 40 G6
Limoges *Town* France 47 E8
Limón *Town* Costa Rica 34 F6
Limpopo *River* South Africa 69 H9
Linares *Town* Spain 45 G9
Lincoln *State capital* Nebraska, USA 25 I14
Lincoln Sea 17 G11
Lindi *Town* Tanzania 67 J10

Linköping *Town* Sweden 42 H7
Linz *Town* Austria 40 E11
Lipetsk *Town* Russian Fed. 58 G7
Lisbon *Capital* Portugal 44 G4
Lithuania *Country* 58
Little Rock *State capital* Arkansas, USA 22 E5
Liuzhou *Town* China 85 I10
Liverpool *Town* England, UK 41 G8
Livingstone *Town* Zambia 69 G8
Livorno *Town* Italy 48 D5
Ljubljana *Capital* Slovenia 48 B7
Lleida *Town* Spain 45 C11
Lobamba *Capital* Swaziland 69 I9
Lobito *Town* Angola 68 F6
Lodz *Town* Poland 57 E8
Logroño *Town* Spain 45 C9
Loire *River* France 46 D7
Lomami *River* DRC 69 D8
Lomas de Zamora *Town* Argentina 37 G8
Lomé *Capital* Togo 65 I8
London *Capital* England, UK 41 H10
London *Town* Ontario, Canada 29 J11
Londonderry *Town* Northern Ireland, UK 40 E7
Long Beach *Town* California, USA 26 F5
Long Island *New York, USA* 21 F12
Longview *Town* Texas, USA 27 G14
Lorca *Town* Spain 45 H10
Lorient *Town* France 46 C6
Los Angeles *Town* California, USA 26 F5
Los Angeles *Town* Chile 36 H6
Los Mochis *Town* Mexico 30 E6
Louisiana *State* USA 22
Louisville *Town* Kentucky, USA 23 B8
Lowell *Town* Massachusetts, USA 21 E13
Lower Hutt *Town* New Zealand 93 F9
Luanda *Capital* Angola 68 E6
Lubango *Town* Angola 68 F6
Lubbock *Town* Texas, USA 27 F11
Lübeck *Town* Germany 51 B10
Lublin *Town* Poland 57 F11
Lubumbashi *Town* DRC 69 F9
Lucknow *Town* India 77 D9
Lüderitz *Town* Namibia 68 I6
Ludhiana *Town* India 77 C8
Ludwigshafen *Town* Germany 51 G7
Luena *Town* Angola 68 F7
Lugano *Town* Switzerland 52 H4
Lugo *Town* Spain 44 B6
Luleå *Town* Sweden 43 D9

Lund *Town* Sweden 42 I7
Lüneburg *Town* Germany 51 C10
Luoyang *Town* China 85 F10
Lusaka *Capital* Zambia 69 F9
Luxembourg *Capital* Luxembourg 50 G6
Luxembourg *Country* 50 G6
Luxor *Town* Egypt 63 G13
Luzon *Island* Philippines 79 E10
Lviv *Town* Ukraine 58 H5
Lynchburg *Town* Virgina, USA 23 B11
Lyon *Town* France 47 F10

Maas (Meuse) *River* Belgium/France/Netherlands 50 E6
Maastricht *Town* Netherlands 50 E6
Macapá *Town* Brazil 37 B9
Macau *Town* China 85 I11
Macdonnell Ranges *Australia* 91 E8
Macedonia *Country* 49
Maceio *Town* Brazil 37 C11
Mackay *Town* Australia 91 D12
Macon *Town* Georgia, USA 23 E9
Ma'daba *Town* Jordan 73 I10
Madagascar *Country* 69
Madeira *River* Brazil 37 B8
Madison *State capital* Wisconsin, USA 20 F5
Madras *See Chennai*
Madrid *Capital* Spain 45 E8
Madurai *Town* India 77 I8
Magadan *Town* Russian Fed. 87 G11
Magdeburg *Town* Germany 51 D10
Magnitogorsk *Town* Russian Fed. 59 G10
Mahajanga *Town* Madagascar 69 G12
Maiduguri *Town* Nigeria 65 H11
Main *River* Germany 51 G10
Maine, Gulf of 21 D14
Maine *State* USA 21
Mainz *Town* Germany 51 G8
Maitri (India) *RS* Antarctica 16 C5
Malabo *Capital* Equatorial Guinea 68 C5
Málaga *Town* Spain 45 I8
Malakal *Town* Sudan 67 D8
Malang *Town* Indonesia 80 H4
Malatya *Town* Turkey 73 D11
Malawi *Country* 69
Malaysia *Country* 80
Mali *Country* 64
Mallorca *Balearic Islands, Spain* 45 E13
Malmö *Town* Sweden 42 I7
Malta *Country* 48
Manado *Town* Indonesia 80 F7
Managua *Capital* Nicaragua 34 E5
Manama *Capital* Bahrain 75 E8

Manaus *Town* Brazil 37 B8

Manchester *Town* England, UK 41 G9

Manchester *Town* New Hampshire, USA 21 E13

Mandalay *Town* Burma (Myanmar) 78 E2

Mangalore *Town* India 76 H7

Manila *Capital* Philippines 79 F10

Manisa *Town* Turkey 72 D5

Manitoba *Province* Canada 29

Manizales *Town* Colombia 35 H8

Mankato *Town* Minnesota, USA 20 F3

Mannheim *Town* Germany 51 G8

Manta *Town* Ecuador 36 B5

Maputo *Capital* Mozambique 69 I9

Marabá *Town* Brazil 37 B9

Maracaibo *Town* Venezuela 35 F9

Maradi *Town* Niger 65 G10

Marajo Island Brazil 37 B9

Marambio (Argentina) *RS* Antarctica 16 D1

Marbella *Town* Spain 45 I8

Mardan *Town* Pakistan 77 B8

Mar del Plata *Town* Argentina 37 G8

Maribor *Town* Slovenia 49 B8

Marie Byrd Land Antarctica 16 F3

Marka *Town* Somalia 67 G11

Marmara, Sea of 72 C6

Marquette *Town* Michigan, USA 20 D5

Marrakech *Town* Morocco 62 E2

Marseille *Town* France 47 H10

Marshall Islands *Country* 93 H12

Martin *Town* Slovakia 57 H8

Martinique *Dep. territory* France 35 E12

Maryland *State* USA 21

Masaka *Town* Uganda 67 G8

Maseru *Capital* Lesotho 69 I8

Mashhad *Town* Iran 75 B11

Massa *Town* Italy 48 C5

Massachusetts *State* USA 21

Massawa *Town* Eritrea 67 C9

Massif Central France 47 F9

Matadi *Town* DRC 68 D6

Matamoros *Town* Mexico 31 E10

Mataram *Town* Indonesia 80 H5

Mataró *Town* Spain 45 C13

Matsue *Town* Japan 82 G6

Matsumoto *Town* Japan 83 G9

Matsuyama *Town* Japan 82 H6

Matterhorn, Mount Switzerland 52 H2

Maun *Town* Botswana 69 G8

Mauritania *Country* 64

Mauritius *Country* 69

Mawson (Australia) *RS* Antarctica 16 E6

Mayotte *Dep. territory* France 69 F12

Mazar-e Sharif *Town* Afghanistan 76 A7

Mazatlán *Town* Mexico 30 F7

Mbabane *Capital* Swaziland 69 I9

Mbandaka *Town* DRC 68 C7

Mbeya *Town* Tanzania 67 I9

Mbuji-Mayi *Town* DRC 69 E8

McKinley, Mount Alaska, USA 25 B11

McMurdo (US) *RS* Antarctica 16 H5

Mecca *Town* Saudi Arabia 74 G5

Mechelen *Town* Belgium 50 E5

Medan *Town* Indonesia 80 E1

Medellín *Town* Colombia 35 G8

Medicine Hat *Town* Alberta, Canada 28 I7

Medina *Town* Saudi Arabia 74 F5

Mediterranean Sea 45, 47, 62, 73

Meerut *Town* India 77 D9

Mekong *River* Asia 78 G5, 85 I9

Melbourne *Town* Australia 91 I11

Melilla *Town* Spain 45 J9, 62 D4

Melville Island Canada 17 E9

Memphis *Town* Tennessee, USA 22 D6

Mendoza *Town* Argentina 36 G7

Menorca Balearic Islands, Spain 45 E14

Mérida *Town* Mexico 31 G13, 44 F7

Mérida *Town* Spain 44 F7

Mesa *Town* Arizona, USA 26 F7

Messina *Town* Sicily, Italy 48 H7

Metairie *Town* Louisiana, USA 22 H6

Metz *Town* France 47 C11

Meuse (Maas) *River* Belgium/ France/Netherlands 50 F5

Mexicali *Town* Mexico 30 B4

Mexico, Gulf of 23 H8, 27 J14, 31 F11

Mexico *Country* 30

Mexico City *Capital* Mexico 31 H9

Miami *Town* Florida, USA 23 I12

Michigan, Lake USA 20 E6

Michigan *State* USA 20

Micronesia *Country* 93 H11

Middlesbrough *Town* England, UK 41 F9

Midland *Town* Texas, USA 27 G11

Milan *Town* Italy 48 B5

Miles City *Town* Montana, USA 25 F10

Milwaukee *Town* Wisconsin, USA 20 F6

Mindanao *Island* Philippines 79 G12

Mindoro Strait South China Sea 79 G10

Minneapolis *Town* Minnesota, USA 20 E3

Minnesota *State* USA 20

Minot *Town* N Dakota, USA 25 E12

Minsk *Capital* Belarus 58 G6

Mirny (Russian Federation) *RS* Antarctica 16 F7

Mirpur Khas *Town* Pakistan 76 D7

Miskolc *Town* Hungary 54 B7

Mississippi *River* USA 20 F4, 22 E6

Mississippi *State* USA 22

Missouri *River* Montana, USA 25 E10

Missouri *State* USA 22

Mito *Town* Japan 83 F10

Miyako *Town* Japan 83 D10

Miyakonojo *Town* Japan 82 I5

Miyazaki *Town* Japan 82 I6

Mobile *Town* Alabama, USA 22 G7

Modesto *Town* California, USA 26 C4

Mogadishu *Capital* Somalia 67 F11

Moldova *Country* 58

Molucca Sea 80 F7

Mombasa *Town* Kenya 67 H10

Monaco *Capital* Monaco 47 H11

Monaco *Country* 47

Monclova *Town* Mexico 31 E9

Mongolia *Country* 85

Monroe *Town* Louisiana, USA 22 F5

Monrovia *Capital* Liberia 64 I4

Mons *Town* Belgium 50 F5

Montana *State* USA 25

Montana *Town* Bulgaria 55 H9

Montauban *Town* France 46 G7

Mont Blanc *Mountain* France 47 F11

Mont-de-Marsan *Town* France 46 F7

Montego Bay *Town* Jamaica 35 C8

Montélimar *Town* France 47 G10

Montenegro *Country* 49

Monterey *Town* California, USA 26 D4

Montería *Town* Colombia 35 F8

Monterrey *Town* Mexico 31 E9

Montevideo *Capital* Uruguay 37 G8

Montgomery *State capital* Alabama, USA 23 F8

Montluçon *Town* France 47 E9

Montpelier *State capital* Vermont, USA 21 D12

Montpellier *Town* France 47 H9

Montreal *Town* Quebec, Canada 29 I12

Montserrat *Dep. territory* UK 35 D12

Monza *Town* Italy 48 B5

Moorhead *Town* Minnesota, USA 20 D2

Mopti *Town* Mali 64 G6

Morelia *Town* Mexico 31 H8

Morocco *Country* 62

Moroni *Capital* Comoros 69 F12

Moscow *Capital* Russian Fed. 58 F7

Mosselbaai *Town* South Africa 68 J7

Mossoró *Town* Brazil 37 B11

Mostar *Town* Bosnia and Herz. 49 D9

Mosul *Town* Iraq 74 B6

Moulmein *Town* Burma (Myanmar) 78 G3

Moundou *Town* Chad 65 I12

Mount Isa *Town* Australia 91 D10

Mozambique *Country* 69

Mufulira *Town* Zambia 69 F9

Mulhouse *Town* France 47 D12

Multan *Town* Pakistan 77 C8

Mumbai (Bombay) *Town* India 76 F7

Muncie *Town* Indiana, USA 20 H7

Munich *Town* Germany 51 I10

Münster *Town* Germany 50 D7

Murcia *Town* Spain 45 G10

Murmansk *Town* Russian Fed. 58 C7

Muroran *Town* Japan 83 C10

Murray *River* Australia 91 H11

Muscat *Capital* Oman 75 F11

Mwanza *Town* Tanzania 67 H8

Mweru, Lake DRC 69 E9

Myanmar *See* Burma

Myrtle Beach *Town* S Carolina, USA 23 D11

Mysore *Town* India 77 H8

Myvatn *Lake* Iceland 43 H13

Nacala *Town* Mozambique 69 F11

Nagano *Town* Japan 83 F9

Nagaoka *Town* Japan 83 F9

Nagasaki *Town* Japan 82 I5

Nagoya *Town* Japan 83 G8

Nagpur *Town* India 77 F9

Nain *Town* Newfoundland and Labrador, Canada 29 G12

Nairobi *Capital* Kenya 67 G9

Nakhon Ratchasima *Town* Thailand 78 G4

Nakhon Sawan *Town* Thailand 78 G4

Nakhon Si Thammarat *Town* Thailand 78 I4

Nakuru *Town* Kenya 67 G9

Nam Dinh *Town* Vietnam 78 E5

Namib Desert Namibia 68 H6

Namibe *Town* Angola 68 F6

Namibia *Country* 68

Nampula *Town* Mozambique 69 F11

Namur *Town* Belgium 50 F5

Nanchang *Town* China 85 G11

Pachuca *Town* Mexico 31 G9

Pacific Ocean 24, 25, 26, 28, 30, 36, 79, 83, 85, 87, 91, 93

Padang *Town* Indonesia 80 F2

Paderborn *Town* Germany 51 E8

Paducah *Town* Kentucky, USA 22 C7

Pakistan *Country* 76

Pakxe *Town* Laos 78 G5

Palau *Country* 93 H10

Palawan Passage South China Sea 79 H9

Palembang *Town* Indonesia 80 G3

Palencia *Town* Spain 45 C8

Palermo *Town* Sicily, Italy 48 H6

Palma *Town* Mallorca, Spain 45 E13

Palmer (US) *RS* Antarctica 16 D1

Palmerston North *Town* New Zealand 93 E9

Palo Alto *Town* California, USA 26 D4

Palu *Town* Indonesia 80 F6

Pamplona *Town* Spain 45 B10

Panama, Gulf of 34 G7

Panama *Country* 34

Panama Canal Panama 34 F6

Panama City *Capital* Panama 34 F7

Pancevo *Town* Serbia 49 C10

Papua New Guinea *Country* 93

Paraguay *Country* 37

Paramaribo *Capital* Suriname 35 G13

Pardubice *Town* Czech Republic 56 G6

Paris *Capital* France 47 C9

Parma *Town* Italy 48 C5

Parnaíba *Town* Brazil 37 B11

Pasadena *Town* California, USA 26 F5

Pasadena *Town* Texas, USA 27 H14

Pasco *Town* Washington, USA 24 E5

Passau *Town* Germany 51 I11

Pasto *Town* Colombia 34 I7

Patagonia Argentina 36 I7

Paterson *Town* New Jersey, USA 21 F12

Patna *Town* India 77 E10

Pátrai *Town* Greece 49 H11

Pau *Town* France 46 G6

Pavlodar *Town* Kazakhstan 86 H4

Pearl *River* Mississippi, USA 22 G6

Pejë *Town* Kosovo 49 E10

Pechora *River* Russian Fed. 59 D9

Pécs *Town* Hungary 54 E5

Pedro Juan Caballero *Town* Paraguay 37 E8

Pegu *Town* Burma (Myanmar) 78 G2

Pekanbaru *Town* Indonesia 80 F2

Pennines *Hills* England, UK 41 F9

Pennsylvania *State* USA 21

Penza *Town* Russian Fed. 59 G8

Peoria *Town* Illinois, USA 20 H5

Pereira *Town* Colombia 35 H8

Perm *Town* Russian Fed. 59 F9

Pernik *Town* Bulgaria 55 I9

Persian Gulf 75 E8

Perth *Town* Australia 90 G4

Perth *Town* Scotland, UK 41 D8

Peru *Country* 36

Perugia *Town* Italy 48 D6

Pescara *Town* Italy 48 E7

Peshawar *Town* Pakistan 77 B8

Peterborough *Town* England, UK 41 G10

Petropavlovsk-Kamchatskiy *Town* Russian Fed. 87 H11

Petrozavodsk *Town* Russian Fed. 58 E7

Pforzheim *Town* Germany 51 H8

Philadelphia *Town* Pennsylvania, USA 21 G12

Philippines *Country* 79

Phnom Penh *Capital* Cambodia 78 H5

Phoenix *State capital* Arizona, USA 26 F7

Phuket *Town* Thailand 78 I3

Piacenza *Town* Italy 48 C5

Pierre *State capital* S Dakota, USA 25 G12

Pietermaritzburg *Town* South Africa 69 I9

Pietersburg *Town* South Africa 69 H9

Pinar del Río *Town* Cuba 34 B6

Pine Bluff *Town* Arkansas, USA 22 E5

Piraeus *Town* Greece 49 H12

Pisa *Town* Italy 48 D5

Pistoia *Town* Italy 48 C6

Pitesti *Town* Romania 55 F10

Pittsburgh *Town* Pennsylvania, USA 21 G9

Piura *Town* Peru 36 B5

Plano *Town* Texas, USA 27 G13

Platte *River* Nebraska, USA 25 I12

Plauen *Town* Germany 51 F10

Plenty, Bay of New Zealand 93 C10

Pleven *Town* Bulgaria 55 H10

Plock *Town* Poland 57 D9

Ploiesti *Town* Romania 55 F11

Plovdiv *Town* Bulgaria 55 I10

Plymouth *Town* England, UK 41 I8

Plzen *Town* Czech Republic 56 G4

Podgorica *Capital* Montenegro 49 E9

Pointe-Noire *Town* Republic of the Congo 68 D5

Poitiers *Town* France 46 D7

Poland *Country* 56

Pontianak *Town* Indonesia 80 F4

Poona *See Pune*

Popayán *Town* Colombia 34 H7

Pori *Town* Finland 43 F9

Port Arthur *Town* Texas, USA 27 H14

Port Augusta *Town* Australia 91 G9

Port-au-Prince *Capital* Haiti 35 D9

Port Elizabeth *Town* South Africa 69 J8

Port-Gentil *Town* Gabon 68 C5

Port Harcourt *Town* Nigeria 65 J9

Portland *Town* Maine, USA 21 D13

Portland *Town* Oregon, USA 24 E3

Port Louis *Capital* Mauritius 69 H14

Port Macquarie *Town* Australia 91 G13

Porto *Town* Portugal 44 D5

Porto Alegre *Town* Brazil 37 F9

Port-of-Spain *Capital* Trinidad and Tobago 35 F12

Porto-Novo *Capital* Benin 65 I8

Porto Velho *Town* Brazil 36 C7

Portoviejo *Town* Ecuador 36 B5

Port Said *Town* Egypt 63 E13

Portsmouth *Town* England, UK 41 I9

Portsmouth *Town* New Hampshire, USA 21 D13

Portsmouth *Town* Virginia, USA 23 B12

Port Sudan *Town* Sudan 67 B9

Portugal *Country* 44

Potosí *Town* Bolivia 36 E7

Potsdam *Town* Germany 51 D11

Poznan *Town* Poland 56 E7

Prague *Capital* Czech Republic 56 G5

Praia *Capital* Cape Verde 64 F1

Prato *Town* Italy 48 D6

Presidente Eduardo Frei (Chile) *RS* Antarctica 16 D1

Presov *Town* Slovakia 57 H10

Prespa, Lake Macedonia 49 F10

Presque Isle *Town* Maine, USA 21 B13

Pretoria *Capital* South Africa 69 H9

Préveza *Town* Greece 49 G10

Prichard *Town* Alabama, USA 22 G7

Prilep *Town* Macedonia 49 E11

Prince Edward Island *Province* Canada 29

Prince George *Town* British Columbia, Canada 28 H6

Pristina *Capital* Kosovo 49 D10

Prizren *Town* Serbia 49 E10

Prome *Town* Burma (Myanmar) 78 F2

Providence *State capital* Rhode Island, USA 21 E13

Provo *Town* Utah, USA 27 C8

Pucallpa *Town* Peru 36 C6

Puducherry *Town* India 77 H9

Puebla *Town* Mexico 31 H10

Pueblo *Town* Colorado, USA 27 D10

Puerto Ayacucho *Town* Venezuela 35 G10

Puerto Montt *Town* Chile 36 H6

Puerto Princesa *Town* Philippines 79 G10

Puerto Rico *Dep. territory* USA 35 D11

Pula *Town* Croatia 48 C7

Pune (Poona) *Town* India 76 F7

Puno *Town* Peru 36 D6

Punta Alta *Town* Argentina 37 H8

Punta Arenas *Town* Chile 36 J7

Puntarenas *Town* Costa Rica 34 F5

Pusan *Town* South Korea 85 E13

Putrajaya *Capital* Malaysia 80 E2

Pyongyang *Capital* North Korea 85 D12

Pyrenees *Mountain range* France/ Spain 45 C11, 46 H7

Qamdo *Town* China 85 H8

Qatar *Country* 75

Qattara Depression Egypt 63 F12

Qena *Town* Egypt 63 G13

Qilian Shan *Mountain range* China 85 F8

Qingdao *Town* China 85 E12

Qom *Town* Iran 75 C8

Quebec *Province* Canada 29

Quebec *Province capital* Quebec, Canada 29 I12

Queen Elizabeth Islands Canada 17 F9

Queensland *State* Australia 91

Queenstown *Town* Australia 91 J11

Quelimane *Town* Mozambique 69 G10

Querétaro *Town* Mexico 31 G9

Quetta *Town* Pakistan 76 C7

Quezaltenango *Town* Guatemala 34 D4

Quibdó *Town* Colombia 34 G7

Quimper *Town* France 46 B5

Qui Nhon *Town* Vietnam 78 G7

Rabat *Capital* Morocco 62 D3

Radom *Town* Poland 57 F10

Ragusa *Town* Sicily, Italy 48 H7

Rainier, Mount Washington, USA 24 D4

Raipur *Town* India 77 F9

Rajshahi *Town* Bangladesh 77 E11

Raleigh *State capital* N Carolina, USA 23 C11

Rancagua *Town* Chile 36 G7

Randers *Town* Denmark 42 I6

Rapid City *Town* S Dakota, USA 25 G11

Rasht *Town* Iran 75 B8

Rat Islands Alaska, USA 25 C8

Ravenna *Town* Italy 48 C6

Rawalpindi *Town* Pakistan 77 B8

Reading *Town* England, UK 41 H9

Reading *Town* Pennsylvania, USA 21 G11

Recife *Town* Brazil 37 C12

Red *River* USA 22 G5

Red Deer *Town* Alberta, Canada 28 H7

Redding *Town* California, USA 26 B4

Red Sea 63 G14, 67 B9, 74 G5

Regensburg *Town* Germany 51 H10

Reggio di Calabria *Town* Italy 49 H8

Reggio nell' Emilia *Town* Italy 48 C5

Regina *Province capital* Saskatchewan, Canada 29 I8

Reims *Town* France 47 C10

Rennes *Town* France 46 C7

Reno *Town* Nevada, USA 26 C5

Republic of Ireland *See Ireland, Republic of*

Republic of the Congo *See Congo, Republic of*

Resistencia *Town* Argentina 37 F8

Resita *Town* Romania 55 E8

Réunion *Dep. territory* France 69 H14

Reus *Town* Spain 45 D12

Reutlingen *Town* Germany 51 I8

Reykjavik *Capital* Iceland 43 I11

Reynosa *Town* Mexico 31 E10

Rhine *River* Europe 50 F7, 52 E4

Rhode Island *State* USA 21

Rhódes *Town* Rhodes, Greece 49 I14

Rhodope Mountains Bulgaria 55 J10

Rhône *River* France 47 F10

Richmond *State capital* Virginia, USA 23 B12

Richmond *Town* Kentucky, USA 23 B9

Riga, Gulf of 58 F5

Ríga *Capital* Latvia 58 F5

Rijeka *Town* Croatia 48 C7

Rimini *Town* Italy 48 C6

Riobamba *Town* Ecuador 36 B5

Río Cuarto *Town* Argentina 37 G7

Rio de Janeiro *Town* Brazil 37 E10

Rio Gallegos *Town* Argentina 36 J7

Rio Grande *Town* Brazil 37 G9

Rivera *Town* Uruguay 37 F8

Riverside *Town* California, USA 26 F5

Rivne *Town* Ukraine 58 G6

Riyadh *Capital* Saudi Arabia 74 F7

Roanoke *Town* Virginia, USA 23 B11

Rochester *Town* Minnesota, USA 20 F4

Rochester *Town* New York, USA 21 E10

Rockford *Town* Illinois, USA 20 G5

Rockhampton *Town* Australia 91 E12

Rocky Mountains Canada/USA 24 F7, 27 D9, 28 G6

Roeselare *Town* Belgium 50 E4

Romania *Country* 55

Rome *Capital* Italy 48 E6

Ronne Ice Shelf Antarctica 16 E3

Rosario *Town* Argentina 37 G8

Roseau *Capital* Dominica 35 D12

Ross Ice Shelf Antarctica 16 G4

Ross Sea 16 H4

Rostock *Town* Germany 51 B11

Rostov-na-Donu *Town* Russian Fed. 58 H7

Roswell *Town* New Mexico, USA 27 G10

Rothera (UK) *RS* Antarctica 16 E1

Rotorua *Town* New Zealand 93 C10

Rotterdam *Town* Netherlands 50 D5

Roubaix *Town* France 47 A10

Rouen *Town* France 47 B8

Rukwa, Lake Tanzania 67 I8

Ruse *Town* Bulgaria 55 G11

Rushmore, Mount S Dakota, USA 25 H11

Russian Federation *Country* 59,86

Rwanda *Country* 66

Ryazan *Town* Russian Fed. 58 G7

Rybinsk *Town* Russian Fed. 58 F7

Rzeszow *Town* Poland 57 G11

Saarbrücken *Town* Germany 50 G7

Saba *Dep. territory* Netherlands 35 D12

Sabac *Town* Serbia 49 C10

Sabah *Region* Malaysia 80 E5

Sabha *Town* Libya 63 F8

Sacramento *State capital* California, USA 26 C4

Safi *Town* Morocco 62 E2

Saginaw *Town* Michigan, USA 20 F7

Sagunto *Town* Spain 45 F11

Sahara Desert North Africa 62 H5, 64 E7

Saiki *Town* Japan 82 I6

St. Augustine *Town* Florida, USA 23 G11

St. Barthelémy *Dep. territory* France 35 D12

St. Eustatius *Dep. territory* Netherlands 35 D12

St. Étienne *Town* France 47 F9

St. George's *Capital* Grenada 35 E12

St. George's Channel 40 G7

St. John *Town* New Brunswick, Canada 29 I13

St. John's *Capital* Antigua and Barbuda 35 D12

St. John's *Province capital* Newfoundland and Labrador, Canada 29 H14

St. Joseph *Town* Missouri, USA 22 B4

St. Kitts and Nevis *Country* 35

St. Lawrence Island Alaska, USA 25 B10

St. Louis *Town* Missouri, USA 22 B6

St. Louis *Town* Senegal 64 F3

St. Lucia *Country* 35

St. Malo *Town* France 46 B7

St. Martin/Sint Maarten *Dep. territory* France, Netherlands 35 D12

St. Moritz *Town* Switzerland 52 G5

St. Nazaire *Town* France 46 C6

St. Paul *State capital* Minnesota, USA 20 E3

St. Petersburg *Town* Florida, USA 23 H10

St. Petersburg *Town* Russian Fed. 58 E6

St. Pierre and Miquelon *Dep. territory* France 29 H14

St. Quentin *Town* France 47 B10

St. Vincent and the Grenadines *Country* 35

Sakai *Town* Japan 83 H8

Sakata *Town* Japan 83 E10

Salamanca *Town* Spain 44 D7

Salem *State capital* Oregon, USA 24 F3

Salerno *Town* Italy 48 F7

Salina *Town* Kansas, USA 27 D13

Salinas *Town* California, USA 26 D4

Salta *Town* Argentina 36 E7

Saltillo *Town* Mexico 31 E8

Salt Lake City *State capital* Utah, USA 27 C8

Salto *Town* Uruguay 37 F8

Salvador *Town* Brazil 37 D11

Salzburg *Town* Austria 40 F9

Samara *Town* Russian Fed. 59 G9

Samarkand *Town* Uzbekistan 86 J3

Samoa *Country* 93 I13

Samsun *Town* Turkey 73 C10

Sanaa *Capital* Yemen 74 I7

Sanae IV (South Africa) *RS* Antarctica 16 C4

San Angelo *Town* Texas, USA 27 H11

San Antonio *Town* Texas, USA 27 I12

San Bernardino *Town* California, USA 26 F5

San Cristóbal *Town* Venezuela 35 G9

Sancti Spíritus *Town* Cuba 34 B7

Sandakan *Town* Malaysia 80 E6

Sand Hills Nebraska, USA 25 H12

San Diego *Town* California, USA 26 F5

San Francisco *Town* California, USA 26 C4

San Francisco de Macorís *Town* Dominican Republic 35 C10

San José *Capital* Costa Rica 34 F5

San Jose *Town* California, USA 26 D4

San Juan *Town* Argentina 36 F7

Sankt Pölten *Town* Austria 40 E12

San Luis Potosí *Town* Mexico 31 F9

San Marino *Capital* San Marino 48 D6

San Marino *Country* 48

San Miguel de Tucumán *Town* Argentina 36 F7

San Miguelito *Town* Panama 34 F7

San Pedro Sula *Town* Honduras 34 D5

San Remo *Town* Italy 48 C4

San Salvador *Capital* El Salvador 34 D4

San Salvador de Jujuy *Town* Argentina 36 E7

Santa Barbara *Town* California, USA 26 E5

Santa Clara *Town* Cuba 34 B7

Santa Cruz *Town* Bolivia 36 D7

Santa Fe *State capital* New Mexico, USA 27 E10

Santa Fe *Town* Argentina 37 G8

Santa Marta *Town* Colombia 35 F8

Santander *Town* Spain 45 B8

Santarém *Town* Brazil 37 B9

Santa Rosa *Town* California, USA 26 C4

Santiago *Capital* Chile 36 G7

Santiago *Town* Dominican Republic 35 C10

Santiago de Cuba *Town* Cuba 35 C8

Santo Domingo *Capital* Dominican Republic 35 D10

Santos *Town* Brazil 37 E10

São Luis *Town* Brazil 37 B10

São Paulo *Town* Brazil 37 E10

São Tomé *Capital* São Tomé and Príncipe 68 C4

São Tomé and Príncipe *Country* 68

Sapporo *Town* Japan 83 B10

Sarajevo *Capital* Bosnia and Herz. 49 D9

Saratov *Town* Russian Fed. 59 G8

Sarawak Malaysia 80 F4

Sardinia *Island* Italy 48 F4

Sarh *Town* Chad 65 H13

Sariwon *Town* North Korea 85 D12

Sasebo *Town* Japan 82 H5

Saskatchewan *Province* Canada 29

Saskatoon *Town* Saskatchewan, Canada 29 H8

Sassari *Town* Sardinia, Italy 48 F4

Satu Mare *Town* Romania 55 C8

Saudi Arabia *Country* 74

Savannah *Town* Georgia, USA 23 F11

Savona *Town* Italy 48 C4

Saynshand *Town* Mongolia 85 D10

Scheldt *River* Belgium 50 E4

Schenectady *Town* New York, USA 21 E12

Schwaz *Town* Austria 40 F8

Schwerin *Town* Germany 51 C10

Scotland *Country* UK 41

Scott Base (New Zealand) *RS* Antarctica 16 G4

Scranton *Town* Pennsylvania, USA 21 F11

Seattle *Town* Washington, USA 24 D4

Ségou *Town* Mali 64 G6

Segovia *Town* Spain 45 D8

Seine *River* France 47 B9

Sekondi-Takoradi *Town* Ghana 64 I7

Semarang *Town* Indonesia 80 H4

Sendai *Town* Japan 83 E10

Senegal *Country* 64

Senegal *River* Senegal 64 F4

Seoul *Capital* South Korea 85 E13

Serbia *Country* 49

Serov *Town* Russian Fed. 86 G3

Sète *Town* France 47 H9

Setúbal *Town* Portugal 44 G5

Sevastopol *Town* Crimea, Ukraine 58 I7

Severn *River* England, UK 41 H9

Severnaya Zemlya Russian Fed. 17 F13, 86 C6

Seville *Town* Spain 44 H7

Seychelles *Country* 69

Sfax *Town* Tunisia 62 D7

Shanghai *Town* China 85 F12

Shannon *River* Republic of Ireland 40 G6

Sheberghan *Town* Afghanistan 76 A7

Sheffield *Town* England, UK 41 G9

Shenyang *Town* China 85 D12

Sherbrooke *Town* Quebec, Canada 29 I12

's-Hertogenbosch *Town* Netherlands 50 D6

Shetland Islands Scotland, UK 41 A9

Shimonoseki *Town* Japan 82 H5

Shinyanga *Town* Tanzania 67 H8

Shiraz *Town* Iran 75 D9

Shizuoka *Town* Japan 83 G9

Shkodër *Town* Albania 49 E10

Showa (Japan) *RS* Antarctica 16 D6

Shreveport *Town* Louisiana, USA 22 F4

Shumen *Town* Bulgaria 55 H12

Sibenik *Town* Croatia 49 D8

Siberia Russian Fed. 86 F7

Sibiu *Town* Romania 55 E10

Sicily *Island* Italy 48 H7

Sidi Bel Abbès *Town* Algeria 62 D5

Siegen *Town* Germany 51 F8

Siena *Town* Italy 48 D6

Sierra de Gredos *Mountain range* Spain 44 E7

Sierra Leone *Country* 64

Sierra Nevada *Mountain range* California, USA 26 C5

Sierra Nevada *Mountain range* Spain 45 H9

Signy (UK) *RS* Antarctica 16 C1

Silver City *Town* New Mexico, USA 27 G9

Sincelejo *Town* Colombia 35 F8

Singapore *Capital* Singapore 80 F2

Singapore *Country* 80

Sinuiju *Town* North Korea 85 D12

Sioux City *Town* Iowa, USA 20 G2

Sioux Falls *Town* S Dakota, USA 25 H14

Siracusa *Town* Sicily, Italy 48 H7

Sittwe *Town* Burma (Myanmar) 78 E1

Sivas *Town* Turkey 73 D10

Skagerrak *Sea* Norway 42 H6

Skellefteå *Town* Sweden 43 D9

Skopje *Capital* Macedonia 49 E11

Slavonski Brod *Town* Croatia 49 C9

Sligo *Town* Republic of Ireland 40 F6

Sliven *Town* Bulgaria 55 H12

Slovakia *Country* 57

Slovenia *Country* 48

Smederevo *Town* Serbia 49 C10

Smolensk *Town* Russian Fed. 58 F6

Snake *River* Idaho/Oregon, USA 24 H6

Snowdon *Mountain* Wales, UK 41 G8

Socotra *Island* Yemen 75 J10

Söderhamn *Town* Sweden 43 F8

Södertälje *Town* Sweden 43 G8

Sofia *Capital* Bulgaria 55 I9

Soledad *Town* Colombia 35 F8

Solingen *Town* Germany 50 E7

Solomon Islands *Country* 93 I12

Solomon Sea 81 G13

Somalia *Country* 67

Songea *Town* Tanzania 67 J9

Songkhla *Town* Thailand 78 J4

Soria *Town* Spain 45 C9

Sorong *Town* Indonesia 81 F9

Sousse *Town* Tunisia 62 D7

South Africa *Country* 68

Southampton *Town* England, UK 41 I9

Southampton Island Nunavut, Canada 29 F10

South Australia *State* Australia 91

South Bend *Town* Indiana, USA 20 G6

South Carolina *State* USA 23

South China Sea 79 G8, 85 J12

South Dakota *State* USA 25

Southern Ocean 16, 90

South Georgia *Dep. territory* UK 37 J10

South Island New Zealand 92

South Korea *See* Korea, South

South Orkney Islands Antarctica 16 C1

South Ossetia *State* Georgia 59 I8

South Sudan *Country* 66

Soweto *Town* South Africa 69 I8

Spain *Country* 44

Spanish Town *Town* Jamaica 35 D8

Spartanburg *Town* S Carolina, USA 23 D10

Split *Town* Croatia 49 D8

Spokane *Town* Washington, USA 24 D5

Springfield *State capital* Illinois, USA 20 I5

Springfield *Town* Massachusetts, USA 21 E12

Springfield *Town* Missouri, USA 22 C4

Srebrenica *Town* Bosnia and Herz. 49 C9

Sri Lanka *Country* 77

Stamford *Town* Connecticut, USA 21 F12

Stara Zagora *Town* Bulgaria 55 I11

Stavanger *Town* Norway 42 G5

Stavropol *Town* Russian Fed. 59 I8

Stewart Island New Zealand 92 J6

Stockholm *Capital* Sweden 43 G8

Stockton *Town* California, USA 26 C4

Stockton Plateau Texas, USA 27 H10

Stoke-on-Trent *Town* England, UK 41 G9

Strasbourg *Town* France 47 D12

Stuttgart *Town* Germany 51 H8

Subotica *Town* Serbia 49 B10

Suceava *Town* Romania 55 C11

Sucre *Capital* Bolivia 36 E7

Sudan *Country* 66

Sudbury *Town* Ontario, Canada 29 I11

Suez, Gulf of 63 F13

Suez *Town* Egypt 63 F13

Sühbaatar *Town* Mongolia 85 C9

Sukkur *Town* Pakistan 76 C7

Sulu Archipelago Philippines 79 I10

Sulu Sea 79 H10

Sumatra *Island* Indonesia 80 F2

Sunderland *Town* England, UK 41 F9

Sundsvall *Town* Sweden 43 F8

Sunnyvale *Town* California, USA 26 D4

Superior, Lake USA 20 C5

Sur *Town* Oman 75 F11

Surabaya *Town* Indonesia 80 H4

Surakarta *Town* Indonesia 80 H4

Surat *Town* India 76 E7

Surgut *Town* Russian Fed. 86 G4

Suriname *Country* 35

Surt *Town* Libya 63 E9

Suwalki *Town* Poland 57 B11

Svalbard *Dep. territory* Norway 17 H12

Swansea *Town* Wales, UK 41 H8

Swaziland *Country* 69

Sweden *Country* 43

Swindon *Town* England, UK 41 H9

Switzerland *Country* 52

Sydney *Town* Australia 91 H12

Syktyvkar *Town* Russian Fed. 59 E9

Sylhet *Town* Bangladesh 77 E12

Syracuse *Town* New York, USA 21 E11

Syria *Country* 73

Syrian Desert Syria 73 G11, 74 C6

Szczecin *Town* Poland 56 C5

Szeged *Town* Hungary 54 D6

Székesfehérvár *Town* Hungary 54 D5

Szombathely *Town* Hungary 54 D4

Tabora *Town* Tanzania 67 H8

Tabriz *Town* Iran 74 B7

Tacoma *Town* Washington, USA 24 D3

Taegu *Town* South Korea 85 E13

Taejon *Town* South Korea 85 E13

Taguatinga *Town* Brazil 37 D9

Taipei *Capital* Taiwan 85 H13

Taiwan *Country* 85

Taiyuan *Town* China 85 E10

Ta'izz *Town* Yemen 74 I7

Tajikistan *Country* 86

Takasaki *Town* Japan 83 F9

Taklimakan Desert China 84 F5
Talcahuano *Town* Chile 36 G6
Taldyqorgan *Town* Kazakhstan 86 I4
Tallahassee *State capital* Florida, USA 23 G9
Tallinn *Capital* Estonia 58 E5
Tamale *Town* Ghana 64 H7
Tamanrasset *Town* Algeria 62 H6
Tampa *Town* Florida, USA 23 H10
Tampere *Town* Finland 43 F9
Tampico *Town* Mexico 31 G10
Tamworth *Town* Australia 91 G12
Tanami Desert Australia 91 D8
Tanga *Town* Tanzania 67 H9
Tanganyika, Lake DRC/Tanzania 66 I7, 69 E9
Tangier *Town* Morocco 62 D3
Tanzania *Country* 67
Taranto *Town* Italy 49 F8
Tarbes *Town* France 46 G7
Târgu Mures *Town* Romania 55 D10
Tarija *Town* Bolivia 36 E7
Tarim Basin China 84 E6
Tarnow *Town* Poland 57 G10
Tarragona *Town* Spain 45 D12
Tarsus *Town* Turkey 73 E9
Tartu *Town* Estonia 58 F6
Tartus *Town* Syria 73 G10
Tashkent *Capital* Uzbekistan 86 I3
Tasmania *State* Australia 91
Tasman Sea 91 I12, 92 F6
Tatra Mountains Slovakia 57 H9
Taupo, Lake New Zealand 93 D10
Tauranga *Town* New Zealand 93 C10
Taurus Mountains Turkey 73 E8
Tavoy *Town* Burma (Myanmar) 78 G3
Tbilisi *Capital* Georgia 59 I8
Tegucigalpa *Capital* Honduras 34 D5
Tehran *Capital* Iran 75 B9
Tehuantepec, Gulf of 31 I11
Tekirdag *Town* Turkey 72 B6
Tel Aviv *Town* Israel 73 H9
Temuco *Town* Chile 36 H6
Tennessee *River* Alabama/Tennessee, USA 23 D8
Tennessee *State* USA 23
Tepic *Town* Mexico 30 G7
Teramo *Town* Italy 48 D7
Teresina *Town* Brazil 37 B10
Terni *Town* Italy 48 D6
Terrasa *Town* Spain 45 C12
Terre Haute *Town* Indiana, USA 20 H6
Teruel *Town* Spain 45 E10
Tete *Town* Mozambique 69 G10
Tétouan *Town* Morocco 62 D3
Texas *State* USA 27

Thailand, Gulf of 78 H4
Thailand *Country* 78
Thai Nguyen *Town* Vietnam 78 E5
Thames *River* England, UK 41 H10
Thanh Hoa *Town* Vietnam 78 E5
The Hague *Capital* Netherlands 50 D5
Thessaloníki *Town* Greece 49 F11
Thimphu *Capital* Bhutan 77 D11
Thiruvananthapuram (Trivandrum) *Town* India 77 I8
Thun *Town* Switzerland 52 G3
Thunder Bay *Town* Ontario, Canada 29 I10
Tianjin *Town* China 85 E11
Tibesti Mountains Chad 65 E13
Tibet China 84 G6
Tibet, Plateau of China 84 G7
Tigris *River* Iraq 74 C7
Tijuana *Town* Mexico 30 B3
Tilburg *Town* Netherlands 50 E6
Timaru *Town* New Zealand 92 H7
Timisoara *Town* Romania 54 E7
Tindouf *Town* Algeria 62 F2
Tiranë *Capital* Albania 49 F10
Tiraspol *Town* Moldova 58 H6
Tiruchchirappalli *Town* India 77 I8
Tisza *River* Central Europe 54 D7
Titicaca, Lake Peru 36 D6
Tocantins *River* Brazil 37 C10
Togo *Country* 65
Tokelau *Dep. territory* New Zealand 93 I13
Tokushima *Town* Japan 82 H7
Tokyo *Capital* Japan 83 G10
Toledo *Town* Ohio, USA 21 G8
Toledo *Town* Spain 45 E8
Toluca *Town* Mexico 31 H9
Tolyatti *Town* Russian Fed. 59 G9
Tomakomai *Town* Japan 83 C10
Tombouctou *Town* Mali 64 F7
Tomsk *Town* Russian Fed. 86 G5
Tonga *Country* 93 I13
Tonkin, Gulf of 78 E5, 85 J10
Tonopah *Town* Nevada, USA 26 D6
Toowoomba *Town* Australia 91 F13
Topeka *State capital* Kansas, USA 27 D13
Toronto *Province capital* Ontario, Canada 29 J11
Torun *Town* Poland 57 D8
Tottori *Town* Japan 82 G7
Touba *Town* Senegal 64 F3
Toubkal, Mount Morocco 63 E2
Toulon *Town* France 47 H10
Toulouse *Town* France 46 G7
Tournai *Town* Belgium 50 E4
Tours *Town* France 47 D8
Townsville *Town* Australia 91 D11

Toyama *Town* Japan 83 F8
Toyota *Town* Japan 83 G8
Trabzon *Town* Turkey 73 C12
Transnistria *State* Moldova 58 H6
Transylvanian Alps Romania 55 E9
Trapani *Town* Sicily, Italy 48 H6
Trencin *Town* Slovakia 56 I7
Trent *River* England, UK 41 G10
Trento *Town* Italy 48 B6
Trenton *State capital* New Jersey, USA 21 G12
Treviso *Town* Italy 48 B6
Trier *Town* Germany 50 G6
Trieste *Town* Italy 48 B7
Trincomalee *Town* Sri Lanka 77 I9
Trinidad and Tobago *Country* 35
Tripoli *Capital* Libya 63 E8
Tripoli *Town* Lebanon 73 G10
Trivandrum *See* Thiruvananthapuram
Trnava *Town* Slovakia 56 I7
Trois-Rivières *Town* Quebec, Canada 29 I12
Troll (Norway) *RS* Antarctica 16 C4
Tromsø *Town* Norway 43 B8
Trondheim *Town* Norway 42 E6
Troy *Town* New York, USA 21 E12
Troyes *Town* France 47 C10
Trujillo *Town* Peru 36 C5
Tshikapa *Town* DRC 68 E7
Tubruq *Town* Libya 63 E11
Tucson *Town* Arizona, USA 27 G8
Tuguegarao *Town* Philippines 79 E10
Tula *Town* Russian Fed. 58 G7
Tulcea *Town* Romania 55 E13
Tulsa *Town* Oklahoma, USA 27 E13
Tunis *Capital* Tunisia 62 D7
Tunisia *Country* 62
Tunja *Town* Colombia 35 G8
Turin *Town* Italy 48 B4
Turkana, Lake Kenya 67 F9
Turkey *Country* 73
Turkmenabat *Town* Turkmenistan 86 J3
Turkmenistan *Country* 86
Turks and Caicos Islands *Dep. territory* UK 35 B9
Turku *Town* Finland 43 G9
Tuvalu *Country* 93 I12
Tuxtla Gutiérrez *Town* Mexico 31 I12
Tuz, Lake Turkey 73 D8
Tuzla *Town* Bosnia and Herz. 49 C9
Tver *Town* Russian Fed. 58 F7
Twin Falls *Town* Idaho, USA 24 H6
Tyler *Town* Texas, USA 27 G14
Tyrrhenian Sea 48 G6

Uberaba *Town* Brazil 37 E10

Uberlândia *Town* Brazil 37 D10
Ubon Ratchathani *Town* Thailand 78 G5
Uchiura Bay Japan 83 C10
Udaipur *Town* India 77 E8
Udine *Town* Italy 48 B7
Udon Thani *Town* Thailand 78 F4
Uele *River* DRC 69 C9
Ufa *Town* Russian Fed. 59 G10
Uganda *Country* 67
Ukhta *Town* Russian Fed. 59 D9
Ukraine *Country* 58
Ulaanbaatar *Capital* Mongolia 85 C9
Ulaangom *Town* Mongolia 84 C7
Ulan-Ude *Town* Russian Fed. 86 H7
Ulm *Town* Germany 51 I9
Umeå *Town* Sweden 43 E8
Umtata *Town* South Africa 69 J8
Ungava Peninsula Quebec, Canada 29 F11
United Arab Emirates (UAE) *Country* 75
Uppsala *Town* Sweden 43 G8
Ural Mountains Russian Fed. 59 F10, 86 G2
Uruguay *Country* 37
Urumqi *Town* China 84 D6
Usak *Town* Turkey 72 D6
Ushuaia *Town* Argentina 36 J7
Usol'ye-Sibirskoye *Town* Russian Fed. 86 H6
Ust'llimsk *Town* Russian Fed. 86 G6
Ústí nad Labem *Town* Czech Republic 56 G5
Ustyurt Plateau Uzbekistan 86 I2
Utah *State* USA 27
Utica *Town* New York, USA 21 E11
Utrecht *Town* Netherlands 50 D6
Utsunomiya *Town* Japan 83 F10
Uzbekistan *Country* 86

Vaal *River* South Africa 69 I9
Vaasa *Town* Finland 43 E9
Vadodara *Town* India 76 E7
Vadsø *Town* Norway 43 A10
Vaduz *Capital* Liechtenstein 52 F5
Valdivia *Town* Chile 36 H6
Valdosta *Town* Georgia, USA 23 F10
Valence *Town* France 47 G10
Valencia, Gulf of 45 F11
Valencia *Town* Spain 45 F11
Valencia *Town* Venezuela 35 F10
Valladolid *Town* Spain 45 D8
Valletta *Capital* Malta 48 I7
Valparaíso *Capital* Chile 36 G6
Van *Town* Turkey 73 D13
Vancouver *Town* British Columbia, Canada 28 I6

Vancouver Island British Columbia, Canada 28 H5

Vantaa *Town* Finland 43 G10

Vanuatu *Country* 93 I12

Varanasi *Town* India 77 E10

Varna *Town* Bulgaria 55 H13

Västerås *Town* Sweden 43 G8

Vatican City *Country* 48

Växjö *Town* Sweden 42 I7

Venezuela *Country* 35

Venice, Gulf of 48 C7

Venice *Town* Italy 48 C6

Veracruz *Town* Mexico 31 H10

Verkhoyanskiy Mountains Russian Fed. 87 F9

Vermont *State* USA 21

Verona *Town* Italy 48 B6

Versailles *Town* France 47 C9

Verviers *Town* Belgium 50 F6

Viareggio *Town* Italy 48 D5

Vicenza *Town* Italy 48 B6

Victoria, Lake Kenya/Tanzania/ Uganda 67 G8

Victoria *Province capital* British Columbia, Canada 28 I6

Victoria *State* Australia 91

Victoria *Capital* Seychelles 69 D14

Victoria Falls Zimbabwe 69 G8

Victoria Island Canada 17 E8, 29 E8

Vidin *Town* Bulgaria 55 G9

Vienna *Capital* Austria 40 E13

Vientiane *Capital* Laos 78 F4

Vietnam *Country* 78

Vigo *Town* Spain 44 C5

Vijayawada *Town* India 77 G9

Villach *Town* Austria 40 H10

Villahermosa *Town* Mexico 31 H12

Villavicencio *Town* Colombia 35 H8

Vilnius *Capital* Lithuania 58 G5

Vina del Mar *Town* Chile 36 G6

Vineland *Town* New Jersey, USA 21 G12

Vinh *Town* Vietnam 78 F5

Virginia *State* USA 23

Virginia Beach *Town* Virginia, USA 23 B12

Virgin Islands *Dep. territory* UK 35 D11

Virgin Islands *Dep. territory* USA 35 D11

Vishakhapatnam *Town* India 77 G10

Vitoria *Town* Brazil 37 E11

Vitória-Gasteiz *Town* Spain 45 B9

Vitsyebsk *Town* Belarus 58 F6

Vladikavkaz *Town* Russian Fed. 59 I8

Vladivostok *Town* Russian Fed. 87 I9

Vlissingen *Town* Netherlands 50 D5

Vlorë *Town* Albania 49 F10

Volga *River* Russian Fed. 59 F8

Volgograd *Town* Russian Fed. 59 H8

Vólos *Town* Greece 49 G11

Volta, Lake Ghana 64 I7

Vorkuta *Town* Russian Fed. 59 C11, 86 E3

Voronezh *Town* Russian Fed. 58 G7

Vosges Mountains France 47 D11

Voss *Town* Norway 42 F5

Vostok (Russian Federation) *RS* Antarctica 16 F5

Vratsa *Town* Bulgaria 55 H9

Vyborg *Town* Russian Fed. 58 E6

Waal *River* Netherlands 50 D6

Waco *Town* Texas, USA 27 H13

Waddenzee *Sea* Netherlands 50 B7

Wadi Halfa *Town* Sudan 66 A7

Wad Medani *Town* Sudan 67 C8

Wagga Wagga *Town* Australia 91 H11

Wakayama *Town* Japan 82 H7

Wakkanai *Town* Japan 83 A10

Walbrzych *Town* Poland 56 F6

Wales *Country* UK 41

Wallis and Futuna *Dep. territory* France 93 I13

Walvis Bay *Town* Namibia 68 H6

Wandel Sea 17 G11

Warren *Town* Michigan, USA 20 F8

Warsaw *Capital* Poland 57 E10

Washington, Mount USA 21 D12

Washington *State* USA 24

Washington D.C. *Capital* USA 21 H11

Waterford *Town* Republic of Ireland 40 H6

Waterloo *Town* Iowa, USA 20 G4

Watertown *Town* New York, USA 21 E10

Wau *Town* Sudan 66 E7

Weddell Sea 16 D2

Weimar *Town* Germany 51 F10

Wellington *Capital* New Zealand 93 F9

Wels *Town* Austria 40 E10

Wenzhou *Town* China 85 G12

West Bank *Disputed region* Near East 73 H9

Western Australia *State* Australia 90

Western Ghats *Mountain range* India 76 F7

Western Sahara *Territory* 64

West Palm Beach *Town* Florida, USA 23 I12

West Virginia *State* USA 21

Whitehorse *Province capital* Yukon Territory, Canada 28 F5

White Nile *River* Sudan 67 D8

White Sea 58 D7

Whitney, Mount California, USA 26 D5

Wichita *Town* Kansas, USA 27 E13

Wichita Falls *Town* Texas, USA 27 F12

Wieliczka *Town* Poland 57 G9

Wiener Neustadt *Town* Austria 40 F13

Wiesbaden *Town* Germany 51 G8

Wilhelmshaven *Town* Germany 51 C8

Wilkes Land Antarctica 16 G6

Williston *Town* N Dakota, USA 25 E11

Wilmington *Town* Delaware, USA 21 G11

Wilmington *Town* N Carolina, USA 23 D12

Windhoek *Capital* Namibia 68 H7

Windsor *Town* Ontario, Canada 29 J11

Winnipeg *Province capital* Manitoba, Canada 29 I9

Winston-Salem *Town* N Carolina, USA 23 C10

Winterthur *Town* Switzerland 52 F4

Wisconsin *State* USA 20

Wloclawek *Town* Poland 57 D8

Wolfsberg *Town* Austria 40 H11

Wolfsburg *Town* Germany 51 D10

Wollongong *Town* Australia 91 H12

Wonsan *Town* North Korea 85 D13

Worcester *Town* Massachusetts, USA 21 E13

Worms *Town* Germany 51 G8

Wroclaw *Town* Poland 56 F7

Wuhan *Town* China 85 G11

Wuppertal *Town* Germany 50 E7

Würzburg *Town* Germany 51 G9

Wyoming *State* USA 25

Xiamen *Town* China 85 H12

Xi'an *Town* China 85 F10

Xining *Town* China 85 F8

Xuzhou *Town* China 85 F11

Yakima *Town* Washington, USA 24 E4

Yakutsk *Town* Russian Fed. 87 F9

Yambol *Town* Bulgaria 55 I12

Yamoussoukro *Capital* Côte d'Ivoire 64 I6

Yanbu *Town* Saudi Arabia 74 F5

Yangon (Rangoon) *Town* Burma (Myanmar) 78 G2

Yantai *Town* China 85 E12

Yaoundé *Capital* Cameroon 68 C5

Yaroslavl *Town* Russian Fed. 58 F7

Yazd *Town* Iran 75 D9

Yekaterinburg *Town* Russian Fed. 86 G3

Yellowknife *Province capital* Northwest Territories, Canada 28 F7

Yellow Sea 85 E12

Yemen *Country* 75

Yenisey *River* Russian Fed. 86 F5

Yerevan *Capital* Armenia 59 J8

Yinchuan *Town* China 85 E9

Yining *Town* China 84 D5

Yokohama *Town* Japan 83 G10

Yonago *Town* Japan 82 G7

York *Town* England, UK 41 F9

Youngstown *Town* Ohio, USA 21 G9

Yucatán Peninsula Mexico 31 G13

Yukon *River* Alaska, USA 25 B10

Yukon Territory *Province* Canada 28

Yuma *Town* Arizona, USA 26 G6

Yumen *Town* China 85 E8

Yuzhno-Sakhalinsk *Town* Russian Fed. 87 I10

Zadar *Town* Croatia 49 D8

Zagreb *Capital* Croatia 49 B8

Zagros Mountains Iran 75 C8

Zahedan *Town* Iran 75 D11

Zajecar *Town* Serbia 49 D11

Zambezi *River* Southern Africa 69 G8

Zambia *Country* 69

Zamboanga *Town* Philippines 79 H11

Zamora *Town* Spain 44 D7

Zanzibar *Town* Tanzania 67 I9

Zanzibar Island Tanzania 67 I10

Zaporizhzhya *Town* Ukraine 58 H7

Zaria *Town* Nigeria 65 H10

Zeebrugge *Town* Belgium 50 E4

Zenica *Town* Bosnia and Herz. 49 C9

Zhangjiakou *Town* China 85 E11

Zhanjiang *Town* China 85 I11

Zhengzhou *Town* China 85 F11

Zhezkazgan *Town* Kazakhstan 86 I3

Zhongshan (China) *RS* Antarctica 16 E7

Zibo *Town* China 85 E11

Zielona Gora *Town* Poland 56 E6

Zilina *Town* Slovakia 57 H8

Zimbabwe *Country* 69

Zinder *Town* Niger 65 G10

Zlin *Town* Czech Republic 56 H7

Zomba *Town* Malawi 69 F10

Zonguldak *Town* Turkey 73 B8

Zrenjanin *Town* Serbia 49 C10

Zug *Town* Switzerland 52 F4

Zürich *Town* Switzerland 52 F4

Zwettl Stadt *Town* Austria 40 D12

Zwickau *Town* Germany 51 F11

Zwolle *Town* Netherlands 50 C7

Index

Acknowledgements

The publishers would like to thank Richard Burgess for his contribution to this book.

All other artworks are from the Miles Kelly Artwork Bank.

The publishers would like to thank the following source for the use of their photographs:
Fotolia.com 10(b) Andrey Mirzoyants, Jean Luc Bohin, Giovanni Catalani, Kárpáti Gábor, Matt Ireland; 20 David Ruderman; 22 Daren Whitaker; 25 Sascha Burkard; 27 Tomasz Kawka; 28 Melissa Schalke; 29 Roman Krochuk; 30 Beatrice Preve; 31(t) Lein De Leon; 34 Françoise Bro; 35 pixphoto; 36(t) urbanhearts; 41(b) C J Photography; 43 Marco Regalia; 44 Hugues Argence; 48 Dubravko Grakalic; 50 Jarno Gonzalez/Fotolia.com; 51 Philip Lange; 52(t) Renato Francia; 54(b) Jozsef Szasz-fabian; 56(b) Bartlomiej Kwieciszewski; 57 Martin Džumela; 58(b) Salazkin Vladimir; 59 Jacek Malipan 65(t) Natasha Owen; 74(t) Richard Connors, (b) MaxFX; 79(c) Dmitry Ersler; 80 Stuart Taylor; 81(b) TAOLMOR/; 83(t) Anna Cseresnjes; 87(b) NFive; 91 Flavia Bottazzini; 92(b) Rico Leffanta; 93 Adam Booth

All other photographs are from: Corel, digitalSTOCK, digitalvision, istock.com, John Foxx, PhotoAlto, PhotoDisc, PhotoEssentials, PhotoPro, Stockbyte

Every effort has been made to acknowledge the source and copyright holder of each picture.
Miles Kelly Publishing apologises for any unintentional errors or omissions.